SLOT'S MASTERSTROKE

A Tactical Analysis of Liverpool's 2024-25 Title-Winning Season

PETER PRICKETT

BENNION KEARNY

First published in 2025 by Bennion Kearny Ltd

Woodside, Oakamoor, ST10 3AE

www.BennionKearny.com

ISBN: 978-1-915855-37-4

Peter Prickett has asserted his right under the Copyright, Designs and Patents Act, 1988, to be identified as the author of this book.

Copyright Bennion Kearny 2025. All Rights Reserved.

No part of this publication may be reproduced, stored in a retrieval system, or transmitted in any form or by any means, electronic, mechanical, photocopying, recording or otherwise, without the prior permission of the publisher.

A CIP catalogue record for this book is available from the British Library.

This book is sold subject to the condition that it shall not, by way of trade or otherwise, be lent, re-sold, hired out or otherwise circulated without the publisher's prior consent in any form of binding or cover other than that in which it is published and without a similar condition including this condition being imposed on the subsequent purchaser.

Bennion Kearny has endeavoured to provide trademark information about all the companies and products mentioned in this book by the appropriate use of capitals. However, Bennion Kearny cannot guarantee the accuracy of this information.

Peter Prickett is the author of multiple bestselling coaching titles, including:

Scan here to learn more

Following Klopp

How do you follow a legend?

In nine years, Jurgen Klopp turned "doubters to believers". He arrived with Liverpool going through what had become a familiar cycle of mounting a title challenge one season, and then falling away badly the next.

Liverpool had sacked Brendan Rodgers, who came within one infamous slip of winning that first league title since 1990, and Klopp slowly helped Liverpool become a team that could keep pace with – and eventually surpass – the riches of Manchester City, creating an era of excellence in the Premier League where 90 points was not enough to guarantee league success. The league was won with 99 points, but a 97-point season and a 92-point season were only good enough for second place. The 99-point season was the second-highest total by any team in an English top-flight season. The 97-point season in 2018-19 was the fourth-highest total ever, whilst the 92-point total ties as the eighth-best tally. Klopp has three of the top ten highest league totals, yet only one Premier League win to his name. He and Guardiola elevated the highest level of English football as they went head to head. That was the perception of the casual fan, but in reality, Klopp was one part of an intricate Liverpool recruitment and management team seeking to find any edge they could. Jurgen was the perfect figurehead for such an operation.

Jurgen helped give the club an identity that the fans could relate to. A man who exuded warmth and charisma; a gregarious, emotional, and excitable man. Everything that the city of Liverpool and its inhabitants have as their own self-image. The charisma of Klopp certainly helped him during the rollercoaster early days of the build.

When Klopp was appointed, he delivered a few quotes that never left him during his time at Liverpool. "Doubters to believers" is one because he absolutely did make everyone believe. No game was ever lost. Anyone was beatable, no matter the circumstance. Just ask Barcelona. That comeback from three goals down will likely be the epitome of Klopp at Liverpool. The "mentality monsters" doing it again, even when star players are unavailable. Mohammed Salah's missing brilliance didn't matter because Divock Origi believed he could win the game for Liverpool. Two goals later, and he was right.

Klopp also famously called himself "the normal one", in a clear reference to Jose Mourinho. However, the quote that had the greatest on-field legacy related directly to Arsene Wenger. "It's like an orchestra… I like heavy metal more".

Like that, Jurgen Klopp's high energy, high pressing, fast counter-attacking style was in place. Over the nine years, more nuance became involved, with Liverpool teams able to slow games down and dominate possession rather than going hell for leather all game, every game. Transition was the identity. Intensity was the identity.

Klopp made the announcement that he was leaving with months of the 2023-24 season remaining. The speculation about his successor was bubbling away for all that time, a quiet effervescence that became a flowing torrent as the season reached a climax. Xabi Alonso was the initial favourite. Alonso had enjoyed an outstanding double-winning season with Bayer Leverkusen, with the team playing dynamic and dominant football to usurp the German giants from Munich. With Alonso would come the romance of a former Liverpool player returning, but the move did not happen.

There were links to many managers but Liverpool took everyone by surprise, appointing Arne Slot. Slot had been successful at Feyenoord, winning a league title, but no one really knew what to expect. How would Slot and Liverpool handle what would surely be a season of transition? When a legend departs, there is usually a huge drop-off in the aftermath. What would the season hold?

Slot At Feyenoord

Arne Slot was a shock. He was not on the radar of anyone outside of Liverpool football club. Really, he should have been.

Slot fitted in many ways. He had restored Feyenoord after years in the doldrums, he was a manager with personality, and had won the Dutch league in 2022-23 and The KNVB Cup in 2023-24. In Europe, he had taken Feyenoord to the Europa League final, losing 1-0 to Jose Mourinho and Roma in a game that Feyenoord dominated in terms of possession and goal attempts.

Slot's Feyenoord had a tactical identity, some of which could be expected to carry over to Liverpool.

His teams generally lined up in a 4-2-3-1 formation, with the two midfielders forming a sold double pivot. The two pivots helped to control possession and cover opposition counter-attacks. Their positioning allowed the full-backs to push high and wide. In prolonged build-up in the opposition half, the wingers positioned themselves wide with the full-backs underlapping into the half-space. In fast counter-attacking phases, the wingers tucked into the half-spaces, running onto forward passes.

In the build-up phase, Slot positioned his pivots beyond the line of the opposition press while keeping the full-backs wide, with the shape switching between a 4-2 and 2-4 depending on how aggressively the opposition press. The right winger tended to come inside and narrow. Along with the attacking midfielder and the pivots, they created a box in midfield to help create or manage overloads. With the right winger tucked in, the right-back had more license to operate wide. On the other flank, the left-back often inverted. There was a symmetry to Feyenoord in their overall structure but not necessarily the roles of the players creating the structure (one full-back inverted, the other wide, for example).

In possession, Slot used lots of passing triangles, rotating movements, and third-man combinations. Midfielders had license to run beyond and receive the penetrating pass of the third-man movement. Essentially, Slot sought to create and find overloads all over the pitch, be that 5v4 against the opposition backline (via the full-backs, wingers and striker positioning), 4v3 in midfield through the box, or small 3v2s and 2v1s created through passing and movement patterns. A favoured scoring method through these overloads and the use of the half-space was to deliver cutbacks and simplify finishing.

Out of possession, Slot looked to press man-to-man but also used a few different pressing shapes. Importantly, the number 10 would step up alongside the striker and wingers to create 4-2-4. In certain circumstances, the 10 would be tasked with marking the opposition pivot. A high backline when in possession helped Feyenoord to counter-press and press in turnover and restart situations. Once the press had been bypassed, Feyenoord slipped into a 4-5-1 mid or low block (depending on how deeply the opposition had made it in Feyenoord's territory).

Once opponents were in Feyenoord's defensive third, Slot sought to be compact defensively – creating a solid central block and encouraging play into wide areas. When Feyenoord regained possession, they would attempt to counter quickly using the wingers.

Similarities and Differences

Arne Slot and Jurgen Klopp's styles mesh in certain respects but diverge in others. During the last season, Klopp inverted one full-back, Alexander-Arnold, with Robertson tucking in at left-back. Liverpool used a full-back to create a midfield box at a time when the box midfield was the most fashionable thing in football. Klopp and Slot were both committed to pressing, but Klopp's best Liverpool sides used a three-player front line to press with three covering midfielders poised to join the press when appropriate, but also cover the space behind the pressing trio.

The midfield is one of the biggest differences between the two teams. Klopp used his midfield in a functional manner, and (aside from the final season) they aided the release of both full-backs to attack in high and wide positions. The midfield was not expected to be creative or play make. Much of this responsibility was passed onto the full-backs and the aforementioned Alexander-Arnold. Remember that Klopp considered counter-pressing to be the best playmaker that any team could have. Only once Liverpool became so dominant in possession did the recruitment team decide they needed a player like Thiago to pull the strings from deeper.

Klopp only used one pivot in midfield because of this. The other two midfielders had responsibilities covering their full-back or stepping higher up the pitch in support centrally. With Slot's liking for a double pivot, the lack of players who are best suited to being a pivot could represent an early challenge for Slot to overcome.

Goodbye to Jurgen

The scenes at the end of Jurgen Klopp's last game showed how much Klopp meant to Liverpool. The man had turned doubters into believers, delivered a Champions League, won the first title since 1990, and fought capitalist oil money to somehow challenge the fiscal beast of Manchester City.

Liverpool is a sentimental club in a sentimental city. The manager needs to fit both the club and the city. The fit has often been a past player, but the eras of Houllier, Benitez, and Klopp slightly skewed the idea of what was a "good fit".

For many, the obvious choice to replace Klopp was Xabi Alonso. A beloved former player who had worked a miracle in Leverkusen, and fought the dominance of Bayern Munich, when Alonso said 'no', nothing was clear any more.

The accounts written in this book will not be a blow-by-blow, linear chronology of the events in each game. Instead, we shall explore the tactical aspects of each game and the principles at play. Let's begin!

Game 1 – Ipswich Away – Premier League – 2-0 win

Liverpool 4-3-3/4-2-3-1

Alisson, Trent Alexander-Arnold (Bradley), Quansah (Konate), van Dijk, Robertson (Tsimikas), Gravenberch, Mac Allister, Szoboszlai, Salah, Diaz, Jota (Gakpo)

Ipswich 4-2-3-1

Walton, Tuanzebe (Szmodics), Woolfenden, Greaves, Davis, Morsy, Luongo (Taylor), Burns (Johnson), Chaplin (Harness), Hutchinson, Delap (Al Hamadi)

Scorers – Jota, Salah

After much anticipation, Liverpool kicked off the 2024/25 season with their first competitive game under Arne Slot at newly promoted Ipswich Town. Ciaran McKenna had worked wonders with the team, dragging Ipswich from the doldrums and back into top-level football.

The Pivot Role

The major story that emerged from the opening game of the season related to Liverpool's well-publicised search for a holding midfielder, or number six as the position is so often referred to.

In the summer of 2024, Spain defeated England in the finals of the European Football Championship. At half-time, Spain were forced to withdraw their number six, Rodri, and – at this stage – English hopes were lifted, then quickly squashed by the excellent performance of his replacement, Martin Zubimendi.

After the tournament, a story gained momentum that Liverpool had secured a deal to sign Zubimendi from Real Sociedad. Indeed, it emerged that all that was required was a signature but – for whatever reason – Zubimendi decided not to sign for Liverpool, leaving a bitterly disappointed taste in the mouths of LFC fans.

So, who would play number six? Alexis Mac Allister and Waturo Endo had performed the role for Jurgen Klopp in the 2023/24 season. However, it was quite clear from pre-season that Mac Allister was intended to be used further forward (number eight), and Endo was not able to progress the ball in the manner that Slot wanted.

Missing out on Zubimendi meant that there were question marks over who would play in the position. The answer turned out to be Ryan Gravenberch, the Dutchman who had largely been a rotation option under Klopp.

In the first half against Ipswich, this was not looking to be a success. Liverpool lacked any real passing flow and Gravenberch was not receiving the ball in pockets of space. He was struggling to find the spaces. In the second half, things changed, though, with Gravenberch involved in the first goal scored under Slot…

Liverpool built up inside their own defensive third. A pass came from the right-back area infield to a central area, in line with the D of the penalty box. Gravenberch received on the half-turn and drove Liverpool forward. Trent Alexander-Arnold played a perfect pass in behind the Ipswich defence to Mohamed Salah, and his low cross was tucked home by Diogo Jota. For the remainder of the game, Ryan Gravenberch would occupy pockets of space and receive on the half-turn as Liverpool found their flow and seemed to find their missing number six.

Releasing The Right Side

Fast forward, flowing attacks were notable from Liverpool. This was visible during pre-season, where Liverpool would play a number of short passes in their own defensive third before hitting a longer ball into forwards; the shorter passes being designed to draw the opposition high up the field to create spaces to flow into when attacking. Against Ipswich, the flow was lacking in the first half. Gravenberch finding pockets of space was one transformative factor; the other was the half-time withdrawal of Quansah for Konate.

Quansah had an okay half, but Konate offered Liverpool a route out of the Ipswich Town press. They pressed in an aggressive 4-2-4 shape (as did Liverpool), which Liverpool struggled to play through. Konate pulled wider on the right side, and it was Konate's pass that found Gravenberch for the opening goal. Konate was generally the player who played the release pass out of pressure (inside when it was available but mainly down the line into Salah or a midfield player pulling across… more often than not Szoboszlai). From here, Liverpool were able to find the necessary flowing football that injected *pace* into attacks.

The 3-2 into 2-3 structure that Liverpool use in possession

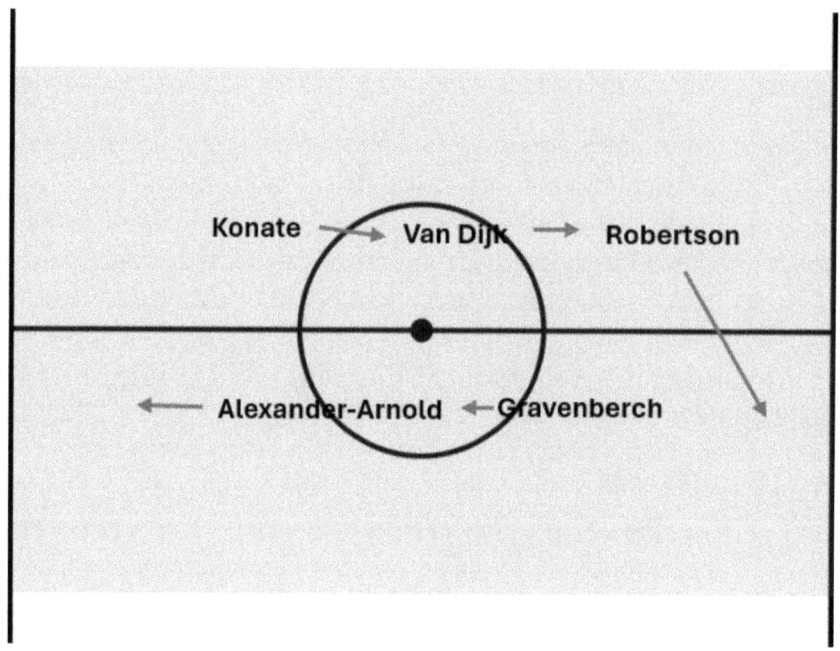

"I don't think our problem in the first half was midfield, our problem is we lost too many duels. A lot had been said about our signings but I saw three or four players coming off the bench and they were already good to play." Slot speaking to TNT Sports

Patterns of Play

Other patterns emerged within the game.

In possession, Liverpool built up in 2-3, 3-2 or 2-4 shape depending on the opposition press. Most common was a "swinging" 3-2/2-3 shape. The opposite-side full-back tucked in close to the central defenders such that when the ball was on the right side, Robertson was alongside Van Dijk and Quansah/Konate. When the ball was on the left side, Alexander-Arnold tucked in higher up, alongside the central midfielders, thus the shape being 3-2 on one side and 2-3 on the other.

Notably, when the ball was in the Ipswich half or final third, the full-backs attacked in different ways. Robertson underlapped aggressively while Alexander-Arnold tucked inside very narrow, sometimes in the number ten position or playing one-two combinations through the middle of the pitch. Robertson underlapped to the by-line, but Alexander-Arnold would be deeper and Szoboszlai drove to the by-line. The Szoboszlai move came as a result of a rotating triangle on the right between Szoboszlai, Alexander-Arnold and Salah.

Szoboszlai's Energy

Szoboszlai used his energy to help create Liverpool's second goal. A long diagonal pass found Salah who passed infield to Szoboszlai who returned the ball to Salah to tuck the ball in at the right-hand near post from six yards out.

The energy of Szoboszlai was also critical to the Liverpool press. As previously alluded to, the shape used was a 4-2-4. The four pressing players were made up of Jota, Salah and Diaz, with Szoboszlai pushing up alongside Jota. Gravenberch and Mac Allister covered the centre but also edged out to their closest flank to assist pressing in those areas. Liverpool pressed more aggressively in the second half than the first, but in general the pressing was far more measured than under Klopp; something that could be said of the performance overall.

Key Points

- Gravenberch shines in the pivot position
- Liverpool used the right side of the pitch to start attacks from their defensive third
- Liverpool used a 3-2 or 2-3 structure in possession
- Szoboszlai's high energy connected attack and defence

Game 2 – Brentford Home – Premier League – 2-0 win

Liverpool 4-2-3-1

Alisson, Alexander-Arnold (Bradley), Konate, van Dijk, Robertson, Gravenberch (Endo), Mac Allister, Salah (Elliott), Szoboszlai, Diaz (Gakpo), Jota (Nunez)

Brentford 4-4-2

Flekken, Ajer, Pinnock, Collins, Roerslev, Lewis-Potter (Damsgaard), Janelt (Onyeka), Norgaard, Jensen (Carvalho), Wissa (Schade), Mbeumo

Scorers – Diaz, Salah

After a successful first competitive game together, Liverpool and Arne Slot faced Brentford at Anfield in their first competitive home fixture. Liverpool once again lined up in the 4-2-3-1/4-3-3 system, with the only change to the starting lineup being Konate replacing Quansah.

Overloads

Brentford lined up in a 4-4-2 system with a clear intention to stay compact and then break out with the pace of Mbeumo and Wissa. The 4-4-2 lining up against 4-2-3-1 creates a midfield overload for Liverpool, but the front pairing asks questions of the two central defenders. Liverpool's preference for a 3-2/2-3 shape when in possession ensures that Liverpool maintained numerical superiority, one of Slot's hallmarks at Feyenoord. In the prior years with Jurgen Klopp in command, he was happy for Liverpool to be 2v2 at the back to get an extra player into midfield or the front line.

In the game against Brentford, Liverpool's build-up shape fluctuated and evolved. Though the shape began in the 3-2/2-3 manner, there were times when a 3-3 was used, with Mac Allister or Szoboszlai creating the additional player in the midfield line. Brentford pressed aggressively in the first half especially and – to counter this – Liverpool deployed the extra player. As the Brentford press became less intense, the build-up became a 3-1 diamond shape. Gravenberch assisting Konate, van Dijk and Robertson. Alexander-Arnold moved into more aggressive attacking areas to receive and offered less assistance in the build-up.

Alexander-Arnold Positioning

Liverpool's shape on the right-hand side is defined by two players: Trent Alexander-Arnold and Mohamed Salah. Alexander-Arnold spends little time outside of the width of the opposition penalty area and a lot of time in a position akin to a central midfielder, sometimes even that of an attacking number 10. Alexander-Arnold possesses exceptional ball-striking ability over a variety of distances, be that crossing, passing or shooting. As such, his career path has taken him away from an overlapping full-back who delivers crosses, and into a player who operates more successfully in the half-space where all of his skills are in play.

Alexander-Arnold's positioning means that Salah is usually the player closest to the touchline on the right side. There are situations where he runs in behind the opposition in central positions, such as the Liverpool second goal against Brentford. An aggressive midfield counter-press ended with Diaz slotting in Salah just to the right of the Brentford goal. Through 1v1 with goalkeeper Flekken, Salah showed great composure to score with a gently flicked curve shot that went over the goalkeeper and bounced into the goal, ever spinning inwards before nestling in the netting.

Salah's wide positioning with the ball situated centrally or on the left side creates opportunities for him 1v1 with the opposition full-back. This gives Salah options. Run at the defender on the outside, a less favoured option but one that is sometimes taken. Cut inside at speed, a favoured option through all of Salah's time at Liverpool. Pass infield or behind. Look for an overlap or underlap. These options bring in the third part of the Liverpool right side, Szoboszlai. It is Szoboszlai who – in the game against Brentford – did much of the underlapping movement on the right side. Szoboszlai is an important part of the dangerous attacking right-side triangle but less definitive than the other two members.

The dynamic on the right side changes when Conor Bradley arrives on the pitch. With Trent Alexander-Arnold not at full fitness (having missed a portion of pre-season due to his summer at the Euros with England), Bradley has come on in both games so far. His involvement is very similar to that of Robertson on the left, explosively underlapping rather than holding outside the box as Alexander-Arnold has.

Passing Combinations

Unsurprisingly, Salah is vital to much of Liverpool's attacking play. He is the target of the release passes from Konate and Alisson that move Liverpool from their defensive third into a state of attacking flow. After three or four short passes, Konate or Alisson will hit a pass into Salah. This might be threaded along the ground or lofted into Salah's chest. Salah will then have a test of strength against the full-back and – when successful – he sets the ball to a supporting player or spins inside to pass. Liverpool attacks are built around short, fast passing. Using one-two passes to play around opponents, setting the ball back to then be punched forward at an angle. Another significant method used by Liverpool players is the one-touch "round the corner" pass that helps maintain or add flow to an attacking move. In many ways, the attacking play of Slot has echoes of Maurizio Sarri at Napoli: short, fast passing designed to lure opponents in, and then create space to flow into. Moving triangles and diamonds are created around the pitch, creating overloads but always looking for opportunities to speed up the attack.

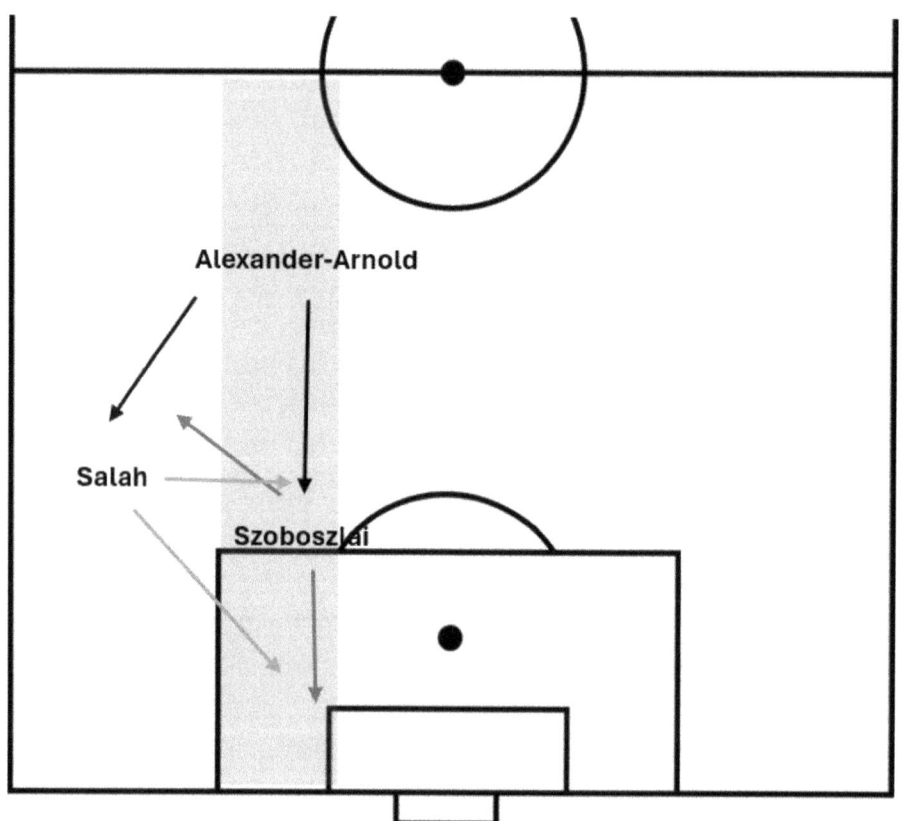

The wide triangle positions and movements between Alexander-Arnold, Salah, and Szoboszlai

Speed of play was a calling card of Klopp's Liverpool, especially on the counter-attack. The opening goal in this match was a throwback to previous seasons as an opposition corner became a dangerous attacking weapon for Liverpool. With the Brentford corner cleared, Jota drove forward from his own half. His pass released Diaz, who drove into the Brentford area and smashed a left-foot shot home. A classic modern Liverpool transition goal showing that the old DNA remains in the team. Slot's teams look for semi-transition moments, where they draw the opponent in to create spaces that look similar to a classic counter-attack. The principles at play in these situations are very similar, which suggests a Slot Liverpool should be proficient when counter-attacking.

"If I'm honest, I think most players are quite used to what we want. But then it has a lot to do with us doing not so many things different to what Jurgen did in the past." Arne Slot speaking to Sky Sports

Key Points
- Slot aimed to have an extra player in and out of possession whenever possible
- Alexander-Arnold positioned in the interior
- Fast passing combinations to play forward

Game 3 – Manchester United – Away – Premier League – 3-0 win

Liverpool 4-2-3-1

Alisson, Alexander-Arnold (Bradley), Konate, van Dijk, Robertson (Tsimikas), Gravenberch, Mac Allister, Szoboszlai, Salah, Diaz (Gakpo), Jota (Nunez)

Manchester United 4-2-3-1

Onana, Mazraoui, de Ligt (Maguire), Martinez, Dalot, Casemiro (Collyer), Mainoo. Fernandes, Garnacho (Diallo), Rashford, Zirkzee (Eriksen)

Scorers – Diaz (2), Salah

A game that should always be one of Liverpool's toughest challenges, and one of the most anticipated rivalries of any season. Last season, an inability to control the transitions cost Liverpool the points and arguably the league title.

Contrasting Pressing

Liverpool's new look 3-2/2-3 shape gives them better "rest defence", protecting against counter-attacks and transitions, and they were able to keep United at arm's length for much of the game. The shape did change on goal kicks, with the full-backs pulled deep. Liverpool used Gravenberch and Mac Allister to build along with the back four and Alisson. A shape of 1-4-2.

With the ball closer to the Manchester United half, the shape was now 3-2 or 2-3, depending on the situation. Slot has said that the shape used is a reflection of the opposition press, and Manchester United's press was somewhat half-hearted, allowing Liverpool's central defenders more time on the ball than against their previous opponents. United had not committed to a high press or a deep block which allowed the Liverpool defenders to slot passes between and through the lines into midfielders to progress the ball downfield securely. Liverpool appeared to be happy to pass into these spaces even when the midfielder receiving was marked, confident that Gravenberch could turn his marker or pass the ball off in one touch.

Liverpool's use of wide release passes was prevalent once more but less successful. Salah was dealt with quite well in the 1v1 situations from the longer release passes into the body, especially in the first half. Liverpool used more release passes on the left than in previous games, but Luis Diaz dribbled into traffic, losing possession. In the second half, Alexander-Arnold moved higher and into the half-space in build-up play, helping Liverpool release down the right side. By that stage, Liverpool had already established a comfortable lead.

Liverpool's pressing shape and Gravenberch jumping to intercept in front of the United midfield

Turnovers

Two first half goals were scored via Manchester United turning the ball over in central midfield. Both were scored by Luis Diaz. Liverpool utilised a strategy of trying to pick the pocket of the Manchester United midfielders. Gravenberch, Mac Allister, van Dijk and Konate were aggressively jumping forward to intercept straight passes into Manchester United midfielders who were not on the half-turn. The positioning of the front line of pressers discouraged passes to Manchester United's full-backs, who were high and wide, in the shadow of the Liverpool wingers with an uninvitingly small passing lane available. For the first goal, Gravenberch pounced to intercept. Driving forward, he found Salah overlapping, and Salah stood up the cross with his right foot to the far post for an unmarked Diaz to head home.

It was Diaz pressing from behind that set in motion Liverpool's second goal. Another midfield turnover. Casemiro attempted to turn but was faced with Mac Allister in front of him as Diaz swooped from behind. Mac Allister found Salah who then provided a wonderful swerved pass with the outside of the foot to Diaz in the United penalty area to sweep in a low finish.

"We always want to press high. That's what Jurgen did. That's what we try to continue. And we scored a few goals from a high press – [including] one disallowed." Arne Slot speaking to Sky Sports

Salah Contributions

Although Salah may not have won the battle with his full-back in the 1v1 and release pass stakes, he came away with two fantastic assists and the third goal of the game. The eulogising of Salah rightly continues as his statistics pile up; if Liverpool score, it seems that Salah must be involved in some way. This is the beauty of having a player like Salah; even when he doesn't appear to be having his best game, he can find a way to score or create. Salah's goal early in the second half came from another midfield turnover, this time Mac Allister jumping to press Mainoo. The pass from Mac Allister found Szoboszlai. With United's fullbacks so high and wide in their build-up, Liverpool were 4v2 with United central defenders. Salah was free to the right and he flashed a left-foot finish low into the near post.

Dynamism

Szoboszlai almost scored a fourth for Liverpool but took too long to get his shot away when in a brilliant position in the middle of the United box. The energy Szoboszlai has shown in being able to be a part of the front four, pressing at one end and then transitioning rapidly to recover and defend his own box, has been eye-catching. This dynamic running power has helped Liverpool to press and regain structure as a feature of dealing with opposition transitions. A structure that focuses on ensuring there is always numerical superiority plus dynamic energy has controlled transitional moments so far this season.

Such dynamism was less evident from the United midfield. Both teams lined up in 4-2-3-1 shape, which should be an equal match-up. Yet Liverpool controlled the midfield and gained transition in part due to the difference between Szoboszlai and Bruno Fernandes when their respective teams were out of possession. Fernandes is a wonderfully gifted attacker, but his work rate and commitment to filling defensive gaps did not match the levels of his Liverpool counterpart. In build-up play, Bruno positioned himself high upfield, away from the ball, unable or unwilling to help prevent the turnovers.

Easing Off?

Manchester United created a few opportunities, showing some potential defensive flaws in Liverpool. Their two best opportunities came from crosses delivered via the right side. For the first opportunity, van Dijk and Robertson managed to end up in the wrong slots, van Dijk at full-back and Robertson at centre-back. The second chance also involved the pairing, with the cross clearing van Dijk and Robertson not reacting at all. The scoreline was comfortably in Liverpool's favour by the time these chances arrived, but the relationship between van Dijk and Robertson did show a crack or two that future opponents could exploit.

Key Points

- Liverpool's structured press was in stark contrast to the half-hearted Manchester United press
- Manchester United turned over possession regularly and Liverpool punished them with swift counter-attacks
- Salah made key contributions on a regular basis
- The Liverpool midfield was far more dynamic, highlighted by Szoboszlai
- Liverpool seemed to ease up a little with the game wrapped up

Game 4 – Nottingham Forest – Home – Premier League – 1-0 loss

Liverpool 4-2-3-1

Alisson, Alexander-Arnold, Konate (Jones), van Dijk, Robertson (Tsimikas), Gravenberch, Mac Allister (Bradley), Salah, Szoboszlai, Diaz (Gakpo), Jota (Nunez)

Forest 4-2-3-1

Sels, Aina, Milenkovic, Murillo, Moreno (Williams), Yates, Ward-Prowse, Dominguez (Hudson-Odoi), Gibbs-White (Morato), Anderson (Elanga), Wood (Jota Silva)

Scorers – Hudson-Odoi

With three wins out of three, and a victory against their fierce Old Trafford-dwelling rivals, a Liverpool victory was expected in a home fixture against a Forest side who were considered by many as relegation candidates.

The reality was that, by the end of the 90 minutes, Forest and Nuno Espirito Santo had produced a masterclass in defensive patience and waiting for the moment to strike.

Early Opportunities Not Taken

The game could have been very different had Liverpool converted opportunities in the first half. Goals change games, as the saying goes, and this is never more true than when two sides have such contrasting game plans. The classic defence vs attack face-off.

Diaz hit the post following a successful counter-press, cutting inside and striking the near post. Jota managed to get between two defenders and squeeze an effort on goal from nigh on six yards out, with the ball seeking out goalkeeper Matz Sels' gloves. Sels then contrived to almost drop a simple catch through his own legs and into the net, but he recovered to prevent an embarrassing own goal. These three moments could all have seen the result end very differently.

So, how were Forest able to prevent Liverpool breaking through?

Forest's Disciplined Shape

They set themselves up in a very disciplined shape when out of possession, and the shape shifted a little depending on Liverpool's movements. In terms of personnel, the system was 4-5-1, although the two players switched roles at times. Morgan Gibbs-White would sometimes step up to make a two-player block at the top end of the shape. From midfield, Ryan Yates would drop in and act as an extra central defender. This meant that – defensively – Forest moved from 4-5-1 to 5-4-1 to 5-3-2. They steadfastly refused to step out of their basic shape, with little to no pressing, asking Liverpool to find a way through.

Gibbs-White and Wood were important in slowing Liverpool's build-up. They created a micro game within a game: a 3v2 with the Liverpool build-up. Ryan Gravenberch was shadowed closely by Gibbs-White, preventing him from turning or playing forward with any ease. Wood blocked a passing line from one central defender to the other. If van Dijk had possession, Wood prevented a simple pass to Konate. With Gibbs-White making Gravenberch an unappealing option in this situation, Liverpool struggled to progress the ball at a fast enough tempo to tempt the Forest players out of their defensive shape.

Forest's Full-Backs Shut Down Salah and Diaz

When Liverpool have been unable to play through the centre in previous games, they used the sides and wings as an out pass. Salah and Diaz have been able to find success against their full-backs most of the time. Against Forest, Moreno marshalled Salah fantastically and Aina suffocated Diaz. Neither Liverpool wide man was able to dominate their 1v1s or sufficiently link play to create the desired forward flow, another reason why Liverpool attacks lacked tempo.

Change of Shape

In an effort to change the flow of the game, Arne Slot took off Alexis Mac Allister to push Trent Alexander-Arnold into midfield. This had little positive impact. Not long after the change, Forest produced a sweeping counter-attack from right to left. Hudson-Odoi dribbled in from the left side to the edge of the box, then planted a right foot shot in off the far post. Alisson could only watch the ball travel. Perhaps Conor Bradley could have been tighter to prevent the shot, but it was an excellent finish.

The goal prompted further changes from Slot, into a system that looked classically Dutch. Liverpool played with three defenders, two of whom were fullbacks. There was a three-player midfield of Jones, Gravenberch, and Alexander-Arnold. Szoboszlai was just ahead of them. Salah and Gakpo were positioned in wide areas, and Darwin Nunez was up front. There was a form of double diamond occurring: Szoboszlai at the upper tip of the tight midfield diamond and at the bottom of the wide attacking diamond. The shape was expansive and also put Liverpool close to a man-to-man match-up with Forest. Unfortunately, the system looked disjointed and under-practiced. Forest were able to see the game out with few late scares.

"We have to find better options than what we found today with the low block of Nottingham Forest." Arne Slot speaking to BBC Sport

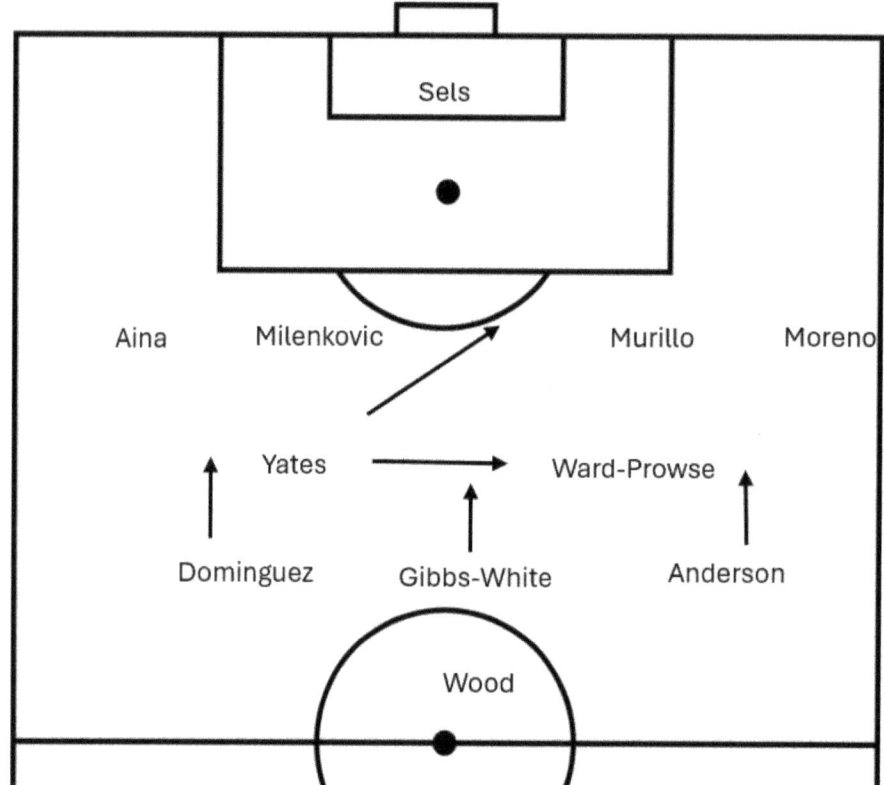

Nottingham Forest's out-of-possession shape(s) switching from 4-2-3-1 to 5-4-1

Key Points

- Take your chances when you are top. It is inevitable that when you don't, you allow the opposition into the game and they will eventually punish you
- Forest used a smart 3v2 game to nullify Gravenberch
- Forest used Yates as an auxiliary central defender
- Forest's full-backs nullified the Liverpool wingers
- Slot tried to change the shape to a classically Dutch system, which felt under-practised and was ineffective

Game 5 – AC Milan – Away – Champions League – 3-1 win

Liverpool 4-2-3-1

Alisson. Alexander-Arnold (Gomez), Konate, van Dijk, Tsimikas, Gravenberch, Mac Allister (Endo), Salah (Chiesa), Szoboszlai, Gakpo (Diaz), Jota (Nunez)

AC Milan 4-2-3-1

Maignan (Torriani), Calabria (Emerson Royal), Tomori (Gabbia), Pavlovic, Hernandez, Fofana, Loftus-Cheek (Abraham), Pulisic, Reijnders, Rafael Leao, Morata (Okafor)

Scorers – Pulisic, Konate, van Dijk, Szoboszlai

A visit to a club of AC Milan's stature in the Champions League is a tough task for any team, let alone a team with a new manager on the back of a surprise home defeat.

Special Treatment For Leao

Milan struck after just three minutes. Portuguese winger Rafael Leao had already menaced the Liverpool defence on the Milan left in the first minute, before Pulisic got in on goal on the Milan right to run into space and fire across Alisson into the bottom corner. Milan played through Liverpool again and again for the first 15 minutes, punching passes through the 4-2-4 pressing structure.

Liverpool's four across the front were quite passive, a flat wall rather than a group of pressing players. In the centre, Mac Allister and Gravenberch were being pulled out of position because of the threat posed by Theo Hernandez from left-back and Leao from the left wing. Alexander-Arnold marked Leao, and Gravenberch had to come out of the middle to mark Hernandez. Slot changed this setup and it stifled Milan from the 17th minute onwards. Konate moved across to mark Leao with Alexander-Arnold pushing onto Hernandez. Now Gravenberch and Mac Allister could cover the centre of the pitch and Milan struggled to play out of their defensive third with penetrative passes.

Leao had been identified as the biggest threat to Liverpool. Other than the first-minute breakaway, and the very last minute, where he cut inside and shot against the post, the Liverpool defence kept him at bay extremely well. Alexander-Arnold did well, but he had ample support. Konate was always within distance to cover or apply pressure, as was Gravenberch, who came across to engage when Leao began an offensive dribble.

Liverpool's right-side passing patterns

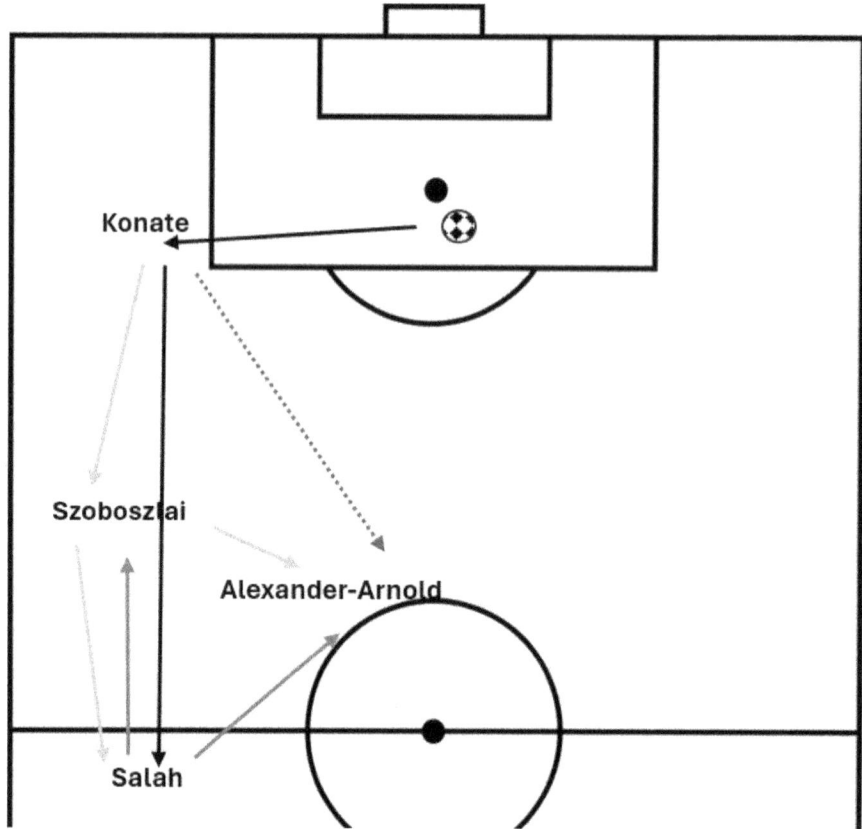

Line Breaking and Diagonal Passes

Once Liverpool asserted themselves on the game, many of their attacking successes came from forward passes and diagonals. One-touch forward passes helped Liverpool to find their forward-flowing football. When Milan committed players to press Liverpool's goal kicks, the one-touch passes out by Konate into Salah were a success, triggering fluid attacking moves. Those one-touch forward passes from midfield did turn over the ball to Milan early on, but these passes also broke defensive lines to progress play into attacking areas.

Diagonal passes into wide players have been a hallmark of Liverpool's attacking play for many seasons. Two players dominate in this area. From left to right, Virgil van Dijk strikes diagonals into Salah or Alexander-Arnold. From right to left, Alexander-Arnold strikes the diagonals into the left-back or left winger. One such diagonal created the free-kick that Liverpool equalised from, and both first-half goals came from set-pieces, with Liverpool crowding the six-yard box and Mike

Maignan, the Milan goalkeeper. Konate was the beneficiary from Alexander-Arnold's free kick, and van Dijk from Tsimikas' corner.

Right-Hand Side Forward Flow

When Liverpool built out from the back, it was noticeable that Alexander-Arnold was positioned narrow, close to the central defenders, while Tsimikas positioned himself closer to the touchline. Szoboszlai provided extra width on the right along with Salah, which was especially prominent when looking for fast-flow football, as the release pass into Salah often resulted in a combination with Szoboszlai. This positioning also enabled Alexander-Arnold to attack the half-space.

Wide Strikers

Arne Slot uses his wingers in a very aggressive manner. There are times that the movement from the central striker and number ten will both be towards the ball to help with build-up play. At those moments, the wingers are Liverpool's furthest players forward, acting as wide strikers running in behind. Liverpool's structure becomes quite fluid, especially as their out-of-possession structure is 4-2-4. At times, Liverpool will appear to have four forwards; at other times, they will appear to have four central midfielders. This fluidity pulls defenders out of position and creates scoring opportunities for wide players, which helps explain why the wingers are the top scorers at present.

Luis Diaz had looked extremely sharp and dangerous, particularly when punishing Manchester United. He was rotated out for Cody Gakpo, who had an outstanding game, dribbling with speed at the Milan defence. He showed a willingness to dribble outside, as well as to cut inside to shoot. Gakpo created the game-settling third goal. Following a Gravenberch interception and quick forward pass, Liverpool found themselves breaking away 3v2. Szoboszlai smartly passed – one-touch – into the forward run of Gakpo before he drove into space and clipped the ball left-footed across the six-yard box. Szoboszlai continued his run from the centre circle and guided the ball home. Another great example of the running power of Szoboszlai capped off with a finish. The goal was possible because of the high, wide positioning of Gakpo and the running power of Szoboszlai.

Key Points
- Slot shows a willingness to adapt for the opposition by giving special treatment to Leao and backing up Alexander-Arnold
- Liverpool used more long passes, especially diagonals
- Liverpool used the right side to release from their defensive third, picking out Salah to combine with Szoboszlai
- Under Slot, the wingers are the real strikers in the team

Game 6 – Bournemouth – Home – Premier League – 3-0 win

Liverpool 4-2-3-1

Kelleher, Alexander-Arnold, Konate, van Dijk, Robertson, Gravenberch, Mac Allister, Salah, Szoboszlai (Jones), Diaz (Gakpo), Nunez (Chiesa)

Bournemouth 4-2-3-1

Kepa, Araujo (Smith), Zabarnyi, Huijsen, Kerkez, Cook, Christie (Scott), Semenyo (Sinisterra), Kluivert (Ouattara), Tavernier, Evanilson (Unal)

Scorers – Diaz (2), Nunez

From the glamour of Milan to the bread and butter of a home win against Bournemouth in the Premier League. The basic statistics of the game suggest Bournemouth matched Liverpool for most of the game. Both teams had 19 shots, though Liverpool had 13 on target to Bournemouth's 6. Liverpool had an expected goals of 2 to Bournemouth's 1.11, according to FBref. The stats suggest that the game was far closer than a seemingly comfortable 3-0 win.

Bournemouth Carry Threats

Bournemouth threatened in the early stages of the game and then again after Liverpool had their three-goal cushion. Bournemouth had an early goal disallowed as they counter-attacked the Liverpool defence following a midfield turnover. Though Liverpool had enough numbers back, the run and cross found Semenyo six yards out to finish. Fortunately, for Liverpool, the goal was ruled out. Late in the game, Kelleher tipped over a powerful shot from a tight angle. From a corner, Bournemouth hit the crossbar and the rebound struck a defender before ricocheting towards goal, and Kelleher reacted superbly to keep the ball out. Bournemouth were certainly worth a goal, but Liverpool were deserving of their three strikes.

Konate The Distributor

The goals all came within 11 minutes of each other, with goals one and two just two minutes apart. Liverpool have already developed a habit of scoring goals in bunches. Against Ipswich, the goals were in the 60th and 65th minutes. Against Manchester United, strikes one and two were just seven minutes apart. All three goals against Bournemouth involved Ibrahima Konate, underlying his status as a key distributor in the games played so far.

Diaz's opening goal owed much to a goalkeeping error from Kepa. Konate played a long ball behind the Bournemouth defence, and Diaz ran onto the ball from the left to control it centrally outside the box. In what could only have been a moment of panic, Kepa rushed from the goal, making it a simple matter for Diaz to take the ball around the now-stranded goalkeeper and stroke the ball into an unguarded net.

Goals two and three were perfect examples of Liverpool using the right-side release pass to combine and score. Konate passed from the right-back area into Salah near the halfway line. His one-touch pass inside set Alexander-Arnold sprinting into space. The defence retreated as Alexander-Arnold's dribble brought him towards the centre of the penalty area, 20 yards from goal. Diaz moved to the left of the area, while Szoboszlai broke forward, drawing the attention of the full-back away from Diaz. Alexander-Arnold passed to Diaz to slide a left-foot finish under Kepa.

"They were really good finishes but it is also important [to look at] what led to the finish. Bournemouth were really aggressive, so [Ibrahima] Konate understood a ball in behind was a good one to take. For the second goal, Trent [Alexander-Arnold] made a good run with the ball. Luis finished both off really well." Arne Slot speaking to BBC Sport

Nunez scored the third after combining with Salah. He received a long ball from Konate wide on the right close to halfway, where he and Salah had switched positions (Salah tucked inside and Nunez closer to the touchline). Konate's long pass found the head of Nunez, then Salah played a one-touch pass to a sprinting Nunez. Nunez dribbled into the box, slowed down the defender, then cut inside onto his left foot, smashing a shot into the far right corner.

Press Baiting

In every game so far this season, Liverpool have sought to play short passes against opposition presses (except for games when there has been no press). Liverpool would ideally like to play line-breaking passes into advanced players, such as Szoboszlai in the ten position or a striker dropping short, as Jota often has. The short, press-baiting passes have rarely succeeded in central areas. From full-back areas, and especially Konate-angled ones, central passes have broken the wide press infield, while the longer pass down the line has released Liverpool into wide areas. Both passes begin fast flow attacks, injecting speed into the play. The line pass has been far more common and more successful.

Liverpool Beat The Bournemouth Press

Bournemouth's presses were aggressive, pushing five or six players onto the build-up. There was no press on Kelleher. When the ball was at his feet, the press seemed to freeze. In these moments, Liverpool might have been stuck but the Bournemouth press was in 50-50 positions, trying to pick off passing lanes and impact more than one player at a time. There were three escape routes. Konate hitting the forward line, an inside pass from the full-back area to find a central midfielder, or a switch from right to left to Robertson. Liverpool were not always successful in their escapes from the pressure, with Bournemouth able to regain possession; however, they could not punish Liverpool.

Liverpool's Quality In Midfield

As the game progressed, Liverpool grew more confident and fluent in possession. They were also able to change tempo, switching from slow, studs-on-the-ball, low tempo into fast-moving triangles. It was said that when the Hungarians came to Wembley in 1953, England could not keep up with their moving triangles. In the middle third, Liverpool used moving triangles to pass their way out of tight areas and around opponents. Vital to this were the midfield trio of Gravenberch, Mac Allister and Szoboszlai. Each brought something different, with their own skill set. Szoboszlai used sharp dribbling skills to extricate himself from tight situations. Gravenberch's ability to turn with the ball and glide past opponents has been a great asset in Liverpool's attacking play. Mac Allister's one-touch passing around corners added flow to the triangles. All passed and moved quickly and were not afraid to pass ahead of teammates so they could surge forward.

Curtis Jones came on for 30 minutes and put in a performance just as accomplished as those of his midfield colleagues. Jones is a technically accomplished midfielder who passes crisply and cleanly. Importantly, he is comfortable in possession under pressure, with excellent tight control and the ability to shield the ball. Jones would appear to be the style of player well suited to playing in a possession-based team.

Key Points

- Liverpool are not perfect; Bournemouth created opportunities at Anfield
- In the early stages of the season, Konate was vital to Liverpool's attacking from deep
- Slot wants his team to use short passes to bait the press and create space to attack in behind

Game 7 – West Ham – Home – EFL Cup – 5-1 win

Liverpool 4-2-3-1/4-4-2

Kelleher, Bradley, Quansah, Gomez, Tsimikas (Robertson), Endo (Morton), Jones, Chiesa (Salah), Jota (Mac Allister), Gakpo, Nunez

West Ham 4-2-3-1

Fabianski, Coufal, Todibo, Kilman, Cresswell. Alvarez, Soucek (Paqueta), Bowen (Kudus), Soler (Irving), Summerville, Ings (Antonio)

Scorers – Jota (2), Salah, Gakpo (2), Quansah (og)

Although this was Arne Slot's first venture into domestic cup competitions and the Carabao Cup, he showed an immediate understanding of how the competition works. Rotate the squad, experiment a little with the team shape, and make it through to the next round.

Change of System

Liverpool changed their attacking shape against West Ham. The lineup featured both Jota and Nunez, two players who had been used in the central striker role in the 4-2-3-1 shape. Lining them both up together was a shift towards a 4-4-2 system, though Jota was more withdrawn than Nunez. The change of formation didn't impact the press shape, as Liverpool had pressed with a wall of four anyway. Their pressing focus showed an attempt to be aggressive when regaining possession in West Ham's full-back areas. At one point, Liverpool created a 5v4 overload in their favour when pressing, and Liverpool had success regaining possession in these zones.

In possession, the Liverpool shape was closer to 2-4-4, especially in West Ham's half. Without Alexander-Arnold and Szoboszlai, the system became more obviously symmetrical. There are times in the 4-2-3-1 when Szoboszlai pushes up alongside the striker, but having Jota and Nunez together meant that – more often than not – two forwards were very close to each other, especially in a sustained build-up. When West Ham's defensive shape was less settled and still in a partial state of transition, there was more licence for the two strikers to depart from their central positions. On the right side, Conor Bradley performed a more similar, dynamic role to Kostas or Robertson at left-back. Alexander-Arnold generally held a position in a half-space or even tucked inside very narrow. Bradley underlapped aggressively, just as the left-backs have done.

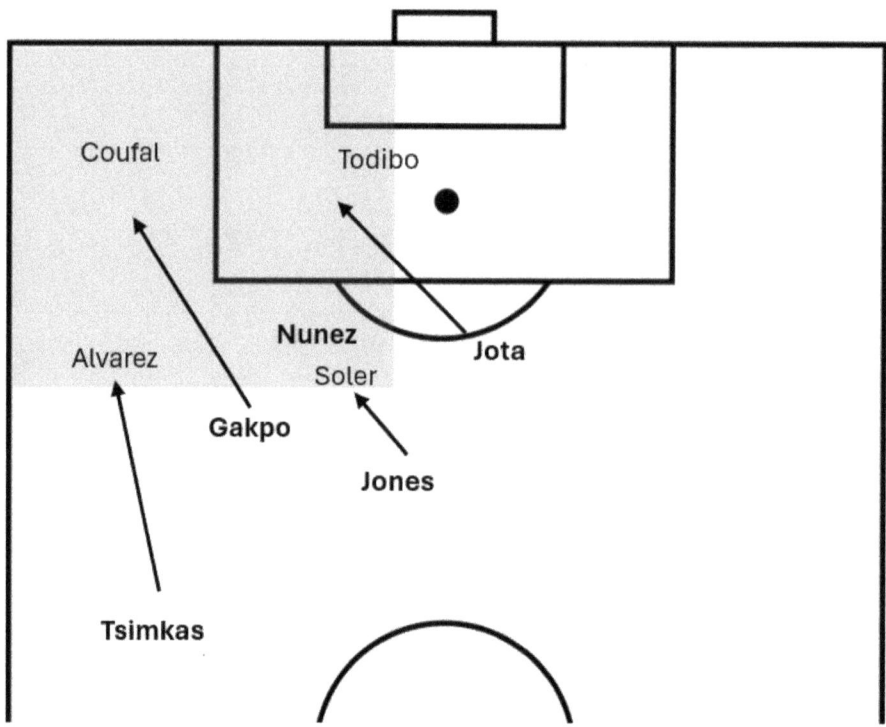
Liverpool pressing aggressively in wide areas

"What pleased me most is that, even if a lot of new players come in, they don't come in and try to have a good individual performance. They tried to work really hard for the team." Arne Slot on BBC Sport

Nonetheless, the full-back roles performed more familiar functions when building up on their own side of the halfway line. The 3-2/2-3 shape was maintained by a full-back staying alongside the central defenders while the other full-back pushed up. Arne Slot's intention to play shorter, quicker passes and bait the press was maintained. Having numbers in such positions also meant that should possession be given away, the likelihood of a counter-attack that overloaded the Liverpool defence remained small.

Jones On Ball Strengths

West Ham did not press the Liverpool back line with real aggression or intent; the Liverpool defenders were allowed plenty of time on the ball. Once more, it was the use of around-the-corner passes and one-twos that injected pace into attacking moves. Wataru Endo started this fixture, and was very secure in possession and won a good number of headers, but he is risk-averse and rather than adding tempo into attacking moves, he would often look to pass sideways or backwards. This 'safety first' style has a place, but it illustrates why Liverpool looked at other options in the defensive midfield position.

Endo's partner in midfield seemed to be able to find the balance between playing safe and taking risks. Curtis Jones was in the starting lineup, and he was outstanding. The dribbling ability he displays draws in multiple opponents, yet Jones seems able to release the ball, rarely turning over possession. The great advantage of having attracted opponents in is that this will mean others are free to receive in more space. Liverpool's second goal involved a Jones dribble in the West Ham half that saw four players come towards him, enabling Jota to run in behind. Once Jones found a nutmeg pass into Jota's run, the position to finish from was an excellent one.

Gakpo Cutting In

It was Cody Gakpo who fed Curtis Jones prior to the magnetic dribble. Gakpo had been a threat to the West Ham defence all game, looking exceedingly sharp with his movement with and without the ball. Gakpo had run behind the West Ham defence following sharp one-two combinations to create the opening goal. Late in the game, he twice dribbled inside to drive right-foot shots home and polish off the 5-1 scoreline. The score flattered Liverpool a little as, at 2-1, West Ham introduced Antonio and Paqueta, who threatened to find an equaliser.

Antonio Troubles Liverpool

Antonio has been a thorn in Liverpool's side for several seasons. The speed and strength on show stretched Gomez and Quansah, and they struggled to contain him. Could similar players be a threat to Liverpool defensively as the season continues? In general, players with these physical attributes will fall into the category often categorised as "a handful". The mitigation for the Liverpool defence is that, after rotation, Gomez and Quansah might not quite be at full speed and, with an eye on future fixtures, Konate and van Dijk are not lacking in the physical departments.

Just as West Ham were building momentum, Liverpool brought on Salah and Mac Allister, then came Alvarez picking up two quick yellow cards. Within minutes, Salah had struck a third, taking all the momentum out of West Ham, and allowing Liverpool to pick them off for a deceptively easy victory.

Key Points

- Slot has quickly learned to use the League Cup to rotate and experiment
- Bradley and Alexander-Arnold play the right-back role quite differently.

- Curtis Jones provides a different option in midfield. A technical dribbler with an eye for a pass.
- Gakpo showed his ability to cut inside and shoot with power and accuracy

Game 8 – Wolves – Away – Premier League – 2-1 win

Liverpool 4-2-3-1

Alisson, Alexander-Arnold, Konate, van Dijk, Robertson (Gomez), Gravenberch, Mac Allister, Szoboszlai (Jones), Salah, Diaz (Gakpo), Jota

Wolves 4-1-4-1

Johnstone, Semedo, Bueno (Doyle), Toti, Ait-Nouri, Andre, Cunha, Lemina, Joao Gomes, Bellegarde (Forbs), Strand Larsen (Hee-Chan)

Scorers – Ait-Nouri, Konate, Salah

Wolves hadn't started the season in great style, meaning Liverpool came to Molineux as heavy favourites. For the first half hour of the game, however, Liverpool fell below that expectation, with Wolves proving to be the better team and getting into promising positions time after time.

Double Width and Playing Out From The Back

Wolves created overloads in wide areas, pushing their full-backs high and wide while Andre dropped from his central midfield position between the central defenders. This created a three-player build-up and double width with the full-backs and wingers. Though Wolves got themselves into threatening positions, they created very little, but they did starve Liverpool of meaningful possession.

Liverpool's press against the Wolves build-up had mixed results. The press was bypassed or played around regularly in the first 30 minutes, but Wolves did give the ball away a few times. The risk versus reward proved to be too weighted towards risk, and Wolves decided to play long from their defensive third around the half-hour mark. Liverpool dominated the first and second balls, and Wolves rarely established consistently threatening field positions for the rest of the game. Though Diaz and Salah adjusted their positioning to better cover the passes into wide areas, the clear choice made by Wolves essentially led to them playing themselves out of the game more decisively than any of the actions taken by Slot and Liverpool.

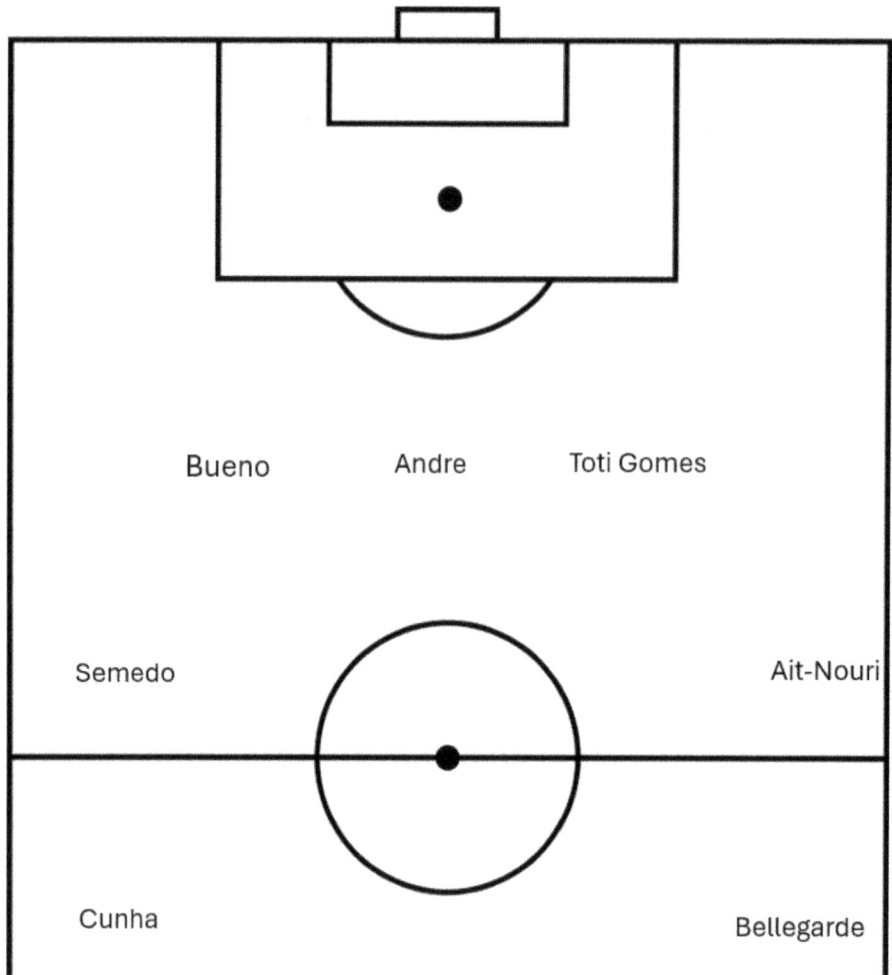
Wolves' use of width to stretch Liverpool

Attacks From The Left

There was little attacking threat from Liverpool in the first half. What there was came on the Wolves left with Robertson overlapping and underlapping aggressively. Dominik Szoboszlai missed a brilliant chance six yards out after a Robertson overlap and cross. The half-volley from the middle of the goal struck Wolves goalkeeper Johnstone's shins and went behind for a corner. Half-volleys are not the simplest skills to execute, but this was an outstanding chance, and adds to a growing list of misses for Szoboszlai. While his mix of technical quality and high energy is important to the Liverpool playing style, it could just be a matter of time before the misses start to be costly.

Diogo Jota crossed from the left side to enable Ibrahim Konate to rise and head home just before half-time. In previous games, the Liverpool attacking threat had focused on the right, but Wolves had kept Salah and Alexander-Arnold quiet in the first half.

Second Half Adjustments

In the second half, Liverpool adjusted by pushing both full-backs very wide in attack against Wolves' narrow defensive block. Jota came deep into midfield to provide the overload, and Liverpool had control of both the possession and the game as a whole. Liverpool had the game in their hands but then made a series of errors in defence that gifted Wolves an equaliser. Robertson slid into a challenge, which ricocheted into the path of a Wolves forward. Konate covered the path of the ball, but a miscommunication between Alisson and Konate meant that neither of them dealt with the ball. The resulting scramble was jabbed in by Alt-Nouri.

Within five minutes, though, Liverpool went back into the lead with Salah blasting home a penalty kick. Another Liverpool cross had created problems for the defenders and, as Jota looked set to attack the cross, he was hauled to the ground.

Key Points

- Liverpool struggled against Wolves' wide overloads
- Wolves played out from the back and dominated the first half hour. Once they stopped playing out from the back, they lost domination
- Liverpool threatened on their left in the first half with Robertson overlapping
- Slot made changes at half-time that improved the Liverpool performance and pushed Wolves' full-backs deeper, lessening their ability to overload in wide areas

Game 9 – Bologna – Home – Champions League – 2-0 win

Liverpool 4-2-3-1

Alisson, Alexander-Arnold (Bradley), Konate, van Dijk, Robertson (Tsimikas), Gravenberch, Mac Allister, Szoboszlai (Jones), Salah, Diaz (Gakpo), Nunez (Jota)

Bologna 4-1-4-1

Skorupski, Posch, Beukema (Casale), Lucumi, Miranda, Freuler (Fabbian), Orsolini, Urbanski (Aebischer), Moro, Ndoye (Iling-Junior), Dallinga (Castro)

Scorers – Mac Allister, Salah

For the second time in the 2024/25 season, Liverpool faced Italian opposition. Bologna were the surprise package of 2023/24 under Thiago Motta, such that Motta's reward was the Juventus job (and Vincenzo Italiano), charged with picking up where he left off. Under Motta, the Bologna style was recognised for patient short passing.

Bologna Use The Goalkeeper To Switch

Bologna were excellent in possession against Liverpool, particularly in their defensive third, using the goalkeeper as the conduit to play from one side of the pitch to the other. Consistently, on the right side, a triangle was made, which resulted in the ball passing into the goalkeeper and then out to the left, where another triangle awaited. From this position, Bologna could combine with one- or two-touch passes to play forward or drive forward with the ball at their feet.

Aggressive Bologna Press

As well as posing Liverpool questions with their build-up, Bologna forced Liverpool to play long with their aggressive pressing. Man-to-man marking blocked many Liverpool passing options (rather than the mixed style of blocking lines and then pouncing upon the pass that Liverpool and others use), and Bologna tightly marked the man before the ball had even arrived. The strategy put Liverpool off from passing into marked players, resulting in overuse of Alisson and long passes behind the Bologna full-backs that were dealt with quite easily.

"It wasn't an easy one, in my opinion Bologna made it difficult. Similar to Atalanta – man-mark all over the pitch. Wait for the right moment if you play through, completely open – it was many times. The last pass could have been better." Arne Slot speaking to TNT Sports

Jota's movement to overload the midfield and push Szoboszlai into the centre-forward position

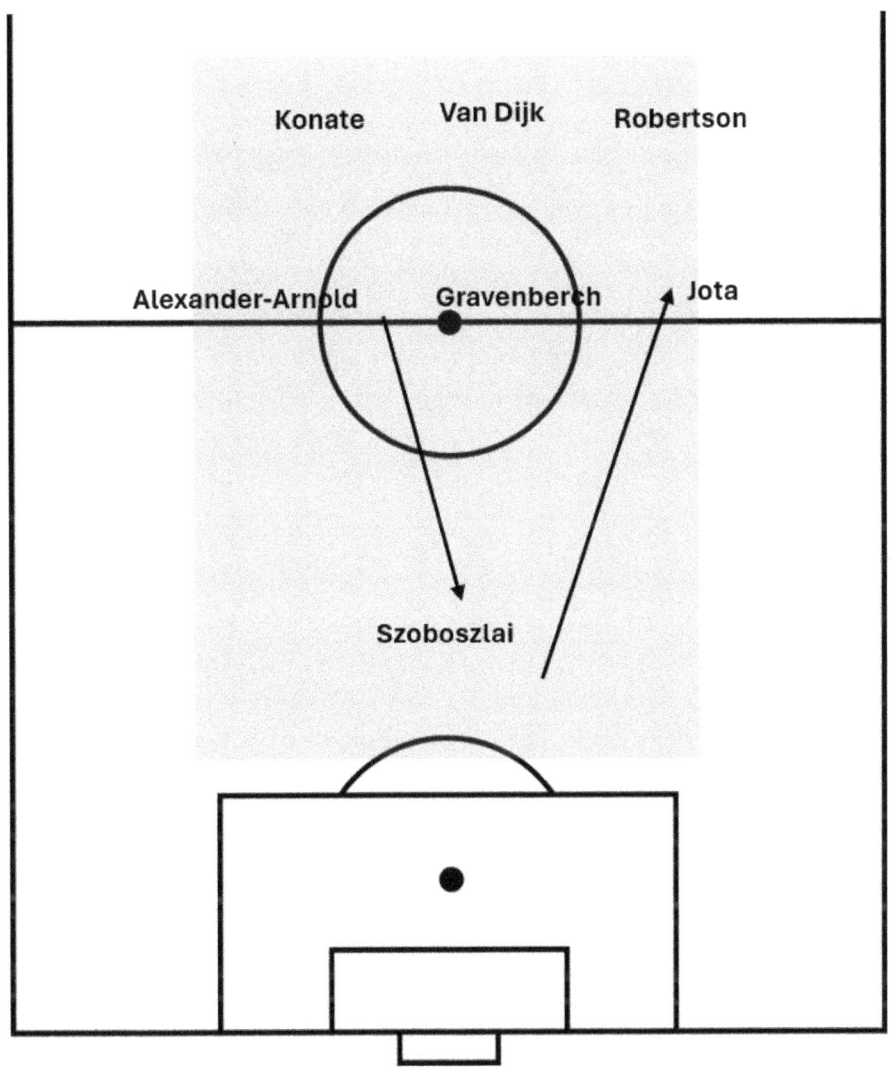

Slot Solving Problems

Darwin Nunez started the game and was positioned up against the Bologna defensive line, rarely coming short. Staying high allowed Bologna to mark man-to-man more easily. In the second half, Liverpool scored their second goal of the game. The move began with a Virgil van Dijk pass forward that picked out Diogo Jota, who was completely free next to the centre spot. He turned and drove forward, collapsing the Bologna defence enough for Szoboszlai and Salah to get free. Jota found Szoboszlai, who swiftly moved the ball onto Salah on the right, creating a 1v1. Salah cut inside as Alexander-Arnold overlapped, and the overlap drew attention away from Salah, giving him just a little extra time to fire his shot into the goalkeeper's top right corner.

Gravenberch Breaking The Press

Jota's movement alone was not enough for Liverpool to break the Bologna press. Ryan Gravenberch's ability to turn under pressure helped Liverpool negate the man-to-man marking. Such a marking style can be very effective, but players who can eliminate opponents in 1v1s can destroy the system and create panic. Suddenly, a player is free and asks players who are marking their man to solve the problem of whether to deal with the man on the ball or stay with their man away from the ball. Gravenberch's use of his hips, outside-of-the-foot turns, no-touch turns, and croqueta moves stir memories of a fully fit Thiago opening up the game for Liverpool. Timing can be everything in football, and one can only imagine how impressive Thiago would be in an Arne Slot Liverpool team!

Pass and Move

When Liverpool progressed into the middle third and higher their confidence to play short combinations was evident. Alexis Mac Allister was outstanding with one-touch passing, both short and long. His close combinations with Szoboszlai broke the man marking higher up the pitch. Mac Allister opened the scoring after his one-touch forward pass found Nunez on the edge of the box. After passing, Mac Allister continued into the box, Alexander-Arnold crossed with his left foot, an inswinging ball that dropped inside the six-yard box. Mac Allister had a simple finish as Liverpool players queued up to score.

Playing In Spells

Worryingly for Liverpool, they continue to play in spells. The first 30 minutes were difficult but Liverpool had control. The next 15 minutes had Bologna causing Liverpool all sorts of problems as the defence lost organisation and concentration. Liverpool then regained control of the game, but in the last ten minutes, Bologna were able to apply pressure and get threatening shots away. Bologna ended the game with more shots than Liverpool, the majority of which came in two periods. Liverpool are winning games, but they continue to have periods where they switch off.

Key Points

- Liverpool were caused problems by Bologna's man-to-man press
- Slot solved the problem of being pressed by switching in Jota to drop off the front line and overload the midfield

- Bologna made it hard for Liverpool to press by using their goalkeeper to switch play
- Gravenberch broke the Bologna press with his ability to turn away from his man-marker
- Liverpool's midfield passed and moved to progress the ball and themselves forward
- The pattern of lulls in performance within games continues

Game 10 – Crystal Palace – Away – Premier League – 1-0 win

Liverpool 4-2-3-1

Alisson (Jaros), Alexander-Arnold, Konate, van Dijk, Tsimikas (Robertson), Gravenberch, Mac Allister (Szoboszlai), Jones (Endo), Salah (Diaz), Gakpo, Jota

Crystal Palace 3-4-3

Henderson, Lacroix, Guehi, Chalobah (Kamada), Munoz (Clyne), Wharton (Hughes), Lerma, Mitchell (Mateta). Sarr, Nketiah, Eze

Scorers – Jota

Crystal Palace had been a tough proposition for opponents in the second half of the 2023/24 season. Oliver Glasner had impressed so much that Bayern Munich tried to lure him away, and at Palace he had organised a side that embodied the qualities of the Bundesliga. Aggressive counter-pressing, fast counter-attacks, and seeking to control territory. At this stage in the 2024/25 season, Palace had not been able to replicate their success, some of which can be connected to the loss of a key central defender (Joachim Anderson) and a key attacker (Michael Olise).

Adaptive Build-Up Shape

Palace's 3-4-3 system caused Liverpool to adapt their stance in the build-up phase during the first half. The trio of forwards created an automatic match-up with the three-player build that Liverpool have preferred for much of the season. Trent Alexander-Arnold did not invert into a midfield position, instead staying closer to Konate, giving four players in the build-up. The auxiliary player in midfield was not required as Liverpool's 4-2-3-1 outnumbered Palace in central midfield, thus releasing the full-backs into wide areas where Liverpool created attacking overloads and 2v1s against the Crystal Palace wing-backs. Liverpool dominated wide areas, especially the left side, with Gakpo often positioned on the touchline and Tsimikas aggressively underlapping.

Liverpool creating a shape with both full-backs wide but deeper/closer to the central defender

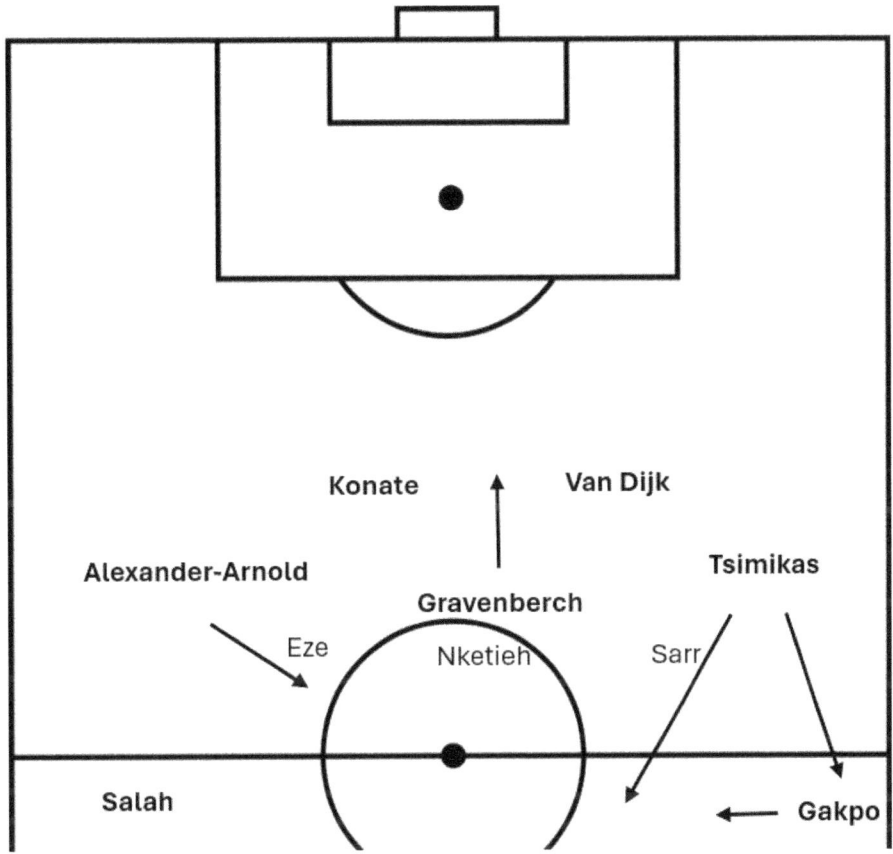

"I think you saw how much we control the first 60 minutes. Then we had 15 to 20 minutes which was a difficult spell. But then, in the last 10 minutes of the game, we took back control of the game. We took control by having a really good build-up and that helps to tire the opposition team." Arne Slot, post-match interview

The only goal came from the left side. After prolonged possession, during which Gakpo and Tsimikas rotated between wide and narrow positions, Tsimikas received the ball deeper, around 40 yards from the Palace goal. He played a straight pass between the wing-back and right-side centre-back that Gakpo ran onto. Gakpo's one-touch was instantly steered in by Jota from close to the penalty spot.

Roles of The Forwards

While Liverpool created the majority of their threat from the left side, it was Salah on the right that provided the release option. Once more, Liverpool favoured picking out Salah with longer balls from their right-back area once the opponents engaged in a high press. Salah uses his speed in behind but also his impressive strength, acting as a form of wide target man to help Liverpool progress downfield.

Diogo Jota has performed mostly in a false nine role to this point of the season. His movement and dropping into midfield manoeuvres opposition central defences out of position, creating spaces for wide players to run into and also for central midfielders to attack. Alexis Mac Allister exchanged with Jota regularly during this game. The role has not diminished Jota's opportunities to score, however, and he is a very effective penalty box finisher although – in this false nine role – his effectiveness seems to come from arriving in the penalty area from deep, in a similar manner to an attacking midfielder. Though he is capable of using his strength and body to hold off defenders, his most effective play is dropping deep to receive and then running into space behind, enabling a midfielder to take that forward position. Jota's ability to link attacks and drop deep has helped Liverpool unlock defences and build out against aggressive pressing. In this game, he had two excellent scoring opportunities on top of his goal. Salah also had an excellent chance, and Liverpool could have put the game away.

Palace Changes Disrupt Liverpool

Liverpool were dominant in possession until Crystal Palace made changes on the hour, bringing on Will Hughes and Mateta. The 3-4-3 switched to a 4-4-2. Where Liverpool had dominated the game – with controlled possession and aggressive regains before the ball could reach the halfway line – Palace now pressured Liverpool. Two strikers meant that Konate and van Dijk were kept busy. Hughes now jumped ahead of the Liverpool midfielders to regain possession, particularly targeting Gravenberch.

When Counter-Pressing Goes Wrong

Palace created opportunities and panic in the Liverpool back line. Alisson rushed a couple of clearances, eventually resulting in a hamstring injury. His regular able deputy Kelleher was not on the bench due to illness, so Liverpool had to turn to young Jaros. Jaros would thwart Crystal Palace's biggest opportunity, and the most interesting part of the opening was that it provided a great example of what can happen when *pressing goes wrong*.

An aggressive counter-press in a central position ended in Palace springing forward upon the Liverpool defence. Konate had been excellent at getting in front of opponents to intercept and maintain attacking pressure, and he attempted to do so here. Unfortunately for Liverpool, this occurred at just the same moment as Alexander-Arnold was also intercepting the ball. Trent got there first, but his control was imprecise, and the ball broke to Will Hughes. Hughes passed with his first touch and went beyond the whole right side of the Liverpool defence, as both Alexander-Arnold and Konate were taken out of position to press the ball. Palace were then 2v1 on the Liverpool right and 1v1 on the left. Mateta released Eze, but his effort proved tame. When people ask, "How can a 3v2 breakaway occur in the Premier League?" this is how!

Jones and Pausa

When Liverpool were on top in the game, Curtis Jones was fantastic in possession. He completed 97.9% of his passes, connecting on 47 out of 48. Jones also helped create the attacking triangle on the right-hand side with Salah and Alexander-Arnold. Liverpool continued their overall pattern of high passing numbers, completing 584 passes in the game. In a previous era, Fabinho and Thiago were noted as the Liverpool players who had "pausa", the ability to hold the ball with calmness before injecting tempo into the game. At present, the whole team seem to have the calmness to play with "pausa". (all stats from FBref)

Key Points

- Liverpool adapted the positioning of their full-backs to help build up against a trio of pressers
- Liverpool created 2v1s in wide areas, especially on their left
- The forwards have different roles and styles that give Slot different options
- Palace changed to two strikers and once again a strong powerful forward caused the Liverpool back line problems
- Counter-pressing carries high risks. When something goes wrong, the chance of the opposition creating a chance is very high

Game 11 – Chelsea – Home – Premier League – 2-1 win

Liverpool 4-2-3-1

Kelleher, Alexander-Arnold (Gomez), Konate, van Dijk, Robertson, Gravenberch, Jones (Mac Allister), Szoboszlai, Salah, Gakpo (Diaz), Jota (Nunez)

Chelsea 4-2-3-1

Sanchez, James (Veiga), Tosin (Badiashile), Colwill, Gusto, Caicedo, Lavia (Fernandez), Madueke (Nkunku), Palmer, Sancho (Neto), Jackson

Scorers – Salah, Jones, Jackson

Chelsea had started the season well and had the Premier League's most in-form player in Cole Palmer. Both teams used a 4-2-3-1 system, but Chelsea dominated Liverpool in terms of possession (57% for Chelsea) and total shots (eight for Liverpool and twelve for Chelsea). However, Chelsea only had two shots on target, and Liverpool produced a 1.9 xG to Chelsea's 1.0.

Cole Palmer's Positioning

There were many similarities in the way that the two teams set up. Chelsea used Reece James as an additional central defender when in possession, creating a 3-2 shape with Caicedo and Lavia in midfield. Gusto operated on the left and overlapped aggressively. Liverpool used their 4-2-4 shape to press, but it was ineffective. The attacking midfielder would join the front three in the press, in this case Szoboszlai. This left Curtis Jones and Ryan Gravenberch to cover the midfield, in theory putting them 2v2 with Caicedo and Lavia with Cole Palmer beyond the two of them. 'In theory' because this is not what Palmer did. Palmer positioned himself in wide areas and quite deep, creating a 3v2 against the Liverpool midfield. Often, Jones or Gravenberch was dragged away from the centre to pick up Palmer whose wide positioning to the right combined with Gusto's positioning on the left. In attempting to cover passes out to Chelsea's wide players, the supposedly compact wall of four Liverpool pressers was split open, creating passing lines that allowed Chelsea to find passes through the centre of the Liverpool team, turning the central 3v2 into a 2v1, and releasing Caicedo or Lavia. Gusto dragged Salah away. When Salah followed Gusto, this created another spare man in Jadon Sancho. Chelsea had multiple avenues out of Liverpool's press.

Cole Palmer's positioning that unbalanced Liverpool's shape

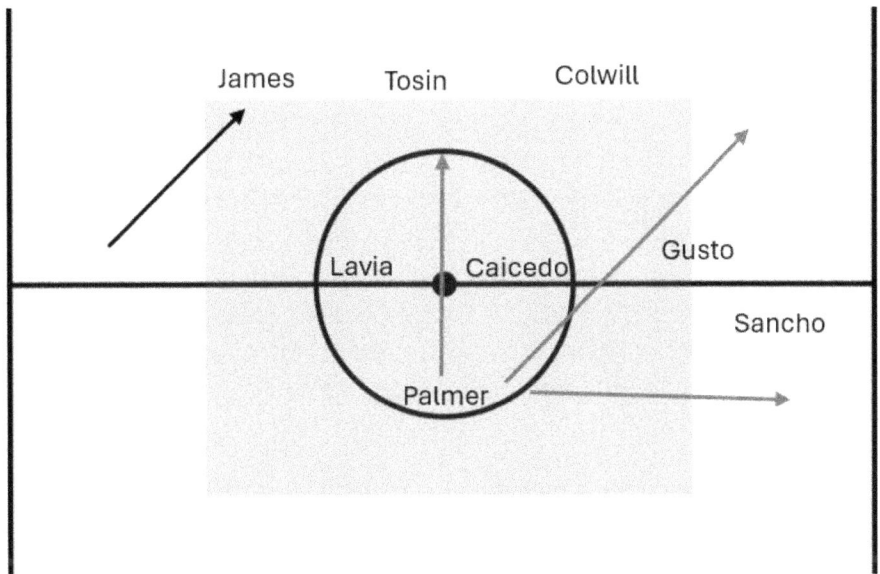

At the start of the second half, Jackson scored for Chelsea. The goal's root lay in Chelsea pulling the Liverpool midfield around and Szoboszlai not covering the centre of the pitch. Chelsea punched a penetrating ball through the open passing lane and were at the heart of the Liverpool defence. Liverpool adapted in the second half, covering the centre of the pitch much more successfully, but the Liverpool press was ineffective throughout the game.

Liverpool Go Long

Liverpool's problems were compounded by a very aggressive Chelsea press, committing as many as six players against the Liverpool build-up. Eventually, Liverpool stopped trying to build from the back and used far more long balls than they had in previous games. Salah was often the outlet, either going into his chest or feet near the halfway line. From these positions, Salah would pass in behind Chelsea. A left-footed trivela pass created an overturned penalty incident for Curtis Jones. Moments after the Chelsea equaliser, Salah and Jones would combine to score, as an excellent pass from Salah – using the inside of his left foot – picked out Jones running in behind the Chelsea defence to score. The run and pass locating a very small channel of space between the edge of the Chelsea box and the six-yard box; the timing and pass had to be executed with outstanding precision.

"Curtis had a difficult job, he had to control Cole Palmer, which is not easy because this player has some quality. It's a team effort but Curtis was mostly responsible for that. He did that really well and he added some really important moments to it." Arne Slot, post-match interview

Jones Impacts The Game

Curtis Jones' general performance was outstanding and different to the performance he gave against Crystal Palace in which he retained possession brilliantly. This time, he was a more direct threat with and without the ball. Running in behind the Chelsea defence and arriving in the box, he won the penalty scored by Salah in the first half as he was fouled in the box. On other occasions, he received the ball and eluded Chelsea challenges to carry Liverpool forward through the centre of the pitch.

Chelsea Substitutions Help Liverpool

This game came after an international break, meaning both managers were very careful with managing the minutes of their players. There were substitutions clearly reflective of international minutes rather than performances. Two Chelsea substitutions, in particular, helped Liverpool more than they helped Chelsea. Noni Madueke had given Andy Robertson a very tough time in the first half but was withdrawn for Pedro Neto at half-time. Neto had a lot of the ball in the second half but didn't really hurt Liverpool. After 52 minutes, Romeo Lavia was withdrawn for Enzo Fernandez. Enzo's positioning did not cause Liverpool the same problems as Lavia and helped Liverpool cover the centre of the pitch more effectively than they had in the first half.

Key Points

- Cole Palmer pulled Liverpool's press apart
- Chelsea pressed Liverpool hard. Liverpool countered by playing long balls and winning the second ball
- Curtis Jones posed Chelsea problems with his dribbling and running off the ball

Game 12 – Red Bull Leipzig – Away – Champions League – 1-0 win

Liverpool 4-2-3-1

Kelleher, Alexander-Arnold (Gomez), Konate, van Dijk, Tsimikas (Robertson), Gravenberch, Mac Allister, Szoboszlai, Salah (Diaz), Gakpo, Nunez (Jones)

Red Bull Leipzig 4-4-2/4-2-2-2

Gulacsi, Geertruida (Bitshiabu), Orban, Lukeba, Henrichs, Vermeeren (Kampl), Haidara (Elmes), Nusa, Simons (Poulsen), Sesko (Baumgartner), Openda

Scorers – Nunez

This was Champions League action against an opponent whose style was a reminder of Liverpool's recent past. The entirety of the Red Bull football family of teams play high-tempo, counter-pressing football in a manner akin to that of Jurgen Klopp. Many former Red Bull players have joined Liverpool, including current players Ibrahima Konate and Dominik Szoboszlai. Jurgen Klopp ended his break from football by becoming Red Bull's head of football.

Twin-Striker Threat

The game was more end-to-end than had been commonly seen with Arne Slot's Liverpool at this stage. Though Liverpool dominated possession, this was to be expected against a Red Bull team who aim to attack quickly as soon as they gain possession, rather than retain and maintain possession. Utilising two strikers for the majority of the game indicated the intent of Leipzig.

Two central strikers is quite rare at the highest levels of professional football. Two strikers up against two central defenders ensured that Konate and van Dijk were always challenged. Brighton would have one or even both strikers drop short to receive or fill in the midfield, but RBL used their strikers in quite an old-fashioned style, one always looking to run in behind (Openda) and another as the target for longer balls (Sesko). Openda's runs in behind caused Liverpool problems for much of the game due to his extreme speed, however he was caught offside often.

How the Leipzig 4-2-2-2 narrow shape enabled them to get multiple players close to the ball in counter-pressing situations

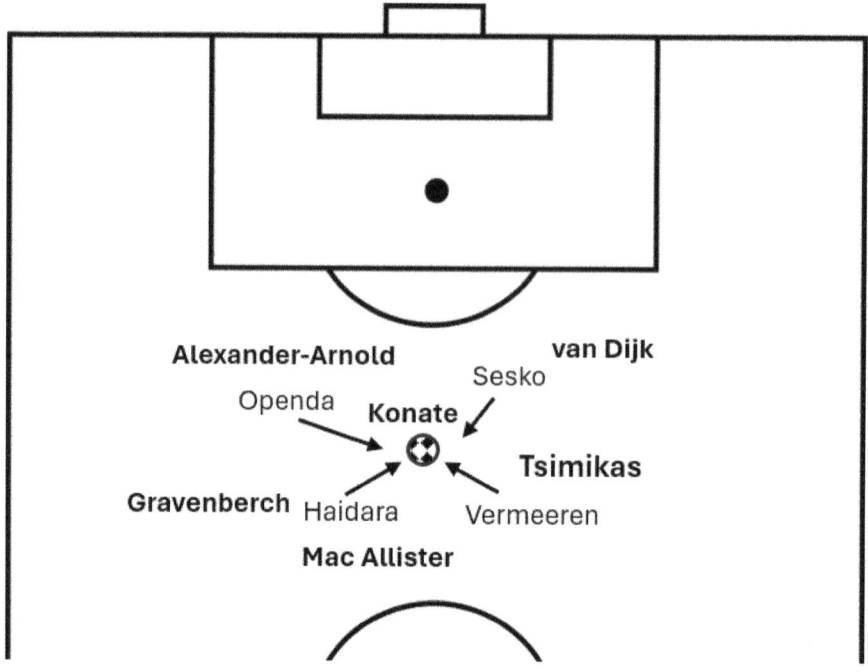

Changing Build-Up Pattern

Counter-pressing is a key part of Red Bull football, and the two strikers created an immediate pair of players to press the Liverpool central defenders. In possession, Liverpool played 3v2 against the strikers using Gravenberch or a tucked-in full-back. The build changed depending on the number of players Leipzig committed to the press. Sometimes, both full-backs tucked in with the central defenders to make four, with the central defenders aligned a few metres closer to the Liverpool goal than the full-backs. At other times, the full-backs were closer to the midfield line. Trent-Alexander Arnold fulfilled multiple roles within this fixture; as well as flexible positioning in the build-up, he exchanged positions with Szoboszlai, particularly when the ball had advanced beyond the halfway line on the Liverpool left side. If Szoboszlai pulled wide, Alexander-Arnold moved infield as a high midfielder. If Szoboszlai was in a more traditional central position, Alexander-Arnold was high and wide on the right, providing a target for van Dijk's long diagonal passes.

Ideal Build-Up Pattern

By this point, Liverpool established an ideal build-up pattern from the defensive third to create attacking openings. With the ball in Liverpool's right-back area, with Konate, the ball would ideally be played infield to Gravenberch to open up the attacking options. The majority of the time, that pass will be cut off, so Konate will instead play a ball towards the halfway line on the right side for Salah or Szoboszlai. The two players will combine with each other or bring Alexander-Arnold into the play. The ball is then switched across to the left, finding Gakpo or Diaz on the left to dribble infield or pass into midfielders. The move then ends with the ball at the feet of Salah to shoot, cross to the far post, or find an overlapping or underlapping teammate. Liverpool needed this pattern against the Leipzig press and also replicated a version of the Konate release on the left side, except with Tsimikas playing from the left-back area into Gakpo close to halfway. Liverpool were able to use a lot of one-two combinations in wide areas to release forward from their own half.

"Many, many, many times we played through their press, opened up their midfield and went for an attack. That led to the first goal, that led to a few chances – more than a few." Arne Slot, post-match interview

Aggressive Pressing

It was not just Leipzig who pressed aggressively. Liverpool used another slightly altered version of their distinct four-man pressing wall (the front three plus Szoboszlai). Against Leipzig, five players pressed high with Nunez leading the press and a wall of five immediately behind him. Mac Allister jumped out from midfield along with Szoboszlai, leaving Gravenberch to cover the middle. This may have been a reaction to both AC Milan and Chelsea exploiting the Liverpool press setup, but it could also have been a tactical response to exploit RBL's build-up system. With only two central midfielders and two strikers who would not drop short, the centre would be relatively empty and Gravenberch was unlikely to be overloaded during the build.

Slot's Substitutions Make An Impact

Arne Slot's substitutions in this game carried tactical or positional changes. When Diaz came on for Salah, this was initially a straight swap. Then came a triple substitution. Jones came on for Darwin Nunez, Gomez for Alexander-Arnold, and Robertson for Tsimikas. Initially, Luis Diaz moved to the left and Szoboszlai to the right, with Gakpo through the middle. After a few minutes, Gakpo moved to the left, and Diaz went through the middle as a central striker, an unusual role for Diaz. The full-backs tucked in and played extremely narrowly. Robertson now inverted in the manner that Alexander-Arnold often does, with license to play midfield, twice occupying a position usually associated with a number ten. Joe Gomez moved in alongside the central defenders, creating a three-man structure. Slot saw an opportunity to experiment in-game with the structure, the back line mirroring its usual form and pushing Diaz into a striking role.

Key Points

- Red Bull Leipzig fielded a twin strikeforce, which posed Konate and van Dijk with different problems to what they usually face
- The game was played at a more frantic pace from the early stages than Liverpool usually desire
- Liverpool adjusted their build-up style in keeping with their "plus one" philosophy
- Liverpool had an ideal build-up from deep, starting on the right, switching out to the left, and ending up on the right

Game 13 – Arsenal – Premier League – Away – 2-2 draw

Liverpool 4-2-3-1

Kelleher, Alexander-Arnold, Konate, van Dijk, Robertson (Tsimikas), Gravenberch, Mac Allister (Szoboszlai), Jones (Endo), Salah, Diaz (Gakpo), Nunez

Arsenal 4-3-3

Raya, Partey, White, Gabriel (Kiwior), Timber (Lewis-Skelly), Rice, Merino, Trossard, Saka (Jesus), Martinelli (Nwaneri), Havertz

Scorers – Saka, Merino, van Dijk, Salah

Possibly the biggest game of the season so far… a well-worn cliché that can be brought out game after game in the world of football! Arguably the next game is always the most important game, but some games carry more context than others. Both Liverpool and Arsenal had started the season well, and both had spent most of the 2023/24 season involved in the race up the Premier League table. Facing each other at this stage offered a measuring stick. A draw away to the previous league runners-up and the team most fancied to displace Manchester City has to be viewed as an affirming result for Liverpool.

Arsenal's Pressing

Mikel Arteta and Arsenal are renowned for their out-of-possession structure and pressing strategies. They are often cited as the exemplar of how modern teams should organise themselves. Their press switches between structures at different stages of the game. A staggered 2-1-3-1 press structure led by Havertz and Trossard was used for the majority of the game, focused on not allowing any spaces through the centre. Arsenal paid Liverpool a lot of respect and had developed plans to limit Liverpool's favoured exit routes.

Arsenal worked extremely hard to prevent Ryan Gravenberch from receiving and turning in deep areas to bring Liverpool forward from their defensive third. A furious reaction from Arteta when Gravenberch was able to turn indicated that Arsenal had worked on this. As the game progressed, Gravenberch was able to turn out of these situations more often, helping Liverpool take control of the latter stages of the match.

How Liverpool attempted to overload the far post of the opposition penalty area

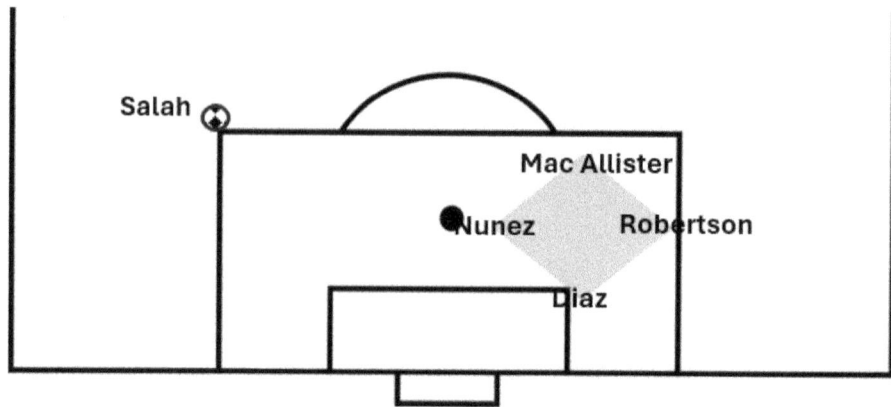

Arsenal Target The Inside Right Channel

Konate and the right-back area was another target for Arsenal. Liverpool have favoured the Konate escape route in the early stages of the season, so Arsenal sent a triangle of pressing players into the right-back area to shut down this exit route. Liverpool had limited success but, vitally, in the 81st minute, they were able to escape through Alexander-Arnold, who found Szoboszlai. Szoboszlai returned a pass to Alexander-Arnold, the one-two method on the flanks often used by Liverpool. Alexander-Arnold found a pass behind Arsenal and into the path of Nunez on the right. Salah ran inside to receive a reversed pass by Nunez and swept a low shot past Raya to level the score at 2-2.

Salah was persistent with his off-the-ball running, seemingly believing that it was just a matter of time before an opportunity would arise. Jurrien Timber stuck with Salah well for the majority of the game, but – eventually – Salah wore him down and Timber was replaced by young Lewis-Skelly. Soon after the change, Salah scored, but Lewis-Skelly recovered to perform steadily for the rest of the game. Injuries were significant in this game. Saliba and Odegaard were already missing for Arsenal from the start, but they also lost Timber and Gabriel during the course of the match.

In the first half, Liverpool bypassed the Arsenal press by playing long from their own defensive third, aiming to use Nunez's physicality, with the wide players narrowing towards Nunez and forming additional strikers. Arsenal handled this and dominated the second ball in the first half. Allied to being able to play through the Liverpool press with comfort, Arsenal were the better team in the first half, and the midway score of 2-1 to Arsenal reflected this.

Havertz Positioning Stretches Liverpool

The movement of Kai Havertz proved a key factor in Arsenal's ability to play through the Liverpool press and into the central third. Perhaps taking a cue from the way that Cole Palmer had stretched the Liverpool central midfield, Havertz positioned himself away from the Liverpool central defenders, pulling wide right. The Liverpool players were unsure who should pick Havertz up, as van Dijk did not want to follow (else he would leave a gap in the centre of the defence). If a midfielder followed, there would be a large gap in the centre of the pitch. During the first half, Gravenberch was left alone to patrol the whole area of the pitch because Havertz's movement pulled Liverpool players out of possession. Trossard had vast amounts of space centrally and a single pass through the press found him, enabling Arsenal to drive at a now exposed Liverpool back four.

Havertz's movement also impacted the goal scored by Saka. Once more, Havertz pulled wide, but this time closer to the Liverpool back line near the halfway line. With van Dijk hesitant to follow, there was a 2v1 scenario against Robertson. A long ball in behind allowed Saka to race with Robertson, a race he won to give Arsenal the lead. The race was made easier because Havertz's movement was enough to lure van Dijk fractionally out of position, just too far away to help cover the space behind Robertson.

Liverpool Pass Through The Press

In the second half, Liverpool changed their approach from playing long in the deep build to passing short. Arsenal switched to playing longer and had less success. Liverpool were able to be brave against the Arsenal press and able to gain a foothold in the game. The Liverpool shape in the build-up changed during the game, which helped them create overloads against the Arsenal press. Alexander-Arnold inverted more to help create an extra man in midfield. Szoboszlai came on as a substitute and dropped closer to the defenders to help overload centrally against the press. Tsimikas was positioned very wide, overlapping Gakpo and delivering crosses from closer to the touchline. Liverpool pinned Arsenal into their defensive third for long periods of the second half, with van Dijk and Konate positioned very high up the pitch to recycle clearances. There was little risk involved in such high positioning as – during this period – Arsenal pulled all eleven players back into their defensive third, meaning there was no target to hit on the counter-attack.

Different Attacking Methods

Liverpool used hitherto unseen attacking ploys in this match, too. In the second half, Nunez positioned himself closer to the right and Salah. Though Liverpool passed shorter in the second half than the first, when they did go long, they could now look for an overload against the full-back or a 2v2 against full-back and central defender. Such a scenario was a part of the previously mentioned equaliser.

When Alexander-Arnold was in possession of the ball – wide on the right or in the right half-space – Liverpool attempted to overload the far post. A diamond of waiting attackers formed, starting with Nunez closest to the penalty spot, joined by Alexis Mac Allister, Diaz, and Robertson. All in a diamond shape and all to the left of the penalty spot and a little wider than the left edge of the six-yard box. This shape formed on a number of occasions, too many to be a coincidence. Liverpool were often 4v4 when a cross came in, and had the delivery been slightly different, there was the potential for a 2v1 at the far post. Robertson has been attacking the far post on crosses for many years for Liverpool, scoring a famous late goal against Aston Villa from such a position. This is an example of Slot taking something that Liverpool already used and adapting it for his own ends.

"They always play 4-3-3, but the way they position themselves they can do – I think he [Arteta] said it once himself – 40 different set-ups. So, you prepare a game plan, you expect something but you cannot tell your players 40 different options." Arne Slot, post-match press conference

Key Points

- Both teams attempted to press aggressively. Whichever team was brave and tried to pass short seemed to be on top during that period
- Konate covered the inside right channel
- Havertz's movements stretched Liverpool's out of possession structure, much as Cole Palmer had for Chelsea

Game 14 – Brighton – League Cup – Away – 3-2 win

Liverpool 4-4-2/4-2-2-2

Jaros, Bradley, Quansah (Konate), Gomez, Tsimikas, Morton (Mac Allister), Endo (Nyoni), Diaz, Gakpo (Salah), Szoboszlai (Nunez), Jones

Brighton 4-2-3-1

Steele, Lamptey, van Hecke (Veltman), Igor, Kadioglu (Estupinan), Moder (Hinshelwood), Wieffer, Gruda (Mitoma), Encisco (Welbeck), Adingra, Ferguson

Scorers – Gakpo (2), Diaz, Adingra, Lamptey

Liverpool were in the unusual situation of facing the same opponent for consecutive cup and league fixtures. Arne Slot previously experimented in the league cup, raising the question of whether the shift to a strikerless 4-4-2 (or 4-2-2-2 with wide strikers?) was a further experiment or double-bluff with the upcoming league game in mind.

Twin Number Tens

Szoboszlai and Jones were listed in the lineup as strikers. In effect, they both played as hybrid false nines or number tens; both with licence to drop short to receive and create space for runners behind the opposition defence. The runners being either the wide players or whichever of the pair of tens had not dropped into midfield. Sometimes, both twin tens did drop into midfield at the same time, at which point both wingers ran in behind the defence. Diaz spent a lot of time in the centre-forward position, either running off the ball into the position or dribbling inside. When a wide player dribbled inside, either Jones or Szoboszlai pulled out into the wide area. The system is extremely fluid.

The Liverpool build-up became 2-4-4, the full-backs higher and wider than usual, with both advancing at the same time. Until this point in the season, the primary build-up shape was 2-3 or 3-2 with a full-back inverting. At times, the positioning of Bradley was so extreme that he was attacking the far post and six-yard box with runs behind the defence when the ball was out on the opposite flank with Gakpo or Tsimikas. This is completely different to the approach taken with Alexander-Arnold in the lineup.

How Szoboszlai and Jones played as twin false forwards in the 4-4-2 shape

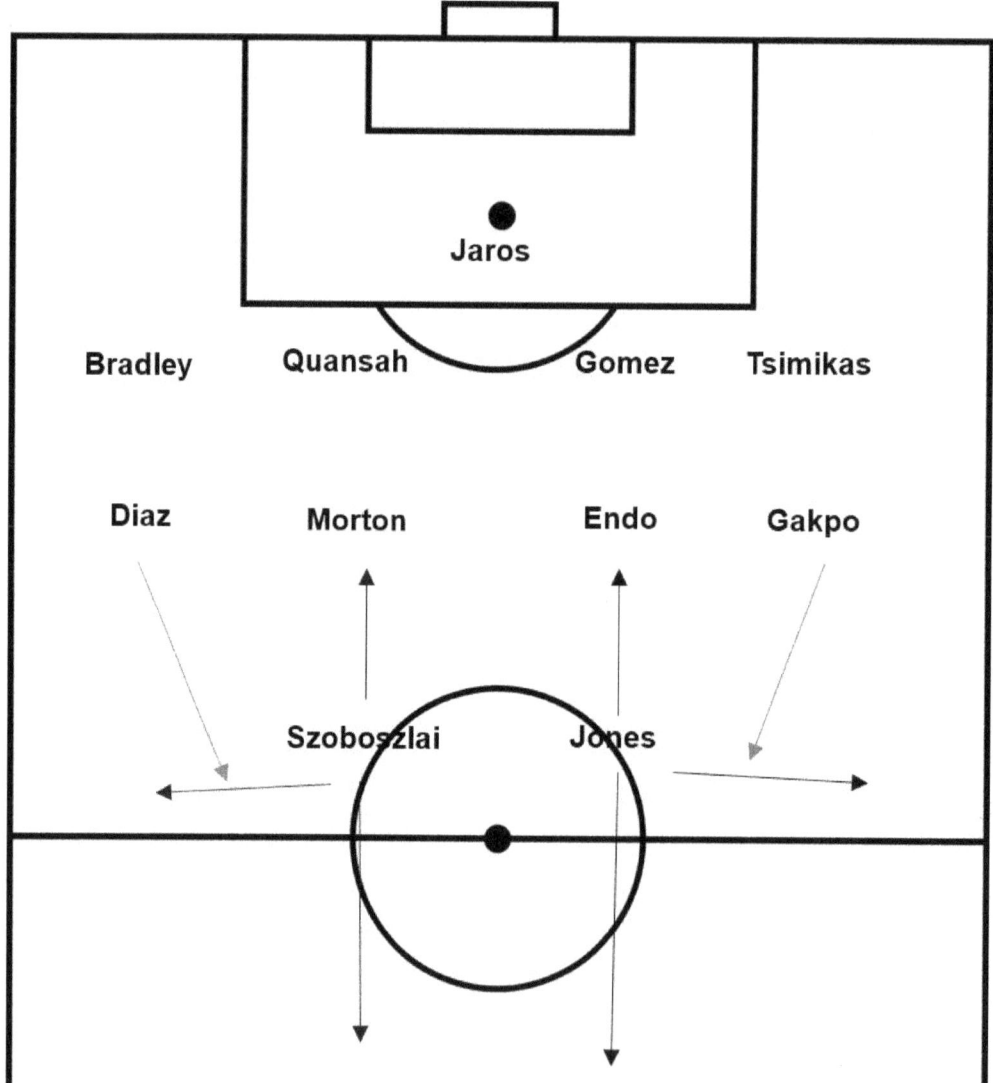

Gakpo's Threat Increases

Cody Gakpo scored two goals in the 3-2. Gakpo aims to receive in one of two positions, either out on the touchline or in the inside left channel. From both positions, he will cut inside and cross or shoot, or control the ball and slot a pass on the outside for runners. For the first goal, Gakpo received out on the touchline before cutting in and firing a shot into the far corner with his laces. The second goal was from a long ball where he got to a loose ball before the defender, drove directly forward and then drilled a low shot into the near bottom corner with his laces. This action all occurred within the inside left channel. Gakpo has grown in effectiveness and threat as the season has progressed.

Liverpool Control The Centre

Unsurprisingly, both teams pressed in an aggressive manner. Both managers would fit into the modern playing style where pressing is key. Liverpool pressed very aggressively in wide areas, very similar to their pressing plan against West Ham in the previous round. Liverpool regularly sent five and six players into wide areas to press the ball from an initial 2-3-1 pressing structure. Though based on a basic principle of the closest players to the ball leading the press when a ball is in a wide area, it doesn't require a lot of movement for 2-4 to become a 2-3-1. Brighton aimed to attack and progress mainly through wide areas, with the attacking midfielder from their 4-2-3-1 formation moving very wide to create overloads in wide areas.

Due to Liverpool committing numbers to wide presses, Brighton had little success passing through the press, but they were able to dribble through the press at times. Endo and Morton in central midfield were rarely overloaded due to Brighton's focus on wide areas, allowing Liverpool to leave spaces between the lines of midfield and defence. The two false forwards were able to cover any threats centrally on the occasions they occurred. Playing without an outright striker who can hold the ball or be an outlet when defending comes from two key Liverpool principles. If the opposition have established a high position in possession, every Liverpool player will be back behind the ball and within ten metres of the penalty area, so a striker is not needed. When Liverpool do play a release pass out of the pressure, the pass goes to a wide player rather than a central player, with the wide players performing one of the functions of a traditional striker.

Key Points

- Slot experimented with double number 10s and no central striker
- Gakpo's influence is increasing with each passing game
- Liverpool were able to control the centre of the pitch

Game 15 – Brighton – Premier League – Home – 2-1 win

Liverpool 4-2-3-1

Kelleher, Alexander-Arnold, Konate (Gomez), van Dijk, Tsimikas, Gravenberch, Mac Allister (Jones), Szoboszlai (Diaz), Salah (Bradley), Gakpo, Nunez (Endo)

Brighton 4-4-2

Verbruggen, Veltman (Gruda), van Hecke, Igor, Estupinan, Kadioglu (Moder), Hinshelwood (Ferguson), Ayari (Wieffer), Mitoma (Adingra), Rutter, Welbeck

Scorers – Gakpo, Salah, Kadioglu

After the phoney war of the midweek cup game came the real business of a Premier League tie. Both teams started with very different formations to those used a few days earlier, but Liverpool showed that perhaps the war was less phoney, reverting to tactics used in the prior clash.

Brighton Press Aggressively

Brighton had the better of the game in the first half. Their aggressive press stifled Liverpool, and their aggression was one of positioning and intent rather than energetically and constantly hunting the ball. Brighton positioned five or six players high in the Liverpool half, blocking passing lanes, with Liverpool unable to find a way through, leading to regular turnovers as they tried to punch through or over the block. One of Liverpool's key principles is numerical superiority, having an extra man in both defence and attack. As Brighton pushed so many players forward, it meant that they were almost man-to-man and able to break the superiority principle. Brighton regained possession near halfway and sprung forward with the advanced players already ahead of the ball, leading to threatening attacks.

When Liverpool did progress the ball beyond the press, a microgame of 3v2 was being played out near the halfway line, with van Dijk, Konate and Gravenberch vs the two Brighton strikers. Liverpool had to work hard against this, with Gravenberch playing one-twos and passing and moving to escape and progress.

Movement of Brighton Strikers

The Brighton 4-4-2 became highly fluid as one or both of the strikers could drop into midfield. When Liverpool pressed in their 4-2-4 shape, a Brighton forward could come into midfield while the other stretched the back line, the system effectively switching from 4-4-2 to 4-2-3-1. Brighton focused their build-up play through the centre, having mainly used the wide areas during the cup game.

Liverpool Change Gears

After being behind at half-time, Liverpool switched gears. Arne Slot has shown himself to be adroit at making adjustments to take the game to opponents in the second half of matches and, once again, the tempo changed in the second half. Liverpool played forward with more speed and bombarded the wide areas. As Liverpool chased the game, there was a stream of crosses from wide areas and half-spaces.

"We changed a bit of tactics, but that had nothing to do with us coming out stronger in the second half. It all had to do with the players showing a different attitude and intensity." Arne Slot, post-match interview

Liverpool dominated from the left side, overloading that wing while leaving Salah in space on the right. Salah had 1 v 1 opportunities, which eventually led to the game-winning goal as Salah was picked out wide on the right to dribble inside, cut in and shoot into the top right-hand corner. This was, at first glance, just another Liverpool counter-attack goal, but the overloading of the left and minimal loading of the right created opportunities for Salah. Salah also requires less support. His strength and ability to pin his full-back means that he can operate with his back to goal and form a wide target man. This has meant that although his pace is slightly diminished, relative to his early years at Liverpool, his strength has increased so he is able to receive passes ahead of him into space, to feet facing towards the opponent's goal, to feet with his back to goal, or a ball anywhere into the body with his back to goal. He has become an all-round outlet on the right side. This is a really interesting development for the modern game, as a traditional central target man will have to deal with two central defenders almost immediately. A wide outlet could have empty space if a full-back has been in an attacking position or have a 1v1 with the full-back until a central defender comes across to engage and double up. The central defender might not be able to engage if the central area is occupied by an attacker, as Liverpool do with the central striker or the attacking midfielder making forward runs.

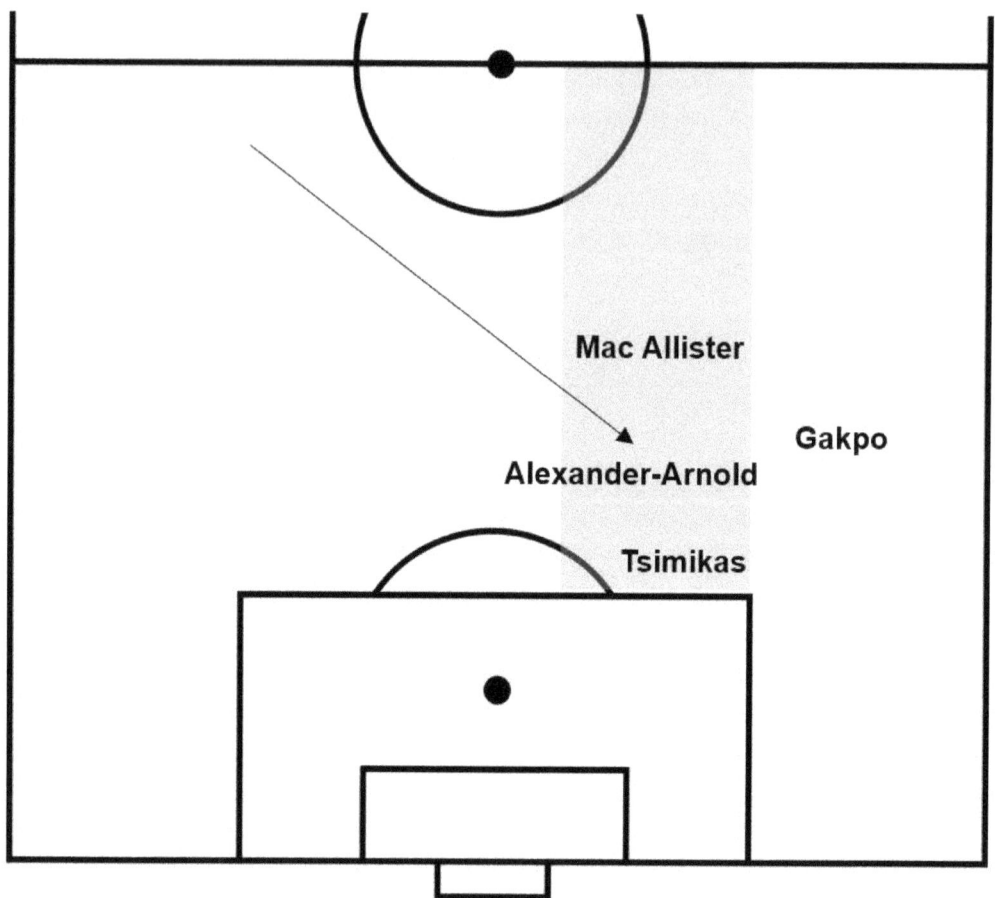

Alexander-Arnold taking up a position close to the Liverpool left side to help overload the half-space

Positioning of Alexander-Arnold

The left side overload was exacerbated by Alexander-Arnold inverting to the extreme. In the second half, he was very narrow, at times almost in the left half-space. His positioning pushed Mac Allister wider. The unusual positioning made it harder for Brighton's press to cut off the passing lines as they had in the first half. The game became 4 v 4 in midfield, with Brighton pulling both of their strikers back and Liverpool using Alexander-Arnold to invert as an extra midfielder. Mac Allister was pushed into closer contact with Gakpo and Tsimikas, who provided crosses. When Mac Allister came off, Curtis Jones took up the same role, overloading the left side. The Liverpool equaliser came as Tsimikas overlapped Gakpo, which created more space for Gakpo to cut inside and strike an inswinging right-footed cross. The cross was missed by everyone and nestled into the bottom corner.

Liverpool's two goals were scored in a quick five-minute burst. Just before the first of the goals, Slot made a tactical switch. The 4-4-2 bluff of the cup tie became the tactic to chase the league game. Diaz was pushed into a central striker role alongside Nunez, with Gakpo and Salah pushing wide. Slot took a risk with 20 minutes to go, giving up his principles of numerical superiority to match Brighton in a 4-4-2. After Liverpool took the lead, Slot reverted to 4-2-3-1, lowering the tempo and trying to control the game for the remainder of the time, replacing Nunez with Endo. Brighton threw attacking players onto the pitch but were unable to threaten sufficiently.

Key Points
- Brighton used an aggressive press in the first half that prevented Liverpool from gaining a foothold in the game
- Brighton's fluid 4-4-2 with double false 9s overloaded the Liverpool midfield
- Liverpool countered the overload created by the Brighton forwards by pulling Alexander-Arnold into midfield, nullifying the overload
- Liverpool once again were able to inject energy after half-time, playing at a higher tempo

Game 16 – Bayer Leverkusen – Champions League – Home – 4-0 win

Liverpool 4-2-3-1

Kelleher, Alexander-Arnold (Bradley), Konate (Quansah), van Dijk, Tsimikas (Robertson), Gravenberch, Mac Allister, Jones (Szoboszlai), Salah, Gakpo (Nunez), Diaz

Bayer Leverkusen 3-4-3

Hradecky, Tapsoba, Tah, Hincapie, Frimpong, Palacios (Hofmann), Xhaka, Grimaldo (Tella), Wirtz, Garcia (Andrich), Boniface (Schick)

Scorers – Diaz (3), Gakpo

On the night a fan favourite returned, Liverpool turned in an outstanding second-half blitz. In many ways, this represented a huge statement from Arne Slot as – on this evening – he defeated the German double winners, who unseated Bayern Munich as champions for the first time in a decade. Leverkusen lost one game all season in 2023/24, which was to an Ademola Lukman-inspired Atalanta in the Europa League final. An Atalanta that had knocked Liverpool out on their way to the final. More decisively, Slot had defeated 'the chosen one'. Xabi Alonso was the romantic and hoped-for choice as the successor to Jurgen Klopp. A Champions League winner with Liverpool, he had started his managerial career so brightly that he had quickly become the one that everyone wanted. In the end, he turned Liverpool down, and Arne Slot was selected, which – to many – felt far less enticing than a returning hero. Yet, here stood Slot, having made a wonderful start and now thumping Alonso's Leverkusen 4-0.

Pressing Problems

At half-time, the game was goalless. Leverkusen had caused problems for Liverpool… a familiar tale of the season as Liverpool have been far stronger in the second half of games. The Liverpool press had been evolving across the season to this point, from one quite fixed 'four-player wall' into a more flexible pressing structure, but the trend remained for there to be problems against teams who used a three-player structure with a full-back or wing-back wide plus a player who has freedom to move centrally. Against Chelsea, it was Cole Palmer; against Arsenal, it was Kai Havertz; and against Leverkusen, it was Florian Wirtz. Wirtz dropped deep from the number ten position to occupy Liverpool players centrally, and the movement triggered a central midfielder to move to a wide position. Liverpool tried to press aggressively, but Leverkusen were willing to drop as many as nine players short to overload Liverpool and play short passes. Wirtz was often free to find teammates with an angled infield pass through the top line of the Liverpool press, from where he could be the launchpad for attacks.

In the first half, Leverkusen sought to use the explosive pass of Frimpong at right wing-back. In their trophy-loaded 23/24 season, the wing-backs had served as wingers or even inside forwards. Frimpong's pace had caused chaos in opposition defences and Leverkusen looked to get Frimpong behind Robertson (this continues another trend in recent games to attempt to exploit the left-back area).

Liverpool Go Long Against An Aggressive Press

Leverkusen pressed Liverpool aggressively. Their 3-4-3 structure allows six or seven players to be involved in the press while still ensuring that there is defensive cover. The front three and midfield two all push up high while the wing-back on the side of the pitch with the ball engages in wide areas, making that escape route unattractive. Liverpool attempted to play longer in the first half. Diaz as the centre-forward was dominated in the air while the passes in behind for Salah and Gakpo were well covered. Liverpool did create some counter-attacking opportunities in the first half. Another pathway to threatening Liverpool attacks were long diagonal passes out to the right side from van Dijk, either to Salah or to Alexander-Arnold. Trent moving infield created space for Salah to receive; likewise, when Salah moved infield, this created space for Alexander-Arnold to receive.

Pushing The Shape Higher Up The Pitch

Liverpool gained control of the game in the second half through possession and more effective build-up, committed to passing short, with fewer long balls in behind when Leverkusen's pressing shape was set. Slot solved the problems posed by Leverkusen's pressure and structure by dropping both central midfielders closer to the centre-backs in the build-up phase. Diaz also came short to receive and, as Slot described after the game, "turn very quickly in the small spaces". In turn, the wide players pushed higher and exploited the classic weakness in a wing-back system, the space outside the central defenders and behind the wing-backs.

Jones Opens Up The Opponents

The breakthrough came in a central area. Curtis Jones and Alexander-Arnold broke the Leverkusen lines and it must be said that Jones had a wonderfully creative game. During the first half, he produced a magical moment, plucking the ball from the air, dribbling away from two defenders, then swivelling to strike a 50-yard left-foot pass to Gakpo. In the second half, the pair took their line-breaking to another level. Alexander-Arnold punched passes infield from an angle on the right to break through the Leverkusen shape. One such pass found Jones in the centre, between the two Leverkusen midfielders. Jones quickly turned to find an accurate 15-yard pass through the defensive line to Diaz, who produced a delicate finish over the goalkeeper.

"Curtis is one of them. When I started off, the first game I played him as a six… but that wasn't his best game. It's one of his qualities that at this moment he can play in every position because he's in a very good place at the moment. So comfortable on the ball, so you can trust him closer to your defence. But like we saw against Chelsea and I saw today as well, he is also able to penetrate inside the 18-yard box and give the last pass." Arne Slot, post-match press conference

Liverpool pushed the tempo in the second half. The press was more aggressive, using a 1-4 shape that pushed both Jones and Mac Allister up with the front three. As has been seen earlier in the season, Alexander-Arnold moved higher up in the press, marking the wing-back early, similar to the way that Leverkusen had in the first half. Effectively, Liverpool pressed in a man-to-man manner during the second half. This discouraged Leverkusen from playing short, and they looked for more long balls. Liverpool won the second balls and attacked swiftly.

Counter-Attacking From Deep

Diaz would score a thrilling hat-trick on the night, with the last two goals scored from counter-attacks. Overall, three of the four Liverpool goals were scored on the counter-attack. The first of the three was scored by Cody Gakpo. A Leverkusen attack was broken up just inside the Liverpool penalty area before Van Dijk found Diaz with a medium-length pass. Jones, Salah and Gakpo were instantly on the move, as was Alexander-Arnold on the right. The pass from Diaz was slightly behind Salah but Diaz had kept running, and Salah's pass to Diaz retained the pace of the counter-attack. Diaz dribbled at the heart of the defence, enabling Salah to overlap him. Diaz then found the overlap, and Salah crossed first time with his right foot, enabling Cody Gakpo to fly in and head the ball home at the far post. The speed of the break and the numbers committed underscored the attitude shown by Liverpool in attacking transitions.

Diaz's second goal and Liverpool's third originated when a Leverkusen shot was blocked and looped into the hands of Kelleher. He quickly released Robertson, and a pass through the lines found Nunez, on as a substitute. Even before the Robertson pass had made it to Nunez, the other Liverpool forwards were sprinting downfield to join the attack. The attack was fast and smooth; out to the right to Salah, who cut inside before picking Diaz out at the far post to score. Goal four followed two Liverpool block tackles in their own box, and one pass set Darwin Nunez away on the break. Leverkusen had pushed attacking numbers up the pitch, giving Liverpool a 4v2 counter-attack. Nunez shot and the strike was saved, but the block dropped to the feet of Diaz in prime position to complete his hat-trick.

Klopp's Liverpool were often considered to be fantastic in transition. Given the number of goals Slot's Liverpool score, added to the sprinting power they show to recover and break up opponent's transitions. Liverpool under Slot remain devastating in transition.

Liverpool crowding the opposition player as they enter a dangerous position, before regaining possession and springing into a counter

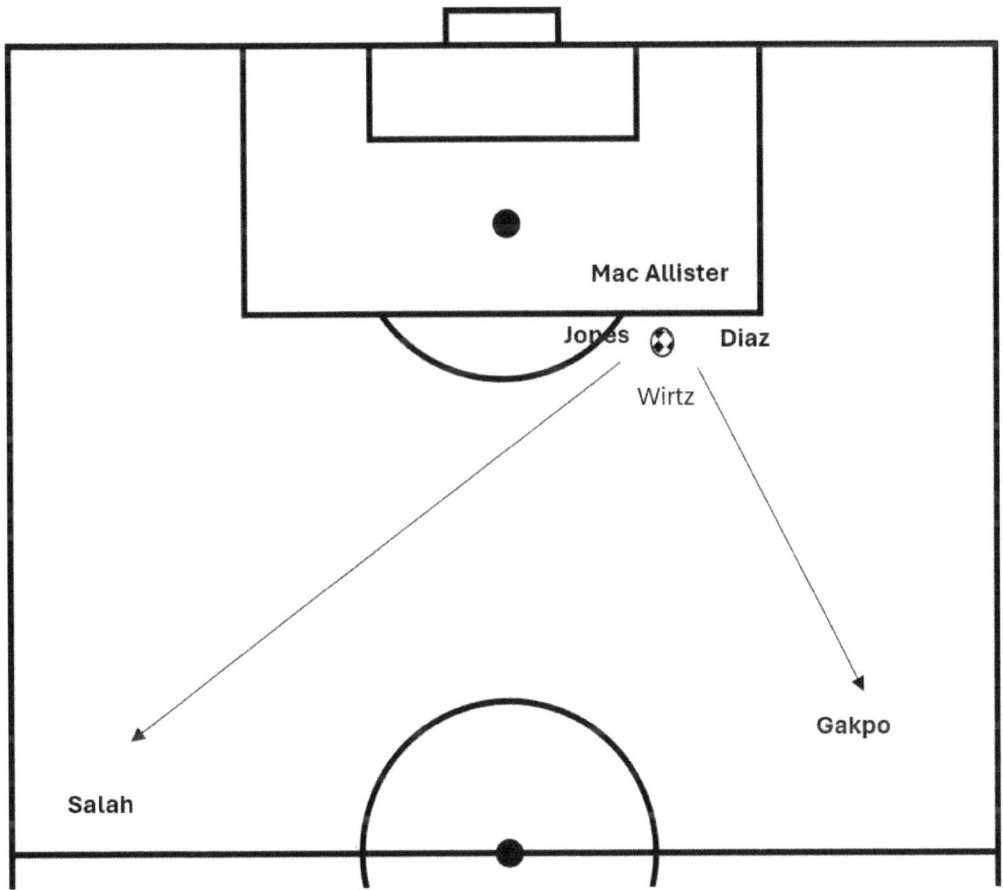

Key Points

- Liverpool have struggled to press against teams who use a three-player structure in the build-up
- Liverpool play long against aggressive pressing initially, but are more successful in the second-half when they commit to shorter passing
- Slot pushed the midfielders higher up the pitch to press, stopping Leverkusen's build-up options
- Curtis Jones was in excellent creative form
- Liverpool defended their box well and are lethal on the counter-attack

Game 17 - Aston Villa – Premier League – Home – 2-0 win

Liverpool 4-2-3-1

Kelleher, Alexander-Arnold (Bradley), Konate, van Dijk, Robertson, Gravenberch, Mac Allister (Endo), Jones (Szoboszlai), Salah, Diaz, Nunez (Gakpo)

Aston Villa 4-2-3-1

Martinez, Konsa, Diego Carlos, Torres, Digne (Maatsen), Onana (Kamara), Tielemans, Bailey (Philogene), Rogers, Ramsey (McGinn), Watkins (Duran)

Scorers – Nunez, Salah

Liverpool relied on counter-attacks to create opportunities against Aston Villa. Villa were well organised when Liverpool had possession, and there were very few open play openings.

Villa Too Open At Their Own Attacking Corners

The organisation in open play was in stark contrast to Villa's organisation when attacking corners. The way that Aston Villa crowded the Liverpool box but failed to cover their own defensive lines was the most startling aspect of the game. Villa aimed to maximise their own goal threat from corners, and there was a first-half sequence that created three goal opportunities within a couple of minutes from two corners and a second-phase cross. The attacking setup filled the Liverpool box, leaving two players on the edge of the box with nobody protecting the halfway line. This might be considered a risk against any side, let alone one as proficient on the counter-attack as Liverpool!

The opening goal came from attacking the vast spaces left by Villa. A corner was blocked and the ball broke to van Dijk. When van Dijk passed the ball forward, Liverpool found themselves in a 3v1 attacking situation. Salah got through ahead of the only defender, was fouled, and the referee waved play on. Fortunately for Liverpool, the ball came to Darwin Nunez, who went around Martinez to score. Nunez had a second opportunity from a Villa corner in the first half that he fired into the Kop End. There were two further breakaways in the second half, one thwarted by a recovery tackle and the last one slowed down by Liverpool with the score 2-0 and minutes remaining.

"We did put effort in defending them from scoring because that was also today – not in general, but today – that was their main threat in my opinion, their set-pieces." Arne Slot talking to Liverpool FC TV

Liverpool Change Pressing Shape

The Liverpool press used differing patterns and shapes as the game demanded. By this stage, Slot and Liverpool have learned from their experiences of the season and also had much more time together. The shape switched between a flat four, 1-3 and 1-4. It was consistent how often Liverpool pressed Villa's left side in the build-up phase, committing numbers to keep their opponents pinned into the corner and preventing Villa from creating overloads in this area.

Liverpool's adjustment in their pressing shape, forming a 1-4 and pulling a second midfielder into the press

Controlling Opposition Transitions

Liverpool were very good at controlling transitions and snuffing out counter-attacks. The distribution of the team in possession helps to prevent opponents from having overloads when counter-attacking. In the defensive and midfield build, one full-back and one central midfielder (at a minimum) will be close to the central defenders, limiting the space teams can transition into should there be a turnover and providing defensive numbers. Liverpool are also very good at pinning opponents into their defensive third once a high position has been established. This is done through a combination of counter-pressing and positioning to recover loose balls. Finally, the team possesses outstanding recovery speed. Konate's ability to control and dominate the space behind the defence, particularly the right channel, was shown by the number of races he won or controlled against Ollie Watkins. As the game progressed, Liverpool's defensive line dropped deeper, 10-15 yards from the halfway line when Villa had possession in their own half, limiting any space in behind. Ryan Gravenberch had an excellent defensive performance, shutting down any threats centrally. He also has fantastic recovery speed and athletic abilities to help defend counter-attacks. Gravenberch is very good at reading forward passes by opponents and cutting them out, creating counter-attacking positions for Liverpool through interceptions.

Penalty Box Defending Creates Counter-Attacks

One of the reasons why Liverpool are such a danger on counter-attacks is their determined and disciplined penalty box defending. Konate and van Dijk position themselves superbly. Neither player goes to ground with ease, and both have the physicality to control most opponents. The defensive work rate of the whole team is also vital. Midfielders track their runners and block potential entry points into the box. Forwards also track back and show great defensive desire. It is common to see Nunez regaining the ball close to his own box. In the second half, Luis Diaz sprinted back to make a challenge that snuffed out a promising Villa attack. The one player who will not be seen doing quite so much defensive work is Mo Salah. He benefited from this for the second goal of the game as he was higher up the pitch and latched onto a loose piece of Villa play to race forward and score.

Finding Ways To Overload The Left

As the season has developed, Liverpool's attacking play has become less reliant on the right-hand side, especially in build-up attacks using Konate and Alexander-Arnold to find Szoboszlai or Salah. By using Diaz as the central striker with Gakpo on the left, there is an exchange of positions that helps the players to find space plus the creation of a left side overload with Diaz going into a winger position and Gakpo the position of an inside forward. When the full-back overlaps, this becomes very difficult for opponents to cover and has the benefit of creating space infield as the defending team drags numbers across to handle the overload.

Key Points

- Villa were very good at attacking set-pieces but they didn't have sufficient cover to prevent Liverpool counter-attacking
- Liverpool have evolved away from almost exclusively using a flat front four to press. In this game, they used a 4-1 and 3-1/1-3 variation
- Liverpool have controlled opposition transitions through their in-possession structure
- Using Diaz as the central forward has enabled Liverpool to overload the left side, with him pulling wide alongside Gakpo

Game 18 – Southampton – Premier League – Away – 3-2 win

Liverpool 4-2-3-1

Kelleher, Bradley, Konate, van Dijk, Robertson, Gravenberch, Jones (Mac Allister), Szoboszlai, Salah, Gakpo (Diaz), Nunez (Endo)

Southampton 5-4-1

McCarthy, Walker-Peters, Harwood-Bellis, Downes, Stephens, Fraser (Sugawara), Dibling, Fernandes, Lallana (Aribo), Armstrong (Archer), Onuachu (Ugochukwu)

Scorers – Szoboszlai, Salah (2), Armstrong, Fernandes

A storm came to the British Isles and tested Liverpool's resolve on the south coast. If you asked those who have coached or played football regularly, they will say that the worst conditions to play in are heavy winds. The wind takes away so much control and brings unpredictability to proceedings. Playing styles can be negated and unexpected challenges presented. This game at St Mary's could be seen as a classic wind game.

Southampton Change of Shape

Though Southampton were newly promoted to the Premier League for the 2024/25 season, their playing style under Russell Martin would not fit with any typical underdog stereotyping. Pep Guardiola complimented their commitment to possession and a short passing approach in all areas. Against Liverpool, a system with three central defenders was used as – perhaps – Southampton had noticed Liverpool's troubles against a back three in the build-up phase. Liverpool were likely not expecting Southampton to start with a three as Arne Slot could be seen signalling to his team with three fingers at kick-off. Flynn Downes moved from central midfield into the centre of the back three, meaning that the team sheet would initially have looked like a back four.

Liverpool primarily had problems pressing the Southampton build-up. The wing-backs again were either free to receive or pulled a player out of the centre to allow a pass through the block into midfield. If the Liverpool wingers pulled wide early and man-marked the wing-back, Downes was able to carry the ball forward and deep into Liverpool territory. Liverpool solved this by not pressing aggressively until the ball went wide or Southampton offered a trigger such as a loose pass or poor touch. There were plenty of these.

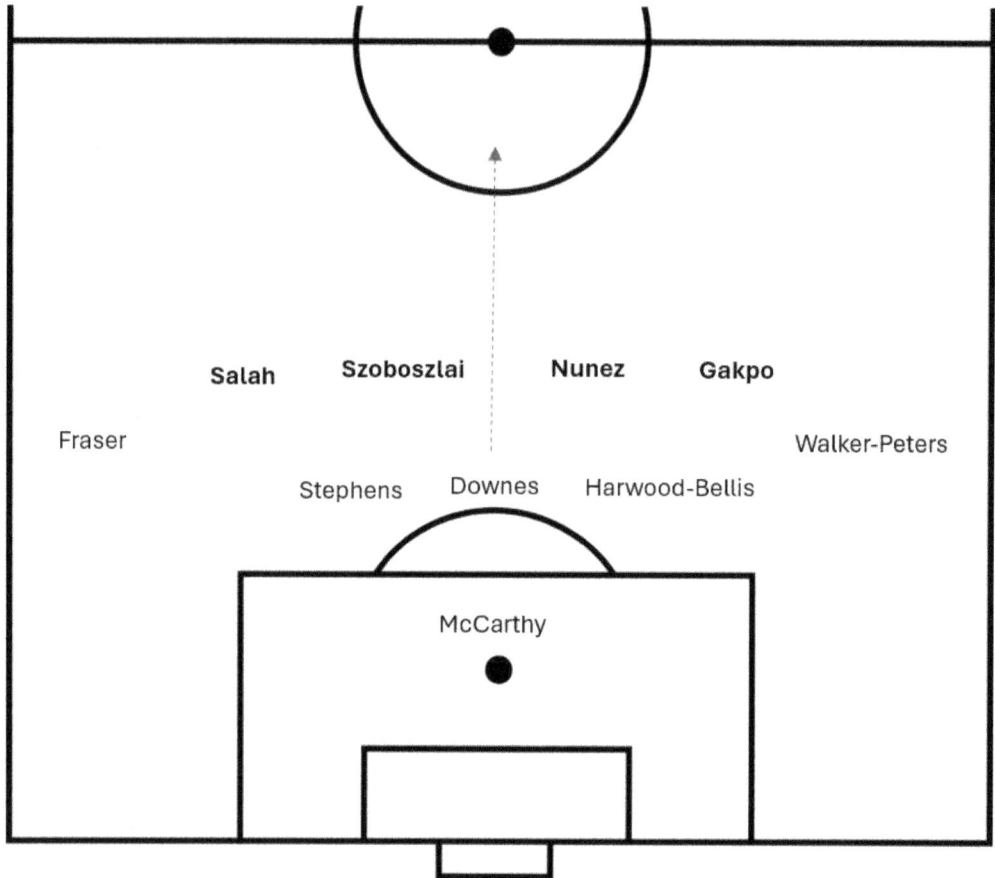

Downes dribbling through the Liverpool press from the centre of a back five

Southampton Playing Into Liverpool's Hands

The first goal came from short Southampton passing in their own box. Their goalkeeper bowled a ball out to a player who had two Liverpool pressers in close proximity. Though he did not turn the ball over immediately, two loose passes later, the ball was at the feet of Szoboszlai on the edge of the area. He curled a finish into the top corner with his left foot.

The Contrast Between Alexander-Arnold and Bradley

Liverpool dominated possession in the first half. With no Alexander-Arnold in the side, the shape was a wide 2-3 when building up, with Gravenberch close to Konate and van Dijk, and the two full-backs higher and wider. Once the ball progressed from close to the halfway line towards the final third, Szoboszlai and Jones both made runs forward, and there were moments when Liverpool created a 5v5 when in possession against the Southampton back line. Robertson was more tucked in than Bradley in the attacking third, making overlaps wide and attacking the far post. Robertson underlapped aggressively as Liverpool peppered crosses in from the left side.

Liverpool Lapses

Liverpool conceded due to a lapse in concentration from van Dijk. He turned over possession in his own half and Southampton gained a penalty. Liverpool have had moments in many games where they have stepped off the tempo or appeared to be finding the game too easy. These lapses have been one of the few vulnerabilities shown by the team.

Liverpool Caught In Transition

At half-time, the score was 1-1 and Liverpool found themselves – once again – having to chase a game in the second half. They upped the intensity in the usual ways, combining with greater speed, getting on the front foot to regain possession, and counter-attacking with more direct passing. Yet it was Southampton who took the lead. As Liverpool had exposed Aston Villa and others this season by breaking forward from set-pieces, it was Southampton who sprung forth from a Liverpool corner to catch the Merseysiders out. Liverpool had three players covering Dibling as he received the ball on the right, but they had over-covered, allowing space centrally. Dibling was able to turn and clip a perfect pass centrally to create a 1v1 situation. Liverpool's excellent recovery speed was on show once again, but they went from over-covering the right to over-covering the left, allowing Alvarez space to finish, having supported the forward run and pass of his teammates. The over-covering comes from recognising the danger but essentially panicking and not fully communicating the threats to teammates.

Liverpool went on to win the game, but they changed very little. Nor did they need to. The flow and run of play had been in their favour all match; it was just that they had been caught out for two goals. What they needed was a strong mentality and a player capable of producing things in the big moments. Step forth Mo Salah, once more! He equalised from a long ball forward that may have also had an assist from the wind. The trajectory of the ball was enough to tempt the Southampton goalkeeper from his line, but he was never going to get to the ball before Salah. Salah touched the ball past the advancing goalkeeper into the net.

As Liverpool continued to apply pressure, Salah then swung in a left-footed cross from the right. The ball swirled and bounced before skidding up into the defender's outstretched hand. Salah converted the penalty. Before the game was done, Salah also hit the post with a volley. Across this season, Salah has grown stronger as games have gone on, scoring and assisting in the second half and in key moments for Liverpool as he wears down opponents – showing outstanding fitness, determination, and mentality.

Key Points

- Southampton changed shape and exploited a weakness in the Liverpool press against ball carriers
- Southampton presented Liverpool with possession in dangerous areas through poor goalkeeper distribution and passing choices
- Alexander-Arnold and Bradley have very different approaches to the right-back role
- Liverpool were unusually caught in transition by Southampton, as their running power to recover became chaotic

Game 19 – Real Madrid – Champions League – Home – 2-0 win

Liverpool 4-2-3-1

Kelleher, Bradley (Gomez), Konate, van Dijk, Robertson, Gravenberch, Mac Allister, Jones (Szoboszlai), Salah, L. Diaz, Nunez (Gakpo)

Real Madrid 4-2-2-2/4-4-2 Diamond

Courtois, Valverde, Asencio, Rudiger, Mendy (Fran Garcia), Camavinga (Ceballos), Modric (Endrick), Guler (Vazquez), Bellingham, B. Diaz, Mbappe

Scorers – Mac Allister, Gakpo

The most enticing name in world football rolled up to Anfield in the Champions League. The defending champions had added Kyliann Mbappe to their ranks of superstars over the summer, but hadn't experienced the best of starts to their season. Nonetheless, they possessed enough shining weapons to hurt any team.

Bradley On The Attack

Liverpool mainly used their 2-3 build-up shape with both full-backs approximately the width of the penalty box. As the ball progressed, Robertson inverted more often, with Bradley taking up wider positions. This changed in the second half when Bradley took up positions in the right-hand half-space, creating more space for Salah on the right.

Conor Bradley's overall performance was much discussed after the game. Without Alexander-Arnold, the young right-back slotted in to face Mbappe. One adrenaline-pumping sliding tackle got the crowd roaring but, generally, the defensive performance was steady and calm. The key to keeping Mbappe quiet was to make it a two-man job. Liverpool had rehearsed for this against Milan and the threat of Leao. Here, Konate supported Bradley just as he had supported Alexander-Arnold against Leao. Any time Mbappe made space against Bradley, there was Konate to close the space. Bradley made lots of adventurous runs off the ball in behind the defence, and Mac Allister picked him out six yards from goal with a cross from the left space. The header was well saved.

Mac Allister and Bradley also combined for the opening goal of the fixture.

Goal of The Season

Alexis Mac Allister's low strike across the goal from just inside the penalty box would not initially appear to be a candidate for Liverpool's goal of the season. If we dig into the manner and construction of the goal, it could be considered the final culmination of combinations Liverpool had been attempting all season without quite finishing them off. Until now! Liverpool had attempted intricate, quick, sharp passing moves around the opposition penalty area, and the moves have drawn ripples of applause without the ball rippling the back of the net. This time, there was no ripple of applause but a roar of excitement. A prolonged period of possession saw Salah receive from Konate on the Liverpool right before he gave the ball back to Konate. Virgil van Dijk then received a 20- yard pass virtually on the centre spot, and with no Real Madrid player within touching distance. Then, Mac Allister received 35 yards from goal, as van Dijk's pass cut out Real's two highest lines of defence. Mac Allister flicked a pass between two Real players to Diaz and his one-touch pass went diagonally backwards to Robertson in space. Curtis Jones had pulled to the touchline. Robertson punched to Jones, who dribbled inside, with Robertson overlapping at speed, attracting the attention of defenders. Jones passed into Mac Allister and drove into the box, injecting pace into the move. Mac Allister then combined with Bradley on the edge of the box, and a swift one-two put Mac Allister in a position 12 yards from goal, just outside the line of the right-hand post. His low shot went through the legs of the defender and into the bottom left corner. An intricate passing move with changes of tempo following a patient period of possession that initially appeared to be going nowhere fast.

Statistical Dominance

Liverpool were statistically dominant against Real Madrid. They had 63% of possession and 16 shots to Real's seven. Liverpool's xG was 2.7 to Real's 1.2 (the majority of the Madrid xG coming from a penalty missed by Mbappe in the second half). A chunk of Liverpool's xG also came from a second-half penalty missed by Salah (all stats from FBref). Real's passive pressing and mismatched shape did not help their cause. Carlo Ancelotti's famed 4-4-2 diamond has the notable natural weakness of no real width in attack or defence. In attack, this can be compensated for by having attacking full-backs, but defensively it can be very hard to prevent overloads in wide areas. The midfield area is packed with four players, but when the ball is passed wide, one of the midfielders has to come out to help the full-back, which can negate the strength initially created by having an extra player in midfield. Liverpool had a lot of possession wide and patiently waited for their moment to play into central players.

"I said: 'I think there's more in you guys than you show at the moment. You can play with more intensity and better with the ball. Forget the shirt that you face, just do what you always do and hopefully we can create more chances than we did in the first half.'" Arne Slot in his post-match press conference

Pincer Pressing

In contrast to Real Madrid, the pressing from Liverpool was highly energetic and intense. Real were able to play out of the initial Liverpool pressure because of the quality of players like Modric and Camavinga, using their intelligence to move into wide positions and create overloads. When that first press was bypassed, Liverpool pressed from both sides in a pincer. The weakness of the press being bypassed is transferred into a strength of being able to pressure players in possession from both sides to force a turnover. Real Madrid simply dropped into a very passive midblock, waiting for Liverpool to make errors that did not come.

Gravenberch Passing and Moving

Liverpool's midfield dominated the game. Gravenberch's position was within the heart of the Real Madrid defensive structure. Gravenberch adapted his style and – rather than receiving, turning and driving forward – he knitted Liverpool's possession together, playing one and two-touch passes to change the angle of the build-up. Alexis Mac Allister's use of one-touch passing was also significant in this fixture. Each Liverpool midfielder brings a slightly different signature to the team, but one of Mac Allister's signatures has been one-touch forward passing. Against Madrid, he used a variety of clips, chips and spins to break lines.

One of Arne Slot's key principles helped a three-man midfield to outplay a four-man midfield. The Liverpool midfielders had license to move and combine. They formed moving triangles in combination. In order to do so, they had to be close to each other, and it is an indication of their energy and intelligence that the midfielders were able to be close enough to each other to combine in midfield triangles and still perform other in-possession duties, such as making runs into the box and supporting teammates in wide areas.

Set-Piece Variations

Over time Liverpool have developed more set-piece routines. Whether these are fixed on the training ground or simply players given license to explore options on the pitch is unclear. In early fixtures, balls were simply delivered into the box, with van Dijk and Konate starting close to the opposition goalkeeper and pulling away to the six-yard box. Short corners have come into play, with the second goal coming from a short corner delivered to the far post by Robertson. Curtis Jones received near the corner of the penalty area, returning to Robertson, who then curved a lofted delivery to the far post and Cody Gakpo headed home.

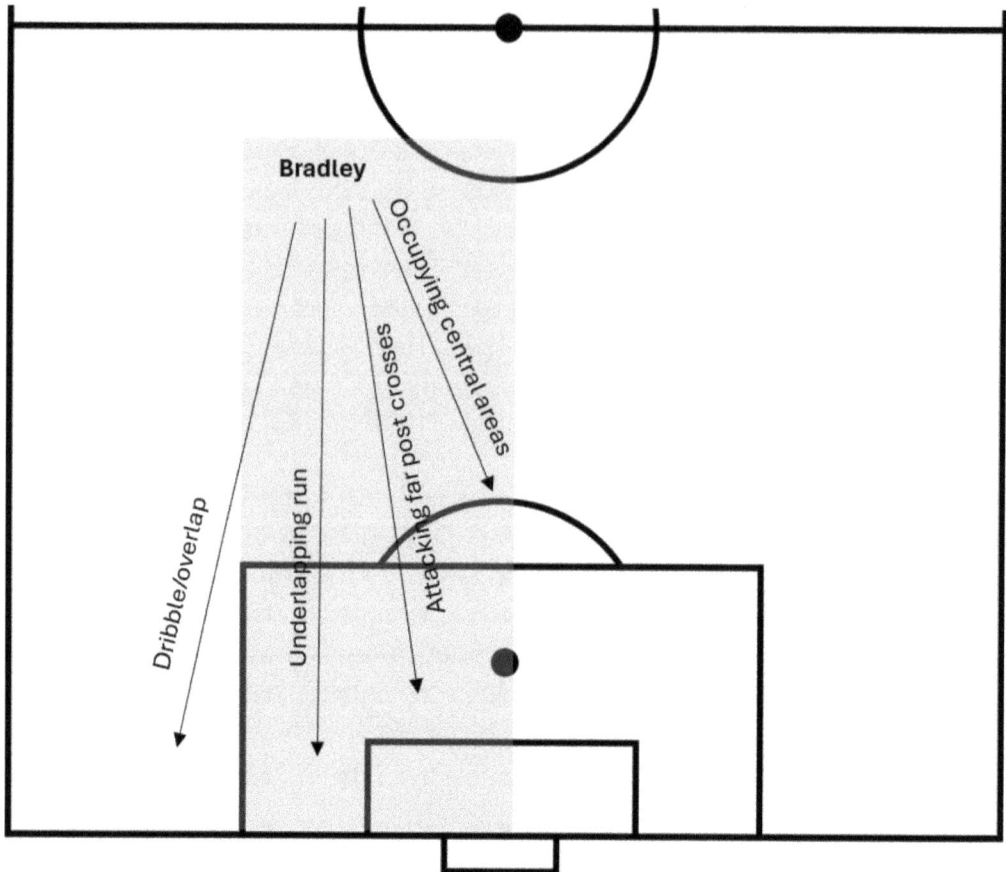
Conor Bradley's attacking movements

Key Points

- Conor Bradley gave a dynamic performance in attack and defence, using his pace to get forward quickly and also recover defensively (as he did in the now-infamous sliding tackle on Mbappe)
- Mac Allister's goal encapsulated everything that Liverpool aim to do in attack, fast flowing one- and two-touch combinations with third-man running
- Liverpool pressed both sides of the ball when the forward pass bypassed the initial press, creating a secondary pincer press
- Gravenberch has progressed the ball by turning and driving forward with the ball at his feet in previous games; against Madrid, he played one- and two-touch passes to knit play together

Game 20 – Manchester City – Premier League – Home – 2-0 win

Liverpool 4-2-3-1

Kelleher, Alexander-Arnold (Quansah), Gomez, van Dijk, Robertson, Gravenberch, Mac Allister, Szoboszlai, Salah (Jones). Gakpo (Nunez), Diaz (Elliott)

Manchester City 4-5-1

Ortega, Walker, Dias, Akanji, Ake, Silva, Gundogan (Savinho), Lewis (Grealish), Nunes (Doku), Foden (de Bruyne), Haaland

Scorers – Gakpo, Salah

Before the season began, this would be a fixture that everyone anticipated. How would Slot's new-look Liverpool cope against the defending four-time consecutive Premier League champions? City had drawn their mid-week Champions League game with Feyenoord 3-3, and did so from a position of being 3-0 in front. Their five previous games before facing Feyenoord had all been defeats. Under Guardiola, a City side had never come into a game with Liverpool in such poor form.

Nonetheless, this game still inspired trepidation. When giants clash, form can count for nothing. During the 2022/23 season, Liverpool had a drop-off in their performances but still found a way to beat City. Many anticipated that Guardiola had something up his sleeve to punish Liverpool.

Liverpool Nail Their Pressing

Liverpool's pressing performance was their best of the season to this point, especially in the first half. In the second half, the pressing was still good but it was much more measured and compact. Liverpool regularly pressed the City build-up in their defensive third with a five-player unit, with Szoboszlai and Mac Allister joining the front three to apply pressure. If City progressed out of their defensive third, the midfielders and central defenders snapped into challenges with an aggressive, front-foot performance. Gravenberch mopped up passes in central areas, also stopping City players from turning and playing forward effectively. The positioning of the Liverpool front five enabled Gravenberch and the full-backs to read and anticipate the next City pass.

In open play, the Liverpool midfield swarmed City, giving no time to play. This swarm was often followed by fast one-touch passing as Liverpool gained field position. Liverpool pinned Manchester City into the corners with an aggressive four-player press. Alexander-Arnold would join the press or position himself to pick off the passes City used to try to escape over or through the pressure. Gravenberch and Alexander-Arnold were able to exchange roles depending on their start positions, remembering that it should always be the closest player to the ball who presses in order to maintain a semblance of structure.

"If you want to win against City, you have to be perfect in every part of the game. High press, low press, build-up. They bring so many problems to you. We came close to perfection. We weren't perfect, but we came close to perfection. That's the only way to beat a quality team like City." Arne Slot speaking to BBC Sport

City's Press Out of Sync

Manchester City were not at their pressing best. The shape was very narrow, with Haaland and Foden looking to create a 2v2 scenario against Konate and van Dijk. As the press was so narrow, it was very easy for Kelleher to find a pass to a free full-back. Nunes was positioned 'half and half' between Alexander-Arnold and Szoboszlai but was too far away to impact either of them; Liverpool were always able to find a free player. In the second half, Manchester City pushed an additional player into midfield and pressed more successfully, able to pin Liverpool in for periods, but this was not enough to fully dominate the game. Liverpool were happy to engage their pressure closer to the halfway line and defend the box to look for breakaways in the second half. As City seemed to be increasing the pressure on Liverpool, some good box defending resulted in a counter-attack and a penalty to make the game 2-0.

Long Balls Against The City Full-Backs

Throughout the game, Liverpool were happy to use long balls to the wingers. Nathan Ake attempted to keep a high line, but Salah's pace continually caused him problems. On the opposite side, Kyle Walker had a torrid time against Cody Gakpo and long diagonals. Often, Gakpo didn't control the diagonal cleanly, but Walker wanted to connect with Gakpo rather than the ball. This created a scrap for a loose, secondary ball that was won by Gakpo who could then drive at the City defence. Walker did not cover himself in glory for either Liverpool goal, switching off at the far post as Gakpo arrived, and then losing possession following a long ball in the build-up to the penalty kick.

Midfield Rotation And Movement

The Liverpool midfield picked up where they left off against Madrid with excellent rotation and movement. Diaz regularly came short to receive from the central striker position, triggering forward runs from Szoboszlai. Trent Alexander-Arnold took up central positions, which triggered Szoboszlai to go wider on the right. Gravenberch was the dominant figure in the game from midfield. In possession, he was able to turn and set attacks into motion. Out of possession, he jumped into presses, coming away with possession and preventing City from playing forward. In the second half, the jump pressure onto forward passes created a chance for Salah as he intercepted a forward pass and raced clear, but put the finish over the bar when 1v1 against Ortega.

How Manchester City tried to create a 2v2 against the Liverpool central defenders. City were very narrow and Liverpool were able to play out to their full-backs with ease.

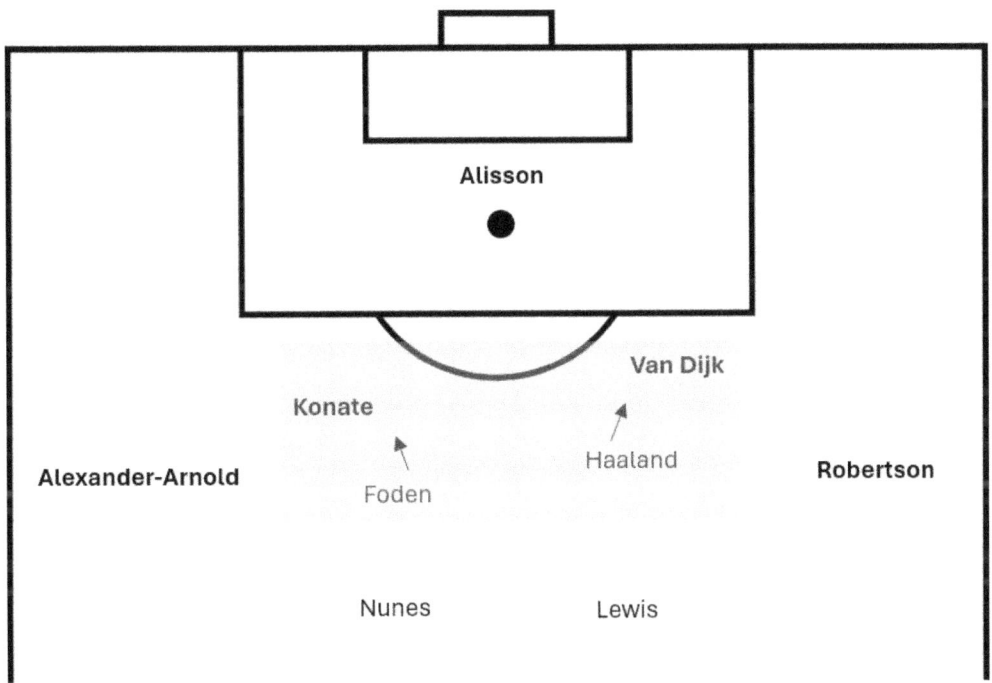

Set-Piece Threats

Liverpool were also a threat from corner kicks. Although he didn't score, van Dijk came close on a number of occasions. Early in the game, van Dijk hit the post with a header at the far post following a short corner. Later in the first half, he headed wide from the centre of the six-yard box, attacking the ball from deep. In the second half, van Dijk glanced a header over the bar at the near post, having started at the far post and moved round to the front post to lose markers.

Van Dijk was also responsible for the only real opportunity Manchester City had in the game. With the score at 2-0, van Dijk took a little too long in possession, and de Bruyne pinched the ball, creating a 1v1 with Kelleher. Fortunately for Liverpool and van Dijk, Kelleher was able to make the save. It is not the first time in the season that van Dijk has had a lapse with Liverpool in a strong position. At Southampton, a similar error created the chain of events that gave away a penalty and would put Southampton ahead. As great as van Dijk is, there are occasionally complacent moments to remind us that no one is flawless.

Key Points

- Liverpool combined a five player press with aggressive secondary pressing from full-backs and defensive midfield
- City tried to create a 2v2 press but couldn't get the balance right, especially in the first-half
- Liverpool used long balls to feed Salah and Gakpo who used their physical attributes to outplay the City full-backs
- Gravenberch, Mac Allister, and Szoboszlai provided an excellent balance in midfield, rotating and covering space
- Liverpool and Slot have developed attacking set-pieces as the season has progressed

Game 21 – Newcastle – Premier League – Away – 3-3 draw

Liverpool 4-2-3-1

Kelleher, Quansah, Gomez (Alexander-Arnold), van Dijk, Robertson, Gravenberch (Szoboszlai), Mac Allister, Jones, Salah, Gakpo (Diaz), Nunez

Newcastle 4-3-3

Pope, Livramento, Schar, Burn, Hall, Tonali (Longstaff), Guimaraes, Joelinton (Willock), Murphy (Barnes), Gordon (Wilson), Isak

Scorers – Jones, Salah (2), Isak, Gordon, Schar

After the two best-sustained performances of the season came one of the toughest challenges… Newcastle.

Newcastle were fantastic against Liverpool, yet Slot's men were able to find a way back into the game when down, and even put themselves into a position where victory was a possibility.

Newcastle Press Man-For-Man In Midfield

Newcastle were by far the better team in the first half of the match. Liverpool created very little in the face of a midfield that had great balance between high pressing and tight mid-block. Newcastle's grip on the game began with the suffocation of the Liverpool midfield, arguably the area where Liverpool have been most expert at controlling opponents.

The midfield trio of Tonali, Guimaraes, and Joelinton went man-to-man with the Liverpool midfield, aggressively attacking passes into the Liverpool players to prevent them turning and playing out of the defensive third with ease. Ryan Gravenberch received special treatment, and if he was able to get away from his midfield marker, Anthony Gordon was never far away and got close, preventing the trademark Gravenberch turns and even impacting his one and two-touch passing. Sandro Tonali went tight to Curtis Jones – the other Liverpool player who has the turning skills to get out of pressure. Jones has been able to affect opponents, memorably Chelsea and Leverkusen, by breaking away with dribbling skills, but Tonali gave him no opportunities. When Liverpool did progress beyond their defensive third, they then faced the challenge of breaking through a tightknit line of five, as the Newcastle midfield barred passing lines and Liverpool were unable to pick out players in the half-spaces between the lines.

"In the first half, we had a lot of problems with their intensity, aggressive playing style without the ball – aggressive in a good way. We tried to cope with it, but every time we touched them, we got a yellow and that doesn't really help for us to be intense then as well." Arne Slot speaking to Liverpool FC TV

The tight 4-5-1 block Newcastle used to prevent Liverpool playing through with ease, while matching up 3v3 in midfield

Newcastle Exploit Liverpool's Right Side

Once Newcastle had picked off possession of the ball, they then fed the brilliant Alexander Isak. Liverpool's starting lineup was without two first-choice players on the right-hand side and Isak picked on that side ruthlessly during the game. Joe Gomez filled in for Konate, while both Alexander-Arnold and Bradley were unavailable at right-back. Jarrell Quansah was chosen to perform in his place, but Isak was more than enough to tie the pair in knots. When you add the presence of Anthony Gordon to that side, then Liverpool found themselves with a severe defensive problem.

Isak opened the scoring with a powerful strike from outside the box from the inside left channel, emphasising his ability to play across the front line and occupy the whole defence on his own. In the second half, Isak smartly created a 2v1 against Quansah to supply Gordon with a chance, which he converted. Gomez dropped very deep, a long way from Isak, whilst Gordon was on the shoulder of Quansah. Isak spotted this and drove at Quansah, drawing the defender closer and giving Gordon more space to receive a pass and score. Gordon had missed a

1v1 with Kelleher just before half-time (that came from an error in this area), but made no mistake with a second opportunity.

Alexander-Arnold Changes The Game

Following the second goal, Gomez was withdrawn and Alexander-Arnold brought on. This substitution was critical. After half-time, Liverpool had already made an adjustment to cope with the Newcastle midfield block by playing forward into wide areas more quickly (thus gaining better field position), but they still struggled to play through the lines and pick out Jones between the lines. The game went from a tactical battle that Newcastle had control of, into a transitional second half, which Newcastle were still winning until the arrival of Alexander-Arnold. With the ball moving into high wide areas early, there came a barrage of crosses prior to the arrival of Trent. Once he came into the game, Liverpool now had a player with the ability to punch passes *through* the Newcastle midfield block and open up attacking opportunities.

Alexander-Arnold picked forward passes from his inverted role. Szoboszlai (on as a substitute) may have made the opportunities to pass through the lines easier, though. Gravenberch had been withdrawn, moving Jones deeper into the holding midfield role, and both Mac Allister and Szoboszlai attacked the spaces between the lines, meaning Newcastle had more potential passing lanes to break. Jones has the dribbling skills to match Gravenberch from deep, while he and Mac Allister could rotate when needed, just as Mac Allister and Gravenberch do. This match saw the rare example of Gravenberch struggling to influence the game, with credit going to the aggressive pressing of the Newcastle midfield. Alexander-Arnold had the quality to pierce even a small line in the block, however, and his ability to fill multiple roles within the one game was to the fore with his two assists coming from low crosses within the half-space but inside the Newcastle block. The double role as a midfield creator and wide attacker proved vital in turning the performance around.

All three Liverpool goals came from their right side. Newcastle defended their left side superbly, paying extra attention to Cody Gakpo. Gakpo had been in excellent form coming into the game, with his ability to dribble down the line and cut inside being especially effective. Newcastle doubled up on Gakpo, just as Liverpool had against wide threats such as Leao and Mbappe. In truth, Gakpo was kept relatively quiet throughout.

Late Error From Kelleher Costs Liverpool Three Points

Liverpool found themselves 3-2 in front late in the game. Newcastle equalised as a freekick from the right drifted out of the reach of Kelleher, and Fabian Schaar –

although operating at a very tight angle – had the quality to steer the ball into the net. Kelleher could have done better for both the Gordon goal (the shot squirmed through his hand) and the late equaliser, and it should be noted that he had made similar misjudgements over the flight of crosses in previous games. It should also be noted that Kelleher had done an *exceptional* job filling in for Alisson, making crucial saves at big moments. He does have these errors in him – all goalkeepers make errors – perhaps they become more noticeable when you are waiting for a world-class goalkeeper to return to the lineup.

Key Points

- Newcastle's midfield dominated with a man-to-man press that reverted into a five-man midblock that proved difficult to punch through
- Newcastle picked on Liverpool's depleted right side, attacking an out-of-position Quansah and an out of practice Gomez
- Trent Alexander-Arnold came on and changed the game for Liverpool with his ability to punch passes through small gaps in midfield
- Liverpool's right-hand side provided all three goals, with Salah involved in all three goals and Alexander-Arnold in two

Game 22 – Girona – Champions League – Away – 1-0 win

Liverpool 4-2-3-1

Alisson, Alexander-Arnold, Gomez, van Dijk, Robertson, Gravenberch, Jones (Elliott), Szoboszlai, Salah, Diaz (Endo), Nunez (Gakpo)

Girona 4-4-2

Gazzaniga, Frances, Krejci, Blind (Solis), Gutierrez, van de Beek (Martin), Romeu, Juanpe, Gil (Portu), Asprilla, Danjuma (Stuani)

Scorers – Salah

Girona were the surprise package of the 2023/24 Spanish season. A small club with little pedigree, they finished third in La Liga, behind only the giants of Real Madrid and Barcelona. Indeed, Atletico Madrid finished five points behind Girona in fourth. Manager Michel took plaudits for a free, attacking system that scored victories against the bigger-name clubs in Spain. One season on, and a number of the players who made a huge impact left, either returning to their parent clubs from which they were loaned or lured away for large fees.

Girona Tactical Flexibility

Against Liverpool, Girona showed flexibility and freedom in their play as they pushed numbers up into their front line; there was freedom of movement from deep. Daley Blind, playing as a central defender, popped up in the centre-forward position. Left-back Gutierrez attacked and underlapped aggressively. The fundamental attacking shape of Girona was a fluid 4-2-4, with an emphasis on the wide players, who aimed to utilise their dribbling skills. Danjuma proved a great threat to Liverpool with his fast, direct 1v1 skills, beating defenders regularly. Unfortunately for him, he lacked the final action to really punish Liverpool.

The 4-2-4 attacking shape allowed Girona to easily shift into a 4-4-2 when out of possession. They attempted to press aggressively, in one instance sending seven players into the Liverpool defensive third to press. Once the press was beaten, Girona looked to get everyone back behind the ball as quickly as possible to create a rigid 4-4-2.

Open Game

Despite Girona's discipline and recovery runs, Liverpool were a counter-attacking threat in an open first half and – at one stage – Liverpool had a 5v4 breakaway that came to nothing. From other breaks, Nunez headed wide when well-placed and shot at the goalkeeper after Salah played him in. When Arne Slot said he was happy with the result but not the performance, he was no doubt displeased with how open the first half was. The first half had many similarities to the game at Red Bull Leipzig earlier in the competition, with both teams having plenty of shots and opportunities. Girona had less possession than Liverpool but used the wings well in the first half. In the second half, Liverpool forced Girona deeper, making them defend their own box more (in the first half, Girona were able to defend 10-15 yards from their own penalty area). The higher regain point meant that when they fed their wingers, the support players were closer and could support the breakaways in numbers. In the second half, the wide players were more isolated and it was easier for Liverpool to contain the counter-attacks of Girona.

Crosses Pin Girona Back

Liverpool used a stream of crosses to pin Girona into their defensive third. The majority of the crosses came from the half-space, either inside or outside the box. Liverpool's crosses from inside the box are usually generated by Robertson underlapping from full-back on the left, and Szoboszlai underlapping from midfield on the right. Against Girona, the crosses came from the half-space outside the box, with the full-backs delivering from balls cut back to them or wingers cutting in and using inswinging crosses. The constant pressure of the crosses created the error that led to the match-winning penalty. Robertson crossed from the half-space, the clearance dropped to Diaz, who was clipped, and Salah then stroked in the penalty.

Differences Between Gakpo and Diaz

Diaz and Gakpo can both play in the wide left position of the 4-2-3-1 system. Both play the role slightly differently, and it would seem that Slot prefers Gakpo on the left when Liverpool are chasing the game. Luis Diaz performs the role as an inside forward who runs in behind, arrives at the far post or cuts inside and shoots. Gakpo has a few more strings to his bow; he can dribble on the outside and cross with his left as well as cut inside. When Diaz cuts inside to cross, his deliveries tend to stay low while Gakpo clears the first defender, floating the ball to the far post. Diaz's attributes have made him a candidate for the centre-forward position, a role that Gakpo sometimes filled under Jurgen Klopp.

Gakpo also presses a little differently. When he plays wide left, and the team presses high on the right, Gakpo staggers his position while still edging wide; by comparison, Diaz tends to come inside very early. Against Girona, there were three different pressing shapes used, but sometimes the differences can be less tactically deliberate and more to do with the way individuals go about their work.

The half-space positions that Diaz and Robertson crossed from, to pin Girona in, and create the penalty kick

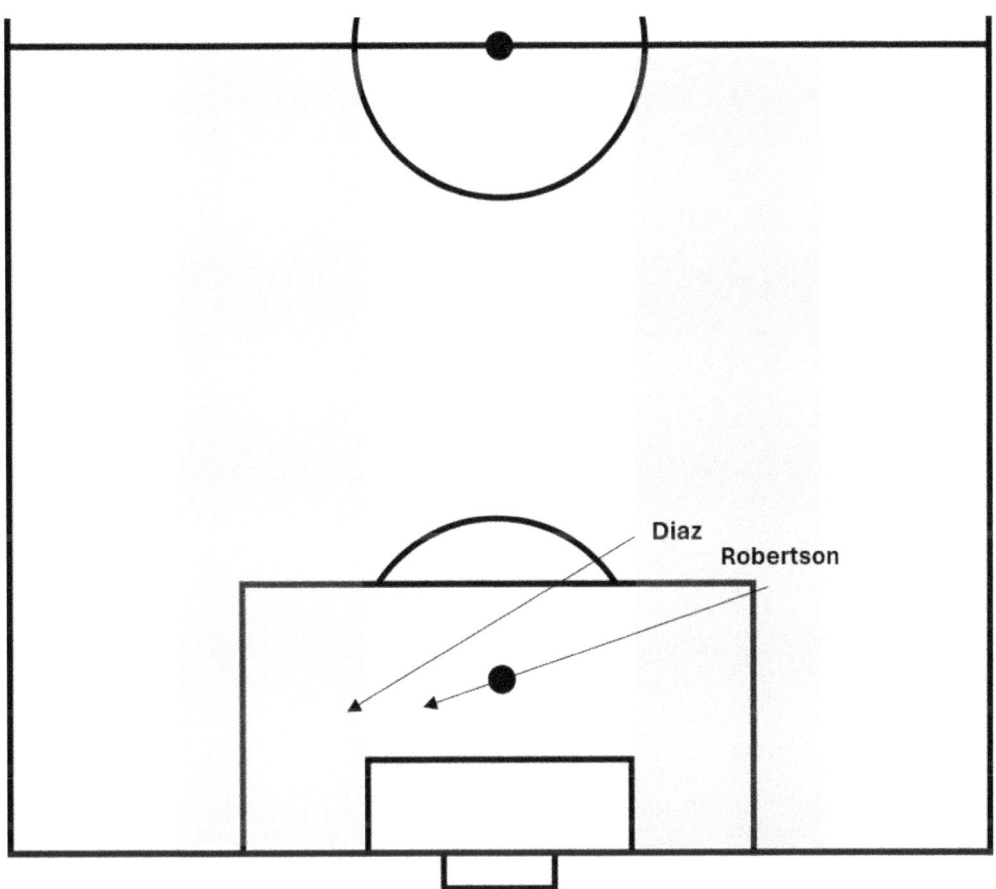

Liverpool Use A 3-5 Press Against Girona Restarts

The 4-2-4 semi-passive press was used, designed to slow ball progression and wait for triggers before pressing. The 4-2-4 can lead to aggressive pressing into wide areas where as many as five players enter the opposition full-back area. Depending on who is closest, Gravenberch or Alexander-Arnold will join the press while the other covers the space behind. Against Girona, it was often Alexander-Arnold pressing with Gravenberch. For goalkicks, Liverpool used a 3-5 pressing shape, with a triangle of forwards around the Girona penalty area. The full-backs were both poised to jump on any attempts at progressive passes down the line, while the midfielders were ready to cover behind the full-backs as well as any passes centrally.

Change Of Tempo

Once in front, Liverpool opted to slow the game down, lowering the tempo of passing and using less aggressive pressing (the flat 4-2-4). They looked to create little triangles to keep the ball away from Girona pressure in midfield and adopted an extremely patient approach in possession.

Key Points

- Girona troubled Liverpool with positional flexibility
- For the most part, the game was open in transitions with both teams threatening on the break
- Liverpool used half-space crosses to pin Girona back and take control of the game
- Gakpo and Diaz played the left wing role differently due to their different attributes
- Liverpool changed tempo according to the game state, happy to slow the game down and be patient when the game called for it

Game 23 – Fulham – Premier League – Home – 2-2 draw

Liverpool 4-2-3-1

Alisson, Alexander-Arnold (Jota), Gomez, van Dijk, Robertson, Gravenberch, Jones (Quansah), Szoboszlai (Elliott), Salah, Gakpo (Nunez), Diaz

Fulham 4-2-3-1

Leno, Tete (Castagne), Diop, Cuenca, Robinson, Berge, Lukic, Iwobi, Pereira (Smith-Rowe), Wilson (Traore), Jimenez (Muniz)

Scorers – Gakpo, Jota, Pereira, Muniz

Red cards change everything. Early on and already behind, the draw became a good result.

Robertson vs Robinson

Robertson was the man sent off. A long ball in behind tested Robertson, and his poor control allowed Wilson to get to the ball. Robertson brought him down, and he was sent off. One perspective is that Robertson had an awful game, but another (kinder) perspective is that the early injury really hindered him, and he never recovered. He received a hard kick very early in the game as he won a race with Harry Wilson, a similar long ball behind to the one that led to the red card. Robertson's tough time continued as Fulham's opening goal deflected in off his knee. His game ended in the 17th minute sending off. How much of his struggles were down to that early kick we will never really know. From here, the real game began.

Fulham's Antonee Robinson was a thorn in Liverpool's side all game. Liverpool have been linked with Robinson as a potential replacement for Robertson and this game certainly helped add fuel to that fire. The perception is that Robertson's performances are dipping below his best, and that age is catching up with him, with errors creeping into his game. Robinson is full of youthful dynamism and creativity, by comparison, galloping up and down the left flank to deliver threatening crosses and create goals. He provided the assist for both Fulham goals, and for the second goal, he started the move by playing out from his defensive third before sprinting forward to join the attack.

Drastic Tactical Change

Arne Slot knew the importance of not dropping points in this fixture. He dug deep into his array of shapes to try to maintain an attacking threat for Liverpool.

Suddenly, all of the experiments in the League Cup and the failed attempt at an Ajax '95 3-diamond-3 (in the Forest defeat) came together. The key was maintaining the principle of an extra man in defence but still being able to attack with numbers and control and utilising Ryan Gravenberch as a half-back.

Out of possession, Gravenberch could drop into central defence, but in possession, he would step forward into the same deep pivot role. When he did this, the full-backs remained tucked in tight, creating a rest defence diamond. The full-backs could push wide and – if they did – Gravenberch remained to create a three. This is reminiscent of the relationship between Blind and Rijkaard at Ajax in the 1995 Champions League-winning side. Given that Alexander-Arnold inverts and the left-back underlaps, the full-backs could remain tight and let the wingers pull wide to stretch the opposition, just as they would with eleven men on the pitch, looking for 1v1 opportunities. Liverpool had to be very careful how they covered the full-back areas. When out of possession, Gakpo was considerably deeper, playing in a position closer to a wing-back. In possession, Curtis Jones often played a role that is called the "false full-back", covering the right-back area in a manner that Henderson, Milner, and Wijnaldum did in the Klopp era.

The initial switch was to a 4-4-1. In possession, this became a 3-3-3, with the front line of three stretching across the pitch and shifting into 3-2-4. After Fulham went 2-1 in front, Slot made two very attacking substitutions, bringing on Jota and Elliott for Alexander-Arnold and Szoboszlai. The system was firmly 3-1-4-1. Darwin Nunez became the focal point through the centre, with Jota joining from deep. Jota and Nunez could rotate, which they did for the equaliser, as Nunez came short to thread a terrific pass into Jota, who skipped past two players and tucked a finish into the bottom corner.

"We just thought [to] bring all the players in that can score a goal. And then to see them working so hard without the ball... so we had five or six players who were mainly offensive players but with ten to keep the other team away from goal and still create chances was great to see." Arne Slot speaking to Liverpool FC TV

*The attacking shape that Liverpool used when chasing the game
and reduced to ten men*

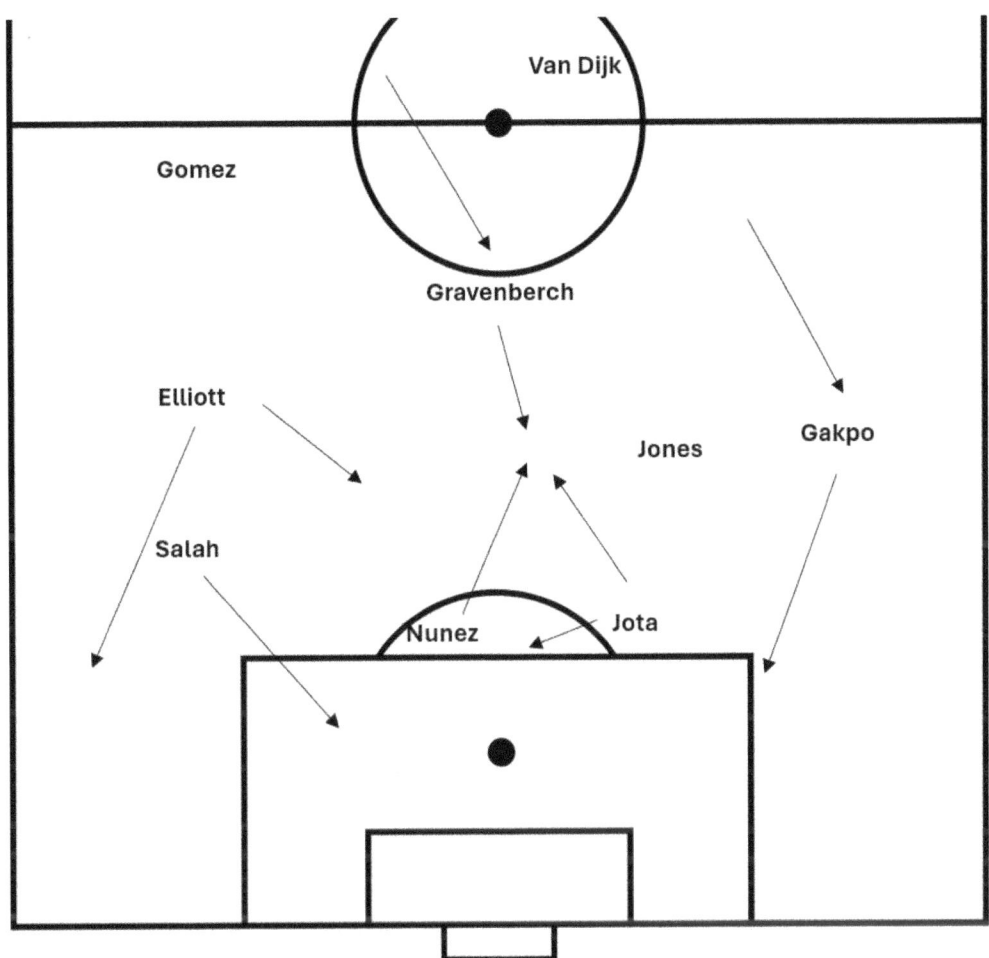

Gakpo Height Advantage

This was Liverpool's second equaliser of the game. The first was just after half-time and came from a now-familiar combination. Salah on the right cut inside and floated a cross to the far post. Gakpo beat his full-back marker to head in. Liverpool are utilising Gakpo at the far post more often under Slot than they did under Klopp. Given that Gakpo is 6'4", this makes a lot of sense; he has a height advantage over the majority of full-backs.

Pressing Despite Being A Man Down

Even when down to ten men, Liverpool pressed aggressively. It can often be very difficult to do when holding a numbers disadvantage but – chasing the game –

Slot decided to take the gamble. The press was the same as it would be in an 11v11 situation, using a 1-4 and 2-1-3 with the full-backs pressing high at goal kicks once the ball moved out to the appropriate side of the pitch. The opposite side full-back tucked inside, and the wide player furthest from the ball dropped deeper and tucked inside, helping to cover the centre but also poised to jump and press if the ball was switched across. This aggression may have been at fault for Fulham's second goal as they were able to play forward from a goal kick, but – overall – the aggression enabled Liverpool to put Fulham under pressure and nullify the man advantage.

Slot went against the accepted norms of how to play when you are reduced to ten men and was rewarded with an energetic performance that could have claimed all three points.

Key Points

- Andy Robertson has been discussed as a point of weakness in this Liverpool lineup. Robinson has been touted as a replacement and each player's impact on the game was vastly contrasting
- The attempted 3-diamond-3 system used when trailing at home to Forest made a return, this time looking far more practiced
- Gravenberch offered an intriguing glimpse of positional flexibility by slotting into a half-back role
- Cody Gakpo has a significant height advantage against most full-backs which can be exploited
- Slot and Liverpool gambled defensively to press even with a man less, being extremely aggressive on the ball side, but withdrawn and cautious on the open side away from the ball

Game 24 – Southampton – EFL Cup – Away – 2-1 win

Liverpool 4-3-3

Kelleher, Alexander-Arnold (Chiesa), Quansah, Endo, Gomez (Tsimikas). Mac Allister (McConnell), Morton, Nyoni (Danns), Elliott, Gakpo (Jota), Nunez

Southampton 5-4-1

McCarthy, Bree (Sugawara), Harwood-Bellis, Bednarek (Brereton), Wood, Manning, Dibling, Downes (Sulemana), Aribo (Lallana), Fernandes, Archer (Onuachu)

Scorers – Nunez, Elliott, Archer

Responsibility for the team passed to John Heitinga for this cup tie as Arne Slot was suspended. The team was rotated heavily, playing a 4-3-3 with Endo in the centre of defence, and this was a version of the half-back system that ended the game with Fulham.

Gelling The Understudies Together

Tyler Morton filled the defensive midfield pivot role and, at times, Endo advanced beyond or alongside him when the team had possession. Joe Gomez dribbled the ball forward from his deeper role, and when this happened, Endo dropped in to cover the space.

Liverpool's possession structure often looked like a 3-1-3 system as both full-backs narrowed and Endo went ahead of the trio of defenders. If a full-back pushed on, Endo slotted in with Morton between the lines of three. The shape shifted in the second half as substitutions were made. Tsimikas came on at full-back, pushing higher and wider. Tyler Morton moved to right-back, playing an extremely inverted role. The system became more akin to the familiar 2-3/3-2 build.

"If I have to give someone a big compliment, it should be Wata Endo because in a different position playing such a good game in these circumstances, that shows you what a quality player he is." Arne Slot speaking in the post-match press conference

Liverpool had a lot of freedom in their defensive structure because Southampton played with just one forward and a deep 5-4-1 system. Liverpool quashed Southampton attacks with ease until Southampton chased the game in the second half, throwing on attacking players to play directly up against the Liverpool line in and out of possession, utilising a press when trying to recover the scoreline that they did not use earlier in the game. The tempo from Southampton became much higher with greater intent in their play; the 5-4-1 shifted to a back three with the wing-backs extremely high.

Pressing Alexander-Arnold Is High Risk

Southampton were perhaps discouraged from pressing by a moment in the first half that led to a goal. Alexander-Arnold received a pass in his own half that was slightly behind him and two Southampton players tried to swarm him, but he dribbled away from both, then struck a ball behind the defence with his weaker left foot. The pass came to Nunez to slot into the net. Teams need to be careful with their choice of player to press. Trent may not be the right press trigger.

Liverpool Play Through Southampton

Southampton's 5-4-1 was quite easy for Liverpool to play through. Some of this was down to the movement from the Liverpool central defenders, but generally, Liverpool's players had license to drop into areas and step away from their nominal positions. Harvey Elliott and Trey Nyoni exchanged from wide and central midfield, and the striker would often come short, allowing midfielders to run in behind, which has now become a hallmark of Liverpool's play. As the season has progressed, Liverpool's rotations and movement triggers have grown. The rotations enable Liverpool to breach opposition defensive lines.

Slot can be characterised as a manager whose teams play more short passes than long passes; they are happy to play long, quickly, and early in behind. Earlier in the season, the long passes into Salah were the main attacking threat of the side. In this game, Liverpool looked for the pass behind the wing-back and outside the central defender to Gakpo time after time. Eventually, Gakpo created a goal for Elliott: receiving wide, dribbling infield, and feeding Elliott after a brief exchange of passes in a central area.

Further Corner Experiments

Liverpool have shown a willingness to experiment with corner kicks from game to game. Similarly, Arsenal have been massively successful with corners where the ball is delivered to the near post with a large number of players coming from outside the far post to attack the zone and block off defenders and the goalkeeper. Liverpool attempted their own version of this corner routine against Southampton with little success.

Key Points

- Slot continues to use the League Cup to experiment and test the capabilities of younger players, players who aren't the number one (or two) choice for their position, or a new system
- The choice to press Alexander-Arnold is loaded with risk as he can break the press and start attacks
- Liverpool's midfield rotation movements are not just limited to Gravenberch, Mac Allister and Szoboszlai, but imprinted upon the whole squad
- Liverpool experimented with the Arsenal corner routine which has led to many goals

Game 25 – Spurs - Premier League – Away – 6-3 win

Liverpool 4-2-3-1

Alisson, Alexander-Arnold, Gomez, van Dijk, Robertson, Gravenberch, Mac Allister (Jones), Szoboszlai, Salah (Eliott), Gakpo (Jota), Diaz (Nunez)

Spurs 4-2-3-1

Forster, Porro, Dragusin, Gray, Spence, Sarr (Bergvall), Bissouma, Kulusevski, Maddison (Johnson), Son (Werner), Solanke

Scorers – Diaz (2), Mac Allister, Szoboszlai, Salah (2), Maddison, Kulusevski, Solanke

The match at Tottenham will go down as one of the more extraordinary clashes of the season. Spurs had been ravaged by injuries, particularly in defence, but Ange Postecoglou had stuck steadfastly to his beliefs in possession-based attacking football and looked defensively questionable. Against Chelsea, four goals were conceded. Against Manchester United, three were conceded. Then, against Slot's Liverpool, six were conceded.

Spurs' Principles Cause Them Problems

Spurs tried to stick to their principles and their identity. Attempting to press in an aggressive 1-4 shape, committing players forward in attack, and using short passing to build out from defence, adherence to these principles gave Spurs problems of their own creation. Fraser Forster (deputising) in goal has been a fine shot-stopper and uses his frame well to dominate balls into the penalty area, but he has never been an expert with the ball at his feet. His inconsistent passing put Tottenham under early pressure, complicating their ability to build out against a Liverpool team that needed no encouragement to apply additional pressure. The whole point of Spurs' (and other teams, including Liverpool) short passing in their own territory is to lure the press to then create space to either pass through or over. With Alexis Mac Allister joining the press, Liverpool were able to create out-of-possession overloads, at one point creating a 4v3. When Spurs went over to relieve pressure, van Dijk dominated in the air.

Liverpool Use Extra Players In The Build-Up

The Spurs press was negated by Liverpool pulling Gravenberch and Mac Allister back to help the build. Spurs pressed with as many as five players, which Liverpool countered with a hexagon (2-2-2) of six, ensuring an overload. They were regularly able to use a combination of Gravenberch and Alexander-Arnold to escape the press on the right, using one-twos and third-man combinations with Mac Allister.

Long Balls In Behind

Liverpool were also happy to put the Spurs full-backs under pressure with long passes in behind, especially for Salah up against Spence. When the ball went behind for Salah, he drove inside, triggering a crossover movement with Szoboszlai. At 2-1 just before half-time, Liverpool sent a long ball forward which was flicked on near the halfway line. Salah ran on to the flick, drove infield, and Szoboszlai crossed over. Salah provided a reverse pass for Szoboszlai to tuck away the opportunity. This was a similar movement to Salah's goal at Arsenal, that time in combination with Darwin Nunez.

Two other significant elements of Liverpool's play came together for the goal. One was the movement of Szoboszlai and Luis Diaz. Diaz playing in the centre-forward position had freedom to float. He often came short to receive or moved out to the left, creating an overload with Gakpo, 2v1 against the right-back, Porro. When Diaz dropped short or moved wide, Szoboszlai pushed into the centre-forward position, making runs in behind, receiving to feet, or attacking the box on crosses. Then, Spurs risked pressing Alexander-Arnold. Spurs had just scored and there were mere minutes until half-time. A slightly loose pass forced Trent to run backwards towards his own goal, take a negative touch, and put the ball onto his weaker foot. All of which is textbook for triggering a press. The problem was that the press came from the Spurs left-back, jumping forward away from Salah, forcing a central defender across to pick up Salah and create a mismatch between Gray and Szoboszlai centrally. The next problem for Spurs is that Alexander-Arnold has a pretty strong weaker foot. He fired a long ball forward to be flicked on, and created the position for Salah and Szoboszlai to combine and score Liverpool's third.

Half-Space Crosses

Back in the 23rd minute, Alexander-Arnold created Liverpool's opening goal. A right-footed half-space cross found the head of Luis Diaz to swoop and head home. Diaz had made a run from outside the penalty area to attack the box, with Szoboszlai, the player in the centre-forward position. Liverpool's second goal also came from a half-space cross, this time from the left and Andy Robertson. Gakpo rolled the ball back into the path of Robertson who clipped a ball towards the far post. Szoboszlai challenged with two defenders, and although he did not win the header cleanly, he kept the ball alive for Mac Allister to attack and score. It must be said that Alexander-Arnold used the half-spaces to deliver an array of brilliantly crafted and shaped passes. One in particular curved around defenders with superb precision to create a shooting opportunity for Salah.

Liverpool had put themselves in a position of dominance in the first half that was almost wasted. Alexis Mac Allister was caught in possession in his defensive third, and this allowed James Maddison to curl in an excellent goal from outside the box. Fortunately for Liverpool, they scored again just before half-time.

Recycling Possession

Liverpool kept Spurs under pressure, pinning them in their own half when possible, with the high positioning of the team and central defenders recycling the ball. Spurs put bodies on the line to block shots and repel Liverpool attacks but refused to give in, continuing to commit numbers forward in attack whenever the opportunity arose. Liverpool's own ability to defend the penalty area enabled them to strike on the counter-attack and exploit spaces behind the ever-high Tottenham defensive line.

Liverpool's fourth, fifth and sixth goals were all scored on the counter-attack. After Liverpool's fourth goal, the game became end-to-end with Spurs still committed. Liverpool seem to come out well in open games because of their powerful recovery running in transition. At this stage of the season, they seem capable of outrunning and out-recovering the majority of teams.

Counter-Attacks

The counter-attack goals were all slightly different. Liverpool's fourth goal came from a Roberston tackle and release pass to find the sprinting Cody Gakpo. Luis Diaz overlapped Gakpo on the outside on the left, an example of the two players creating 2v1s. A low cross created chaos which eventually led to Salah tapping into an unguarded net.

Goal five involved Diaz once more. This time, he came short to receive the forward pass and set the ball back. A long pass put Szoboszlai away through the middle, and – as Salah found Szoboszlai with a reverse pass in the first half – now Szoboszlai found Salah with a reverse pass and Salah slipped the finish under the goalkeeper.

Goal six was scored by Diaz. After he and Jota (on for Gakpo) created a 2v1 wide, the ball was passed infield. Diaz continued his run infield as the ball was worked to Szoboszlai and out to Salah, approximately five yards in from the right corner of the box. Diaz underlapped Salah and fired in a right-foot finish across the goalkeeper. It was a finish that was very similar to the goal controversially disallowed by VAR in this fixture last season.

"If you watch the goals back, they mostly started with centre-backs or full-backs. Every lead-up involved multiple passes and contributions from the entire team." Arne Slot speaking in the post-match press conference

Spurs scored three goals but did not have that many shots in the game. Spurs had nine shots with five on target, while Liverpool had 24 shots with 11 on target. Spurs generated an xG of 1.3, while Liverpool had an xG of 5.6 (all stats from FBref). Liverpool have conceded more shots in games with opponents scoring fewer goals. Maddison scoring from long range probably impacted the xG weighting.

How the movement of Diaz helped Liverpool create overloads on the left

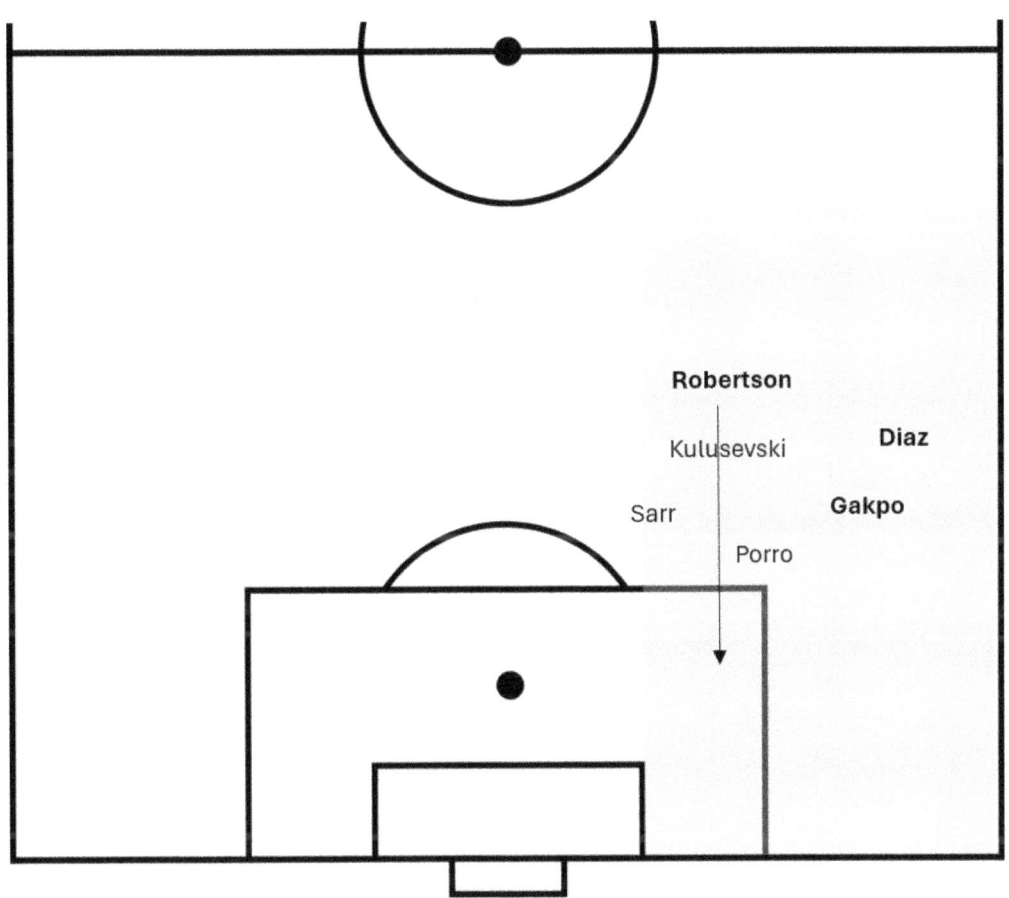

Increasing Rotations

Arne Slot appears to build Liverpool on blocks. With each passing week, the team evolves a little more. It is apparent that Slot did not attempt to work on all the principles at once in the beginning. He picked out key areas to work on and has added to them as the season has progressed. This began with the principles of third-man runs and passing triangles, using the right side to release when playing out, building through the defensive midfielders, the four-player pressing line, Alexander-Arnold inverting with the 3-2/3-2 build shape, and the left-back underlapping. This appears to be quite a lot, but in the context of footballing actions, this is a very light load.

At this stage of the season, we see the addition of the central striker dropping deep and the midfielders running forward to fill the position. There have been more rotational elements added, with a central defender sometimes acting as a half-back. There is more variety and experimentation with set-pieces, taking short corners, and having players attack the front post from a far post starting position. This might be one of the reasons why Slot has been so successful so quickly. He retained key elements of Klopp's playing style, especially rapid counter-attacks, while slowly adding his own ideas without overloading the players with too much information.

Key Points

- Liverpool were able to use their pressing to overload Tottenham's build-up play
- Liverpool countered Spurs' pressing with additional players in the build-up and long passes in behind
- Liverpool used half-spaces, with central midfielders the primary targets
- Counter-attacks were explosive and manyfold
- The rotations used by Liverpool have increased as the season has progressed, particularly the movement of Diaz as the striker, triggering movements from midfielders

Game 26 – Leicester City – Premier League – Home – 3-1 win

Liverpool 4-2-3-1

Alisson, Alexander-Arnold, Gomez, van Dijk, Robertson (Tsimikas), Gravenberch (Endo), Mac Allister (Elliott), Jones (Szoboszlai), Salah, Gakpo, Nunez (Jota)

Leicester City 4-2-3-1

Stolarczyk, Justin, Coady (Okoli), Vestegaard, Kristiansen, Winks (Skipp), Soumare, Ayew, El Khannouss (Buonanotte), Mavididi (de Cordova-Reid), Daka

Scorers – Gakpo, Jones, Salah, Ayew

Liverpool went into the traditional Boxing Day fixture against a Leicester team that was embroiled in a relegation fight. Liverpool had stepped up their attacking intent, with the front line at its most potent, in comparison to the beginning of the season, which had been more dependent on defensive solidity. Liverpool have experienced similar circumstances before. When they finished second in the 2013/14 season, the opening fixtures were three successive 1-0 victories, playing in a restrained and controlled manner. That team ended with 101 goals scored and 50 goals conceded. The style went from conservative to wild, illustrating how a team's early playing pattern and style can change drastically as the season progresses.

Leicester Low Block and Counter-Attack

Leicester began the game in the manner that would be expected of a team from the lower reaches of the league facing the team in top spot. They were very compact centrally, getting everyone back behind the ball. Up front, they had selected the pace of Patson Daka in an obvious effort to try to catch Liverpool on the counter-attack. Leicester took the lead early in the game, and Daka was involved in the goal. Leicester counter-attacked, but Liverpool were well positioned as the Midlanders attacked on the right. Daka held his run, and van Dijk stayed with Daka and did not occupy his usual central position (when the ball is on the LFC right side). This put Ayew 1v1 with Robertson as the cross came in low. Ayew took the ball well, swivelling to strike a shot low into the bottom corner.

The right and left half-spaces Liverpool cross from, plus the positioning of the defensive midfielder and central defenders to pin the opposition in

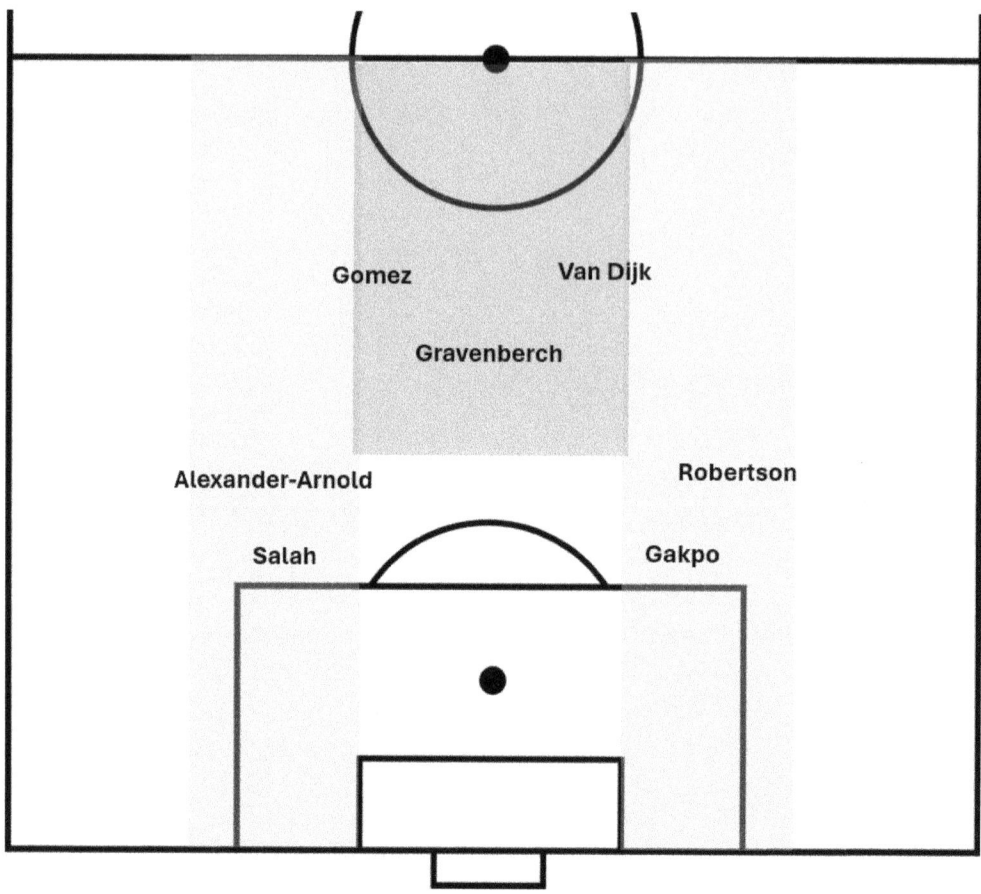

Liverpool Focus On Left-Side Attacks

The goal only persuaded Leicester to double down on their defending. They sat with three screening at the front of the team, attempting to prevent line-breaking passes. Salah was often doubled up on the right, forcing Liverpool to use the left side more. A switch of emphasis from the right to the left has been notable in Liverpool's play as the season has progressed. Robertson or Tsimikas provide a stream of crosses, mixing underlaps with overlaps depending on the opponent. Gakpo has received a lot more of the ball and his confidence and output has grown as the season has progressed. With Liverpool looking to break Leicester down, Robertson and Gakpo both provided crosses from the half-space in their own manner, one cross in towards the far post and one curving away.

Hard To Stop Gakpo

Gakpo's ability to put dangerous crosses into the box is made easier for him because of the multitude of threats that he carries when on the ball. The modern trend for wingers is for them to invert, playing on the opposite side. Traditional wingers will play with their strong foot on the same side. The objective for such players is that they beat the defender on the outside, creating space to cross or get to the line and cut the ball back towards the penalty spot. Stanley Matthews, winner of the very first Ballon d'Or, specialised in low cutbacks. Steve Heighway, part of the great Liverpool teams of the 1970s, would get to the line. John Barnes, though he rapped about getting to the line on the 1990 England World Cup song *World In Motion,* was a player who signalled a shift. Capable of crossing in the air and getting to the line, Barnes' right foot was strong enough that he had the dual threat of going outside and cutting in. Perhaps no player had a greater double threat, however, than Marc Overmars, the Dutchman who could take corners with both feet, such was the equality in strength. Overmars could cut in and score or drive to the line. Gakpo has much in common with his compatriot. Many commentators note that we all knew what was coming, yet defenders failed to stop it. Why?

Why is Gakpo proving so hard to stop? Gakpo can go both inside and outside onto his weaker left foot. He has scored goals in previous seasons where he has shot low across the goalkeeper with his left, plus he can clip a cross or cut the ball back from the line. This makes it very hard to commit to stopping the shot. Looking deeper into the technical detail, Gakpo likes to dribble with the ball positioned towards the outside of his right foot, and from this position, he can push the ball inside. The touch can be diagonally away from the defender, which creates separation and space to wrap his foot around the ball. The distance is too great for a defender to cover, making it very difficult to prevent a shot or cross.

The same initial touch can also act as a feint, beginning a drive down the outside of the defender. Liverpool's opening goal came when Gakpo received the ball at speed and drove down the outside. The defender went with him, but Gakpo used the momentum of the defender to go against the flow and nudge the ball at the right angle inside the pitch. He knew he had space to bend a shot into the far top corner.

"I think the main difference maybe is that the set-up of the front three was a bit different [in the past] than the set-up now. We expect a bit from our wingers to keep it wide, to try to get them in 1v1 situations. Cody has done this really well. Lucho has done this really well when he played from the left but Lucho is, in our opinion, also capable of playing as a nine; he did that really well against Spurs.

Against Spurs, it was mainly maybe Lucho and Mo that were dominant, now it was Cody again, together with Mo. It's just nice to have so many options, in every position actually, but also in the front three." Arne Slot speaking at the post-match press conference.

Learning From Forest Defeat

Liverpool's experience against Nottingham Forest early in the season can be seen whenever they face an opponent who packs the defence. Liverpool aren't reluctant to put in crosses regularly and they load the penalty area. There is often a diamond of attackers around the far post poised to attack crosses, particularly half-space crosses bending away. The left-side diamond is especially prominent as Robertson and Gakpo attack the ball in a manner that Salah and Alexander-Arnold do not. If the ball is being crossed from the left, it is more likely that the players attacking the ball will be Szoboszlai and Mac Allister.

Liverpool are also very good at maintaining the pressure after a cross. In the early days of the Fenway Sports Group takeover, Liverpool looked to use the Moneyball methods that had helped the Boston Red Sox become Major League Baseball champions for the first time in 86 years. They identified that crossing and scoring with headers were undervalued in the market. The method was evident in games, but the issue Liverpool had was that – with wingers and full-backs high up the pitch and midfielders attacking the box – any time a cross was cleared, there was a counter-attacking opportunity. Liverpool of modern times are much better at controlling the spaces that come from pushing central defenders high up the pitch, along with a holding midfielder to regain any second balls and keep the pressure on, as well as aggressive counter-pressing. Curtis Jones' goal to put Liverpool ahead came after a cross was half cleared and the team counter-pressed on the edge of the box. A narrow overlap by Mac Allister put the ball across the six-yard box for Jones to score.

Liverpool Press With Five

Once Leicester went behind, they showed an unsurprising shift in their pressing. Their line of engagement shifted higher up the pitch, using a 4-2-4 shape. Liverpool pressed all game. They began the game with four players positioned on the edge of the Leicester box on goal kicks, and the 'standard' line of four was rarely seen against Leicester. The shapes were 2-3, 3-2 and 1-4, adding Mac Allister into the pressing mix for an aggressive five-player high press, particularly focused on high and wide positions. One regain created a 6v5 attack in Liverpool's favour. In the first half, Leicester eventually stopped playing out from the back and went long when the ball was with the goalkeeper.

Another Counter-Attack Goal

Liverpool sealed victory with another fast attack goal. With Leicester pushing forward more, the opportunities to counter increased. One particular move was extremely slick. A one-touch forward pass from Mac Allister was flicked backwards by Gakpo to Robertson. This strung together two of the season's hallmarks, Mac Allister's one-touch passes and the use of a backward pass after a forward pass. The initial forward pass extends the spaces between the lines; the backwards setting pass enables more runners to get ahead of the ball. At other times, the setting pass triggers rotation between the centre-forward and central midfielders, switching positions. Robertson had three runners on the right and Gakpo running centre left. Robertson found Salah to then feed a pass into the channel where Nunez' shot was well saved. The move for 3-1 came from a quick pass by Gakpo, wide to Salah, who then dribbled infield and curved a shot into the far corner, using the Leicester defender's body to block the vision of the goalkeeper.

Key Points

- Arne Slot learnt a lot from the defeat against Forest at Anfield. When opponents have used a low block, Liverpool have adopted a high tempo, put in lots of crosses, and flooded the box early in the game
- Liverpool have developed the ways they attack on the left side, especially using the central striker to create an overload
- Gakpo is hard to stop for defenders. Teams know that his preference is to cut inside but he is also capable of going outside on his left
- Liverpool's pressing has evolved as the season has progressed. Slot started with the four-player press, then added the five-player pressing structures

Game 27 – West Ham – Premier League – Away – 5-0 win

Liverpool 4-2-3-1

Alisson, Alexander-Arnold, Gomez (Quansah), van Dijk, Robertson (Tsimikas), Gravenberch (Endo), Mac Allister, Jones (Elliott), Salah, Gakpo (Jota), Diaz

West Ham 5-3-2

Areola, Coufal (Todibo), Mavropanos, Kilman, Wan-Bissaka, Emerson, Paqueta, Alvarez (Fullkrug), Soler (Irving). Kudus (Guilherme), Bowen (Summerville)

Scorers – Diaz, Gakpo, Salah, Alexander-Arnold, Jota

West Ham, in many ways, epitomise Premier League clubs. All the way down the league, teams are loaded with players of international quality. It is not too much of an exaggeration to say that if you play Premier League football, you are in international squads or in consideration for international squads. This means that every team in the Premier League has a couple of players who – if both have a day that is at or close to the apex of their ability – they can beat you. West Ham have Kudus, Paqueta, and Bowen – all of whom played against Liverpool and, at various points in the game, threatened. Yet Liverpool came away with a win and scoreline that looked very comfortable.

West Ham Attacking Threats

West Ham had an opportunity to open the scoring. In the 5th minute, Kudus caught Robertson in possession and poked the ball to Bowen. Bowen ran at the defence, squared the ball, and Paqueta sprinted in. Fortunately for Liverpool, he was off balance and sliding to get contact, and sliced the ball high and wide. For much of the game, West Ham carried a threat when they went forward, especially the excellent Kudus with his energy and dribbling skills. One run and shot from range that hit the post was particularly eye-catching.

Liverpool Carve West Ham Open

Yet Liverpool always created more chances than West Ham. The minute after Paqueta had a chance to score, Salah almost scored after a dribble and pass from Gakpo cut open the defence. Diaz made a smart run across the defence to open the passing line, which Gakpo threaded diagonally from left to right. Salah's shot was saved. Incredibly, in a game that finished 5-0, Salah could have been accused of being wasteful. He scored and made two goals, yet a five-goal haul was there for the taking.

In the second half, he missed an early one-on-one after a brilliant piece of play by Mac Allister. Later, an extraordinary swerved pass by Alexander-Arnold put Salah in, but the shot was blazed over the crossbar. When the missed chances are only the difference between a 5-0 win and 8/9-0, then it makes little difference. Should the wastefulness spill over into closer games, then Liverpool could have problems.

Full Throttle Pressing vs An Empty Tank

The contrast in pressing between the two teams was stark, West Ham were extremely passive, while Liverpool were aggressive. The West Ham shape was not designed to press Liverpool high. Using a 5-3-2 (with quite defensive-minded wing-backs) allowed Liverpool to control the wide areas. The two forwards lacked support when they had opportunities to press, but West Ham did not engage Liverpool with any pressure on the ball until possession had progressed to close to the halfway line. Liverpool could easily create overloads against the wing-backs with their full-backs pushing up. The lack of pressure on the central defenders when in possession allowed long diagonals, especially from van Dijk to Salah or Alexander-Arnold to move Liverpool into West Ham territory with ease. Liverpool were able to structure themselves in a 3-2 or 2-3 shape without pulling any additional players back to help the build-up due to the lack of press from West Ham. As the game progressed, Liverpool could play create 2v1s at the back, with one of the West Ham forwards dropping into midfield, creating a 5-4-1. This released Gravenberch, Alexander-Arnold, and Robertson higher up the pitch.

Liverpool pressed with the 4-2-4 shape once again and put additional energy into pressing in wide areas. Against West Ham in the League Cup at Anfield, there was a lot of success pressing wide. In this game, Liverpool were able to either win the ball wide or pick off attempted passes into midfield to then counter. Gravenberch moved across to help the press while Joe Gomez jumped across to the right to get in front of forwards to regain. This was made easier for Gomez as there was little danger if he missed the regain due to a lack of forward numbers from West Ham. The pressing from Liverpool created their third goal, with three players surrounding two West Ham midfielders as they tried to play out from a goal kick. Gakpo and Mac Allister leapt onto the pass, stabbing the ball to Curtis Jones. His pass allowed Salah to sweep in a low shot at the near post from just inside the penalty area.

Jones' Tactical Flexibility

Curtis Jones's forward running was vital in this victory. When Diaz moved short, Jones moved into the centre-forward position. Jones made runs in behind, when Salah was on the ball, into the half-spaces and channels in a similar manner to

Szoboszlai. It was Jones' movement that helped drag the West Ham defence away and opened up the centre for Gakpo to create the early Salah chance. Later in the half, Jones made a forward run into the half-space (picked out by Salah), but his shot was saved.

Jones also moved into the deepest pivot role at times, enabling both Mac Allister and Gravenberch to move further forward. With this selection, Slot had three midfielders who were all capable of performing in the pivot role, with two able to move into the penalty area to fill the forward position when Diaz dropped deep. The additional rotation was a tweak in his role. Why make this change? As West Ham didn't press, Gravenberch wasn't required to help the two central defenders in the build-up as much as against other teams. West Ham didn't even stop the pass into midfield by effectively blocking the passing lines. The movement of Jones in behind meant that he wasn't in wide areas to help create the wide triangle as he or Szoboszlai usually do; in this game, it was Gravenberch pulling wide to help create the shape.

West Ham were quite competitive for much of the game. It took Liverpool 30 minutes to score. Where they looked to be levels behind Liverpool was in the transition. They did not seem to have the energy or desire to keep up with the Merseysiders. As the game went on, the effort levels decreased further, with Liverpool completely in control of transition and outrunning West Ham as their performance collapsed in on itself. The cup game at Anfield earlier in the season was quite similar, with the game being close for a large period, but then Liverpool completely taking over and punishing West Ham to end with a large winning score.

Key Points
- Liverpool used a variety of passes from short and long range to get in behind West Ham and open them up
- Liverpool pressed aggressively, creating multiple turnovers. West Ham barely pressed at all, giving Liverpool time and space to play
- Curtis Jones showed tactical flexibility in his midfield role, running in behind West Ham and also covering deeper spaces to enable others to run in behind
- Liverpool used runners from midfield and wide to push the opponent's defensive lines deeper

Game 28 – Manchester United – Anfield – Premier League – 2-2 draw

Liverpool 4-2-3-1

Alisson, Alexander-Arnold (Bradley), Konate, van Dijk, Robertson, Gravenberch, Mac Allister, Jones (Jota), Salah, Gakpo (Elliott), Diaz (Nunez)

Manchester United 3-4-3

Onana, de Ligt (Yoro), Maguire, Martinez, Mazraoui, Ugarte, Mainoo (Garnacho), Dalot, Diallo, Fernandes, Hojlund (Zirkzee)

Scorers – Gakpo, Salah, Martinez, Diallo

Liverpool versus Manchester United is always a huge clash. With ten Hag now relieved of his duties and Ruben Amorin coming in, expectation was briefly heightened before coming crashing down. The Manchester United players appeared to be struggling to play in Amorim's 3-4-3 system, and it looked like a mismatch of squad and styles. However, United were able to find cohesion and compete with Liverpool at Anfield, which came as a surprise to many pundits who were simply wondering how many United would lose by!

Manchester United's Shape

The criticism of Amorim's insistence on 3-4-3 looked misplaced after this fixture. United deployed the system to perfection, making it tough for Liverpool to break them down, while also providing enough attacking opportunities to score twice. A three-at-the-back system is well suited to causing Liverpool issues when pressing. The four-player press is stretched by the wing-backs with twin pivots to also attempt to cover. Liverpool's wingers could not cover the wide players, and United often had Dalot spare to find as an out ball. When a 2-3 or 3-2 press was used, United could still find overloads. As well as the two pivots, Fernandes and Diallo could drop in to create a midfield box or pull wide to create an overload in midfield. United had periods of possession that were far too comfortable for Anfield's liking.

United Attacking Success

Liverpool were exposed on their right side with concerning regularity. The balance on the right is very delicate as two of Liverpool's biggest creative influences are on the right side, Alexander-Arnold and Mo Salah. Salah is largely excused from defensive duties, and while Alexander-Arnold has shown signs of improved defensive work this season, he can still be troubled. To counter this, Gravenberch operates more to the right to offer cover in front, while Konate covers the right channel expertly. Usually.

On this occasion, the balance was not right. Konate looked very rusty, having not played since the Real Madrid game and was unable to marshal his space as effectively as usual. This compounded the struggles of Alexander-Arnold. Dalot constantly beat Alexander-Arnold in 1v1s, and Manchester United were able to create more of these through the positioning of their midfielders, taking his support away. Alexander-Arnold gave the ball away regularly in possession and seemed slow to respond to the situations. Much of the noise post-game surrounded Alexander-Arnold's poor game, yet it might all have been different had a shot during the early stages hit the back of the net. Instead, it was superbly blocked by a defender.

Midfield Off The Pace Too

Not only did Liverpool's right side of defence struggle, but there were issues in midfield too. Curtis Jones was closed down and marked extremely tightly by Mainoo and Ugarte. He was unable to turn and drive away to carry the ball forward, instead turning possession over. These off days were compounded by the lack of options on the Liverpool bench. There was no Bradley to replace Alexander-Arnold, and Jones had his off day when Szoboszlai was out of the picture due to illness.

Liverpool React To United

Lisandro Martinez put Manchester United in front early in the second half. Bruno Fernandes dribbled infield from the left into the half-space before passing into the channel that was not sufficiently protected by Konate and Alexander-Arnold. This allowed Martinez the space to score.

From a position of being behind, Arne Slot responded in what has become typical fashion, shifting the team shape into a 4-2-4 shape. Jota was brought on to play as an additional striker, and Gakpo scored to equalise before Salah put Liverpool in front with a penalty. Slot took a risk to get into the lead but, once in front, retained the attacking 4-2-4 formation. Endo was available on the bench. Slot could have changed back to a more balanced system to see out the game.

Attacking Midfielders

Liverpool and Slot have become less conservative with their movement and spacing as the season has developed. Liverpool have scored more goals in the last month but also conceded more. More freedom has been granted to the midfielders. Early in the season, when the striker dropped deep, only Szoboszlai pushed forward. This has evolved into two midfielders attacking the space opened up by the striker's movement. Gravenberch has been less limited by the duties of protecting the defence and has been able to take up positions closer to the penalty area. Alexis Mac Allister can rotate in to cover him, but that moment of rotation can be pivotal to controlling the transition or losing control. With fewer players pushing forward, Liverpool had more players protecting the defence but fewer players flooding the box.

The 4-2-4 shift illustrated the transference from control into risk-taking. In the 4-2-3-1 shape, Liverpool kept the full-backs both closer to the central defenders with a double pivot to create a 2-4 shape. The full-backs – being deeper – were used to counter the United front three in the Liverpool build-up phase. In the second half, a full-back would invert while the other pushed forward. The inverted full-back countered the United midfield, creating a 4v3 when Fernandes and Diallo tucked in. Alexander-Arnold coming inside created parity and 4v4. When it came time to roll the dice and take more risks, the full-backs were pushed high and wide in a bid to create overloads, overlaps, and a stream of crosses.

Further Ploys

Both teams made some specific adjustments at restarts for their opponents. Manchester United did not play short on goal kicks. Liverpool were unable to press high as often as they did in the game at Old Trafford, where all three Liverpool games came from pressing or counter-pressing.

Liverpool attempted to take advantage of a possible Manchester United weakness at corners. In a previous game, Wolves had scored directly from a corner, so Liverpool crowded Onana and tried to bend corners in. Later, Liverpool would attempt the Arsenal corner routine of starting outside the far post and taking up positions to block the goalkeeper at the last moment. United survived these attacks but it was the barrage of crosses that created the penalty with a handball blocking a cross and Salah converting the penalty.

It looked as though this would be the winner, but Dalot exploited the Liverpool defensive right to cross low. The ball made it across to Diallo to scuff a shot low past Alisson.

"What affected him is that he had to play Bruno Fernandes and Diogo Dalot, two starters for Portugal, great, great, great players. That tells you how much quality United have." Arne Slot discussing Alexander-Arnold's performance (from Reuters)

How Manchester United shifted their 3-4-3 shape into a 4-5-1

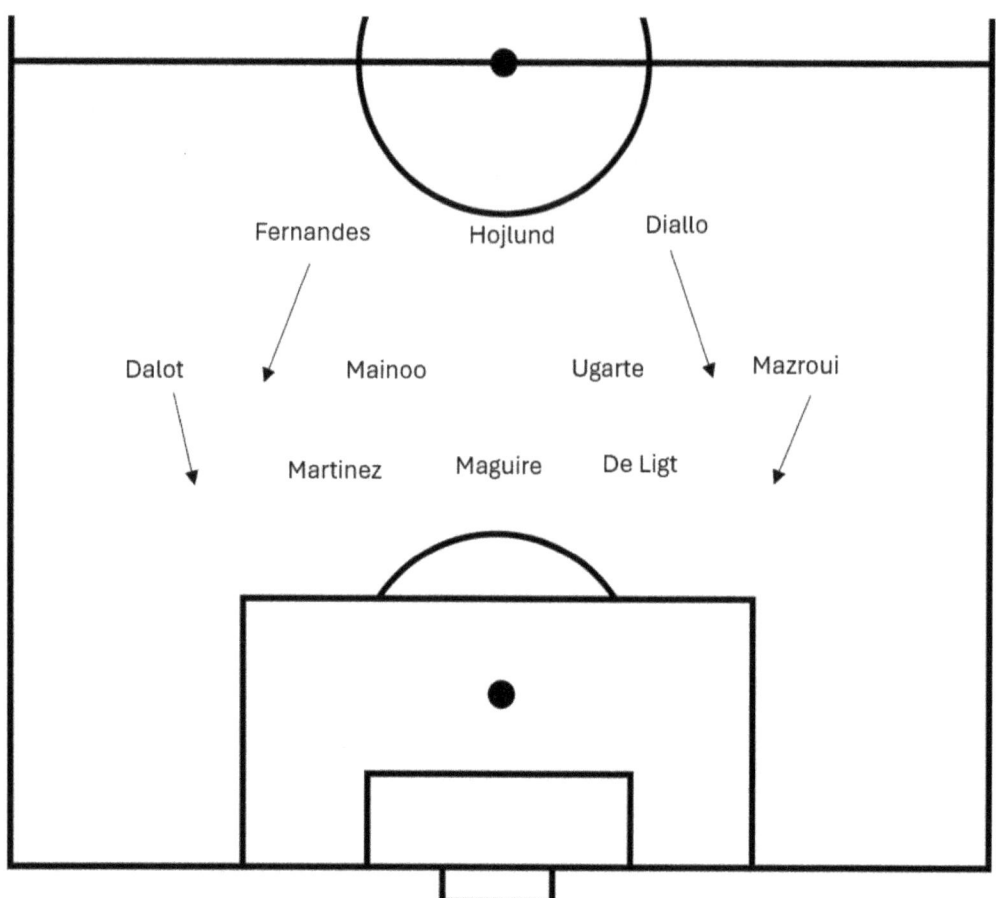

Key Points

- Manchester United's use of 3-4-3 proved very difficult for Liverpool to break down
- Slot, yet again, showed his willingness to take risks but this time didn't turn the dial back down once going in front
- Liverpool suffered through players having poor performances and lacking alternatives in their roles

Game 29 – Spurs – Away – League Cup – 1-0 loss

Liverpool 4-2-3-1

Alisson, Bradley (Alexander-Arnold), Quansah (Endo), van Dijk, Tsimikas, Gravenberch, Mac Allister (Konate), Jones, Salah, Gakpo (Diaz), Jota (Nunez)

Tottenham 4-3-3

Kinsky, Porro, Dragusin, Gray, Spence, Bissouma, Bentancur (Johnson), Bergvall, Kulusevski, Son (Werner), Solanke

Scorers – Bergvall

Two games without a win for Liverpool and a rare loss. This defeat was the equivalent of being 1-0 down at half-time as the second leg at Anfield was to come. Tottenham and Liverpool played out this fixture mere weeks earlier, and the game could not have been more different. A goal-fuelled encounter, previously, made way for a far tighter game that was goalless until very late on.

Frequent Transitions

The game was transition-heavy, with both teams pressing and counter-pressing aggressively. Usually, Liverpool come out on top when the game becomes highly transitional, but on this occasion, they could not find the final pass to capitalise on being in good positions. Tottenham did an excellent job with their recovery runs when Liverpool counter-attacked, focusing on being compact centrally, and they crowded the box with defenders, making it very hard for Liverpool to create decisive opportunities.

Spurs Press Impressively

Spurs put Liverpool under a heavy press throughout the game. In the first half, Liverpool misplaced seemingly simple passes in their own defensive third whilst, in the second half, they didn't give the ball away in their own third but misplaced the passes from the defensive third into the midfield third. Spurs were often able to push players into 3v3 and 4v4 situations, so Liverpool did not have a free player to play out with ease.

Liverpool's structures did not differ wildly from the normal, despite some rotation in the lineup. The general build-up shape remained a variation on 2-3/3-2, moving into 2-4 or 2-2-2 close to the halfway line. Liverpool attempted to get forward using one-two combinations on the right side (as did Spurs) with mixed results. There were times when the initial Spurs press was bypassed either through the one-two or a line-breaking pass, but Spurs flooded their own penalty box to deny Liverpool.

Liverpool Caught Out of Position

The key moments in the game involved Lucas Bergvall. The teenage midfielder came on as a substitute during the 6-3 game and helped Spurs gain better possession, picking up pockets of space to knit play together. In this game, he scored the only goal after a controversial incident. Liverpool were furious that Bergvall was not sent off for a forceful foul on Kostas Tsimikas. He already had a yellow card to his name, and there was a clear belief that this foul was worthy of a second card. Arguably, a bigger issue was that Tsimikas was forced off of the pitch for treatment. Spurs played a long pass into the vacated left-back area, the central defenders were pulled across to cover the space, but this – in turn – created a space in the middle of the box, where Bergvall arrived to score. Perhaps Endo and Alexander-Arnold could have reacted more quickly to the threat, but there is no denying the circumstances that created the scenario.

Key Points

- A transition-heavy game
- Spurs got their pressing right
- Tsimikas was injured and off the pitch in the challenge from Bergvall. Tottenham played the ball into the vacant left-back area and Liverpool failed to organise well enough to prevent the only goal of the game

Game 30 – Accrington – FA Cup – Home – 4-0 win

Liverpool 4-2-3-1/4-3-3

Kelleher, Alexander-Arnold (Bradley), Quansah, Endo (Nyoni), Tsimikas, Morton (McConnell), Elliott, Szoboszlai (Chiesa), Jota, Ngumoha (Danns), Nunez

Accrington 4-2-3-1

Crellin, Love, Rawson, Awe, B. Woods, J. Woods (O'Brien), Khumbeni (Coyle), Martin (Conneely), Hunter (Henderson), Walton (Mooney), Whalley

Scorers – Jota, Alexander-Arnold, Danns, Chiesa

Underdogs come to Anfield in the FA Cup third round. This is no ordinary underdog, though; this underdog has a special association with Liverpool thanks to a famous milk advert in the 1980s. You know the one.

Slot Rotates The LineUp and The Formation

Arne Slot rotated the lineup. The shape in midfield has been getting harder to pigeonhole as the season has progressed. Earlier in the season, the positioning and role of Szoboszlai made it very difficult to definitively state the system as 4-2-3-1 or 4-3-3. With Mac Allister, Jones and Szoboszlai all making forward runs into the position vacated by the striker, the system could be described as 4-1-4-1, but that implies that the wide players are much deeper when, in fact, they are often the highest players in the team. It might be that the reality of the system is that it is a form of 4-4-2 diamond once the striker withdraws from the front line and the wingers behave as split strikers. Even then, if you consider the average position of Alexander-Arnold, the system could be considered as three at the back, with two holding players. The levels of fluidity meant that Liverpool switched from one structure to another with ease. The lineup against Accrington used Morton as the holding midfielder, while Elliott and Szoboszlai filled the other roles. Jota was the central forward, while Ngumoha and Chiesa took the wing positions.

Back-Up Players Enjoy This Moment

This was Rio Ngumoha's first-team debut, having been called up from the academy. Ngumoha played 72 minutes, showing Anfield his close control and tight dribbling skills. His replacement was Jayden Danns, who would score within four minutes of coming off the bench, pouncing on a rebound to guide home from eight yards. The rebound followed a Chiesa shot.

Chiesa has been searching for full fitness since arriving at Liverpool, and he seemed determined that he would score his first Liverpool goal. In this game, he registered six shots with three on target (according to FBref). His dribbling and running off the ball were a constant threat, and he was eventually rewarded with a 90th-minute goal, low into the bottom left corner from outside the box.

How Liverpool use the wide players as strikers

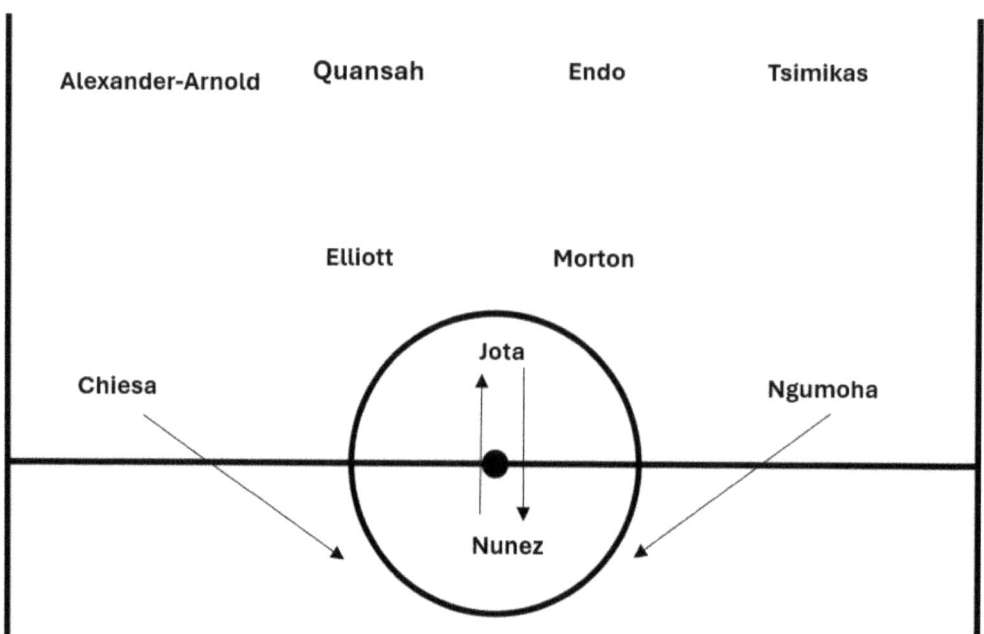

Fitness Tells

Accrington were well organised for most of the game, but ultimately fitness told. Liverpool's first goal came in the 29th minute. The third goal came in the 76th minute. Goals two and four were scored in stoppage time at the end of each half. Accrington dropped into a tight defensive block, only looking to press in Liverpool's half if there was a trigger. At goal kicks, they went long, avoiding the pressing of Liverpool. As each half progressed, the defensive structure formed more slowly as their energy levels began to dip. Liverpool were able to play through and create more easily.

"They are not afraid to press high, they're not afraid to play 1v1, but then you wonder, will they do this at Anfield as well? But they definitely did. They were not afraid." Arne Slot speaking about Accrington Stanly (from Reuters)

Alexander-Arnold Plays Himself Back Into Form

Trent Alexander-Arnold was selected to start at right-back, most likely a response to his below-par performance against Manchester United. An opportunity to regain some form and confidence that was taken in style. He netted the second goal of the game from outside the penalty area and – after an hour – was withdrawn, with Conor Bradley substituting. Bradley showed his usual high energy but played a more inverted style than usual, tucked inside. He took up unusual positions during the build-up in Liverpool's defensive third. The initial position would be in the shadow of Accrington's players, preventing a narrow passing lane from opening. Bradley quickly moved out to the right, orienting his body side on to receive and then drive forward with the ball. This is an alternative to the usual in-possession build structure.

Key Points

- Against opponents from lower down the league, Slot rotated heavily and gave fringe players the opportunity to shine
- Slot is comfortable changing the basic formation but retaining the playing principles
- Accrington were well organised but fell away in the latter stages of the game
- Trent Alexander-Arnold was given the opportunity to play himself into some form after recent below-par displays

Game 31 – Nottingham Forest – Premier League – Away – 1-1 draw

Liverpool 4-2-3-1

Alisson, Alexander-Arnold, Konate (Jota), van Dijk, Robertson (Tsimikas), Gravenberch, Mac Allister, Szoboszlai, Salah, Gakpo, Diaz (Jones)

Nottingham Forest 4-2-3-1

Sels, Aina, Milenkovic, Murillo, Williams (Moreno), Yates (Dominguez), Anderson, Gibbs-White (Morato), Elanga, Hudson-Odoi (Jota Silva), Wood (Awoniyi)

Scorers – Jota, Wood

"In your head, Arne, Arne, Arne", sang the Forest fans. Perhaps they were correct. Forest gave Slot a lot to think about, and he undoubtedly learned a lot of lessons from the loss at Anfield. Liverpool have learned to load the box, cross the ball often, and crank up the tempo. Against Nottingham Forest at Anfield came the first attempt – in-game – at using a back three, which bore fruit against Fulham when Liverpool were down to ten men. Liverpool used these lessons from the off, with plenty of rotating movement, and crosses and shots to attempt to disrupt and draw out the Forest defence.

Gravenberch Switches To Half-Back

The half-back switch was required against Forest once again, as Liverpool found themselves a goal behind in the second half, prompting Slot to make the switch. Chris Wood was playing as a lone striker, one who never really wanted to receive a ball played in behind, so Slot decided to have Virgil van Dijk play man-to-man against him. Gravenberch then moved into a role alongside van Dijk when Forest had established possession, but when Liverpool had possession, Gravenberch fulfilled his most established role in front of the defensive trio. Indeed, Liverpool switched to a system reminiscent of Ajax in 1995. There were hints of it against Fulham, but with the full complement of players, the system was fully formed. One central defender, two full-backs, and a half-back. The central defender was the most fixed of the group. Out of possession, this was a regulation back four, but in possession, Gravenberch stepped forward, Tsimikas could overlap, and Alexander-Arnold patrolled the right in both wide and inverted positions. The key to playing such a fluid system is being able to read each other's actions and respond accordingly – a far easier task after 31 games than after a mere handful!

How Slot used Gravenberch and van Dijk to create a midfield overload while maintaining attacking numbers

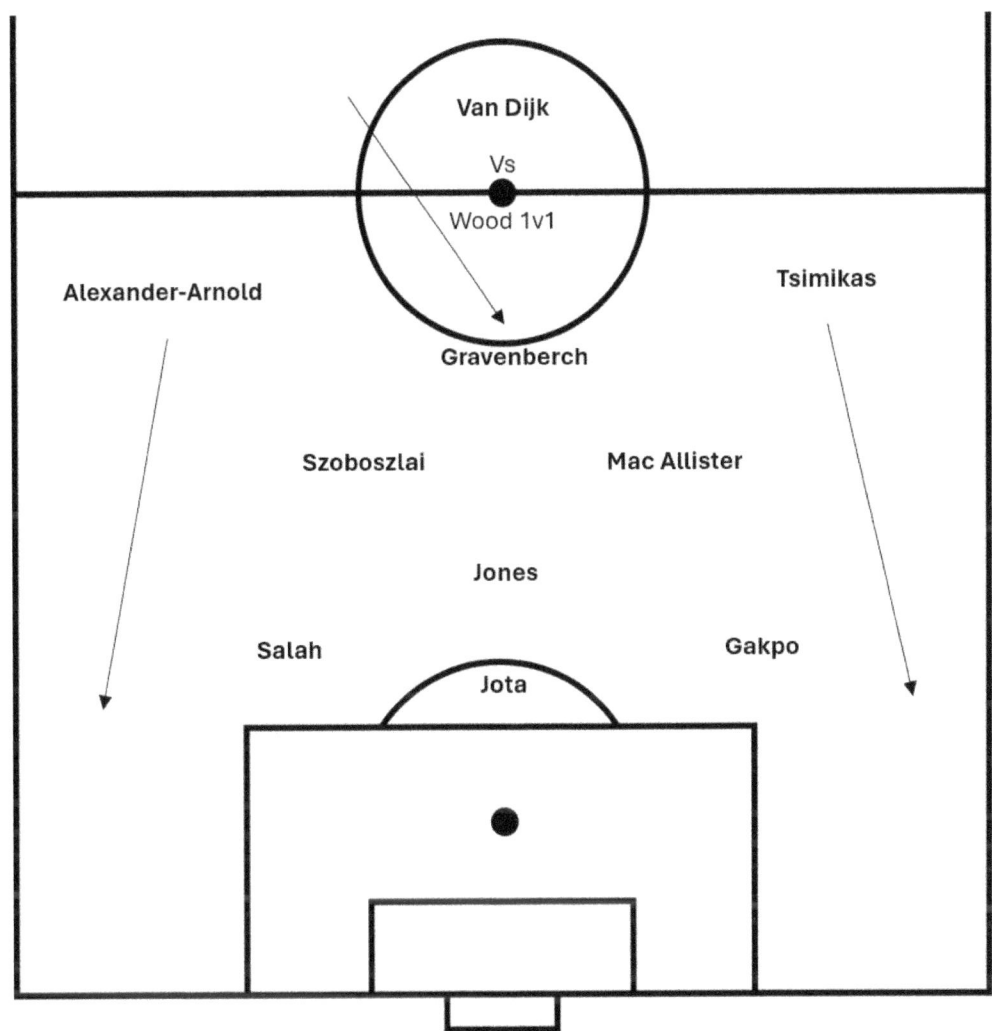

Slot Trusts van Dijk To Play 1v1

Wood's lack of running onto long passes in behind was not the only factor that enabled the change. Forest didn't press or apply pressure to Liverpool players until the ball was well within their territory. Konate and van Dijk were both able to carry the ball a long way forward before being pressured. From a Forest perspective, these two players carried less open play goal threat than the other Liverpool outfield players. Switching Gravenberch for Konate combatted this strategy as Gravenberch's dribbling and passing are a considerable threat, and it is a huge risk to give Gravenberch time on the ball. The switch drew Forest's line of engagement a little higher, creating more space between the lines.

Forest Counter-Attacking Style

Nottingham Forest have defended with a low to mid-block all season. Their strength has been their defensive discipline and fast counter-attacks using their wide players. Forest defend the box well, getting bodies back while Murillo and Milinkovic repel crosses. Their depth means that opponents have a lot of possession in front of a packed Forest defence, a problem that Liverpool needed to solve. Chris Wood might not seem the ideal player for a team that wants to break at speed, though (Vardy at Leicester is more likely to come to mind). Wood is adept at holding up the ball and linking with the wide players or the supporting runs of Morgan Gibbs-White. Gibbs-White and the wide players make the runs in behind, onto longer balls, but Liverpool had this covered with Konate looking back at his sharpest to cover the channels in behind Alexander-Arnold. Wood also moves intelligently onto the shoulders of defenders and has just enough speed to receive in small spaces and get a shot away. He did just this when Forest opened the scoring following a regain. Two forward passes got Wood into position to shoot low into the bottom corner.

Risk Takers

Forest play a style that limits risk and, in turn, limits errors. An example of this was how rarely they pass short at goal kicks. Aside from some early short kicks with the Liverpool press nowhere near, everything else went long, a tactic we have seen from many teams seeking to avoid Liverpool's intensive pressing.

Arne Slot does take risks. Jurgen Klopp was notable for his willingness to risk losing a game in order to have a chance of winning it. Slot is clearly similar. Over the last 10-12 games, the central midfielders have run in behind far more, not just one at a time, but two at a time, flooding the spaces with runners. He has taken off central defenders and put on additional forwards in the search for goals – risking going behind or further behind in the quest for the goal they need. So far, the willingness to take risks has been rewarded, none more immediately than in this game. Tsimikas and Jota were brought on and their first touches resulted in a goal, with Tsimikas curling in a corner and Jota heading in.

Liverpool Pile On The Pressure

In the last quarter of the game, Liverpool created a number of good chances, but a mixture of excellent goalkeeping, brave defending, and slightly below-par finishing prevented a Liverpool winner. Forest had an xG of 0.3, while Liverpool created an xG of 2. Certainly enough to win the game. Jota is considered to be

Liverpool's most efficient finisher but he missed a very presentable chance from eight yards, smothered by Sels. Salah then struck a curving effort from just inside the box that looked destined for the top corner, but Sels tipped it over. Liverpool kept the pressure on, moving the ball quickly and regaining possession after attacks were repelled to build another attack. Against Forest, at home, Liverpool kept the ball but didn't move the ball quickly enough or have enough attacking patterns to keep Forest under intense pressure. Liverpool have evolved with many more methods of creating chances than in those early stages of the season.

"I couldn't have asked for more today. I think most people talk about the second half – that they are really positive about the second half. If you ask me, I am also more positive about the second half than the first half, but if you play at this ground against this team, who are in such good form, hardly concedes a chance in every single game... so many counter-attack threats, almost every game they have counter-attack after counter-attack after counter-attack. We conceded only one counter-attack here today in 98 minutes of football of total domination. Unfortunately for us, that ball immediately went in." Arne Slot speaking at the post-match press conference

Key Points

- With Liverpool chasing the game, Arne Slot was willing to task risks to get level and attempt to get ahead
- Ryan Gravenberch's flexibility and intelligence enabled Liverpool to make drastic positional switches
- There are very few central defenders who can cope playing 1v1 for a prolonged period in the Premier League, Virgil van Dijk is certainly one of them
- Liverpool were able to visit one of the most in-form teams in the league and statistically dominate them, and only be denied a victory by an outstanding goalkeeping performance

Game 32 – Brentford – Premier League – Away – 2-0 win

Liverpool 4-2-3-1

Alisson, Alexander-Arnold, Konate, van Dijk, Tsimikas (Robertson), Gravenberch, Mac Allister (Jones), Szoboszlai (Elliott), Salah, Gakpo (Chiesa), Diaz (Nunez)

Brentford 4-3-3

Flekken, Roerslev, Collins, van den Berg, Lewis-Potter, Norgaard, Janelt (Schade), Damsgaard (Jensen), Mbuemo, Yarmolyuk, Wissa

Scorers – Nunez (2)

Brentford and Nottingham Forest take quite similar approaches. Their strengths are to counter-attack, though Brentford rely on the speed and elusiveness of Mbuemo and Wissa.

Special Plans For Mbuemo

Liverpool acknowledged the special threat of Mbuemo as – when he received the ball in a period of established build-up – Liverpool ensured that he was doubled up against to deny him space to dribble into. In counter-attacking situations, Brentford looked to pick Mbuemo out with long diagonals to create 1v1s against the full-back. A similar ploy to that used by Liverpool with Salah. Liverpool were very quick to get tight to Mbuemo and prevent him from attacking open spaces.

Brentford Set Up To Find Space Behind

Brentford defended extremely deep. Whether this was because of a game plan to hit Liverpool on the counter-attack or because of Liverpool's excellence at pinning Brentford in is open to discussion, though the likelihood is that the two combined to emphasise one another. The majority of the game, especially the more structured passages of play, was played out in the Brentford defensive third. From early on in proceedings, Brentford dropped very deep, very quickly, with every player inside their defensive third. This created situations where a defensive triangle of Konate, van Dijk and Gravenberch were well placed to pin Brentford in but were little more than 15 yards outside the Brentford penalty area.

In one situation, Konate took on a shot from 25 yards out, which flew high over the bar. Another instance saw him find a defence-splitting pass to create a chance for Diaz. Though Brentford were under pressure, the flip side of this was that if they did gain possession, there were vast swathes of space to attack into, suiting their speedy forwards. Everything Brentford did was designed to hit the spaces behind Liverpool. At goal kicks, they passed short to invite a few Liverpool players to press and then looked to hit long into the space behind.

Brentford's deep compact defensive shape

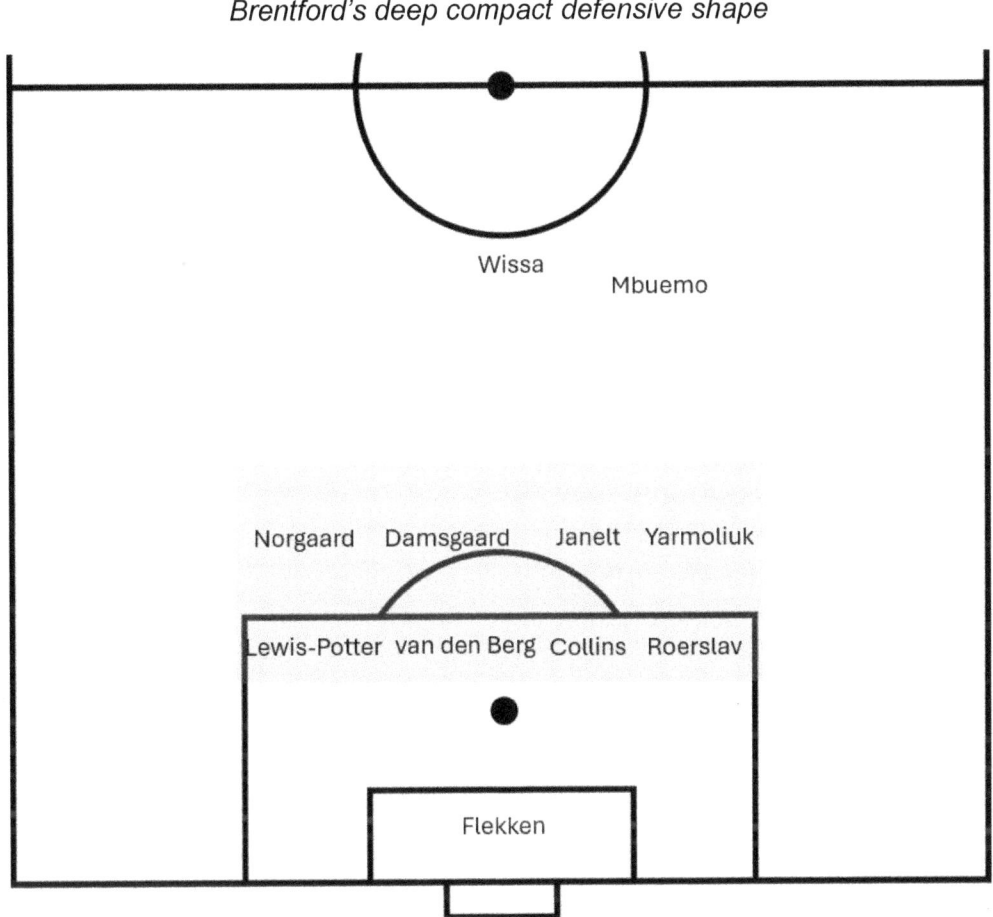

Brentford Press High

Unlike Forest, there was a press at Liverpool's goal kicks. When Brentford first came into the Premier League, one of the hallmarks of their play was their fierce pressing and counter-pressing. The press has become more measured, and against Liverpool, the press from goal kicks was a trapping press rather than an ultra-aggressive one. The press didn't last very long, and after a few passes, Brentford dropped back into their shape. Liverpool used one of their escape patterns to get out of the press, but rather than Konate and Alexander-Arnold linking with Salah on the right, it was Tsimikas releasing on the left to Gakpo, who came inside to set Szoboszlai away. This move created an opening as Szoboszlai found Salah who passed behind the defence to Gakpo. His attempted lifted finish trickled wide of the far post.

Szoboszlai The Attacking Threat

Brentford frustrated Liverpool for most of the game, keeping them at bay. Overlaps, half-space crosses, underlapping runs into half-spaces, fast combinations and long shots. Szoboszlai was prominent in the first half with some spectacular and powerful long-range shooting. He came to Liverpool with a reputation for ferocious ball striking, but his main utility for the team has been his lung-busting energy. Against Brentford, he moved into pockets of space around the half-space and central zone. One movement and shot of his crashed against the crossbar. There have been glimpses of his power, at times, and with Liverpool facing packed defences, a long-range weapon can be highly useful. Even if the shot doesn't go in, it can earn set-pieces and another scoring opportunity.

Substitutions Change The Game

For the second game in a row, it was Slot's substitutions that changed the outcome of the match. Against Forest, there was the instant impact of Jota and Tsimikas. At Brentford, Darwin Nunez struck a quickfire stoppage time double, one tucked in low from six yards after an Alexander-Arnold cross; the second fired high into the roof of the net following a counter-attack that involved fellow substitutes Chiesa and Elliott.

"Darwin is always having a lot of impact when he comes in. Brings energy and power. Most of our games are the last half hour in control around 18 yards, and that's where he's at his best. The first hour is often open but the last 30 minutes dominant. Then to have someone like Darwin is nice to have." Arne Slot speaking to BBC Sport

Key Points

- If opponents have a clear key attacking player, Slot will make plans to help neutralise that threat
- Brentford set up to defend very deep. Liverpool also pinned Brentford back through their midfield and defence positioning
- Szoboszlai's long-range shooting power can be an effective weapon against a low block
- Slot will make changes to tactics or personnel (or both) and has been rewarded for his proactivity

Game 33 – Lille – Champions League – Home – 2-1 win

Liverpool 4-2-3-1

Alisson, Bradley (Alexander-Arnold), Quansah, van Dijk, Tsimikas, Gravenberch (Mac Allister), Jones (Elliott), Szoboszlai (Endo) Salah, Diaz (Chiesa), Nunez

Lille 4-2-3-1

Chevalier, Mandi, Diakite, Alexsandro, Gudmundsson (Ismaily), Mukau (Bouaddi), Andre, Bakker (Meunier), Haraldsson, Cabella (Sahraoui), David

Scorers – Salah, Elliott, David

A win in game seven out of eight in the new version of the Champions League group stage, as Liverpool eased to a 2-1 win against 10-man Lille to all but guarantee a first-place finish.

Slot took the opportunity to rotate while retaining a strong lineup, with Bradley, Tsimikas and Quansah starting in defence, Jones restored to the starting lineup, and Diaz taking Gakpo's place wide left. Nunez was rewarded for scoring his late double with the start at centre-forward.

Lille Press Well

Liverpool's regular build-up patterns were on show, using a 2-3 shape. Both full-backs inverted early on to help establish possession against a well-organised Lille press. Lille used a narrow, disciplined 2-2-2 shape that focused on cutting out passing lanes and preventing central passes into Ryan Gravenberch. Liverpool needed the two full-backs to be narrow to avoid an overload when van Dijk or Quansah had possession. The full-backs being narrow triggered Liverpool's central midfielders to pull wide, outside of the full-backs to help Liverpool progress the ball downfield. Liverpool had a lot of possession, but the progression was slow, as Lille were able to make the patterns of progression relatively predictable. Even after the red card, Lille tried to press, removing one player from the pressing unit and creating a 2-3 or 3-2 pressing shape.

When in possession, Lille played slick, short passing football, getting into wide areas well, but were not able to penetrate centrally. They put in a number of crosses but came up against the wall that is Virgil van Dijk.

Virgil van Dijk: The Formidable Barrier

When Jose Mourinho and John Terry were an item at Chelsea, it was Terry's job to repel crosses, especially crosses into the front post area. This position was roughly on the corner of the six-yard box and came to be known by many as the "John Terry position". With Liverpool, this is the "Virgil van Dijk" position, where he forms an intimidating block to anything at the near post and deals with high or low crosses. Lille got into good wide positions, but van Dijk was there to see off any threat. His body shape is often perfectly positioned, with his shoulders open to see as much of the pitch as possible, including the area the ball is coming from and the immediate attacking threat to his zone. Lille did score an equaliser from a cross as the ball was cut back all the way to the edge of the box, the shot was blocked by Robertson on the six-yard line, and the rebound dropped to Jonathan David to strike. Parity lasted just five minutes before Harvey Elliott hit a deflected volley.

Long Diagonal Passes

Virgil's importance to the team is not just his defensive skills and organisation. He is an important attacking weapon from deep. His long-range diagonals are prominent in the way that Liverpool can stretch and switch the play, and against Lille, these passes created direct opportunities for Salah. In the first half, he showed exceptional control under pressure to get away from the defender and slot a shot just wide of the far post. In the second half, Salah pulled a long pass out of the air and immediately ran at the defender, creating a shooting opportunity blocked by the feet of the goalkeeper. A low ball behind created Salah's first-half goal, however. Following a regain in Liverpool's half, Curtis Jones threaded a ball through that Salah ran onto and lifted over the advancing goalkeeper from outside the box.

Different Tempo After Half-Time

Liverpool upped the tempo in the second half. A common occurrence in all fixtures, but especially in their Champions League games. The standout alteration came through the full-backs, where Bradley and Tsimikas pulled wider and drove into the space. Lille were narrow in their pressing structure, allowing space on the outside. The midfielders dropped deeper to allow the full-backs to push on, in contrast to the first half positioning. Conor Bradley, in particular, attacked at high pace from wide on the right side.

How Liverpool use diagonals from van Dijk to either Alexander-Arnold or Salah. When one is wide the other moves infield.

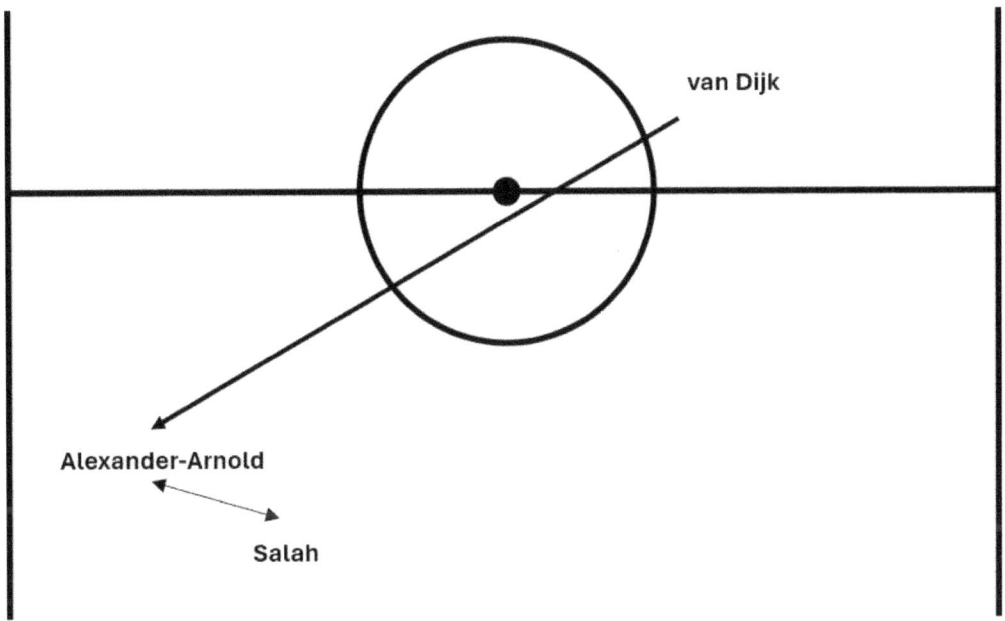

Key Points

- Lille pressed well, making Liverpool drop their full-backs deeper and hit long passes
- Virgil van Dijk was key in this performance, cutting out Lille crosses and striking excellent long passes
- The van Dijk to Salah diagonal pass has been a key feature in Liverpool's play under both Slot and Klopp
- Liverpool's full-backs carried the ball forward in wide spaces created by Lille's narrow out-of-possession shape

Game 34 – Ipswich – Premier League – Home – 4-1 win

Liverpool 4-2-3-1

Alisson, Alexander-Arnold, Konate, van Dijk, Robertson, Gravenberch (Endo), Mac Allister (Danns), Szoboszlai (Elliott), Salah, Gakpo (Nunez), Diaz (Chiesa)

Ipswich 4-2-3-1

Walton, Tuanzebe, O'Shea, Greaves, Davis (Townsend), Morsy, Phillips, Burns (Johnson), Hutchinson (Enciso), Philogene (Broadhead), Delap (Hirst)

Scorers – Szoboszlai, Salah, Gakpo (2), Greaves

A comfortable win against relegation-battling Ipswich Town. For the third Premier League game in a row, Liverpool came up against an opponent who chose to sit very deep in an effort to be compact and hard to break down. In the fixture before this, Ipswich had faced Manchester City and been beaten 6-0 at home. They did not want a second successive pummelling.

Liverpool Expressing Themselves

Liverpool had the luxury of breaking the deadlock relatively early. Szoboszlai scored in the 11th minute after an excellent line-breaking pass from Konate enabled him to evade a defender and strike a low, hard left-footed shot into the bottom corner. Liverpool could then enjoy themselves. In no other game to this point have there been so many flicks and tricks on show. Szoboszlai received one ball in the air near the halfway line and rapidly controlled then flicked the ball to start and attack. The crowd gasped, everyone smiled, and on Liverpool went. Later, Alexander-Arnold and Salah combined with a double one-two, which culminated in a low cross being cut out. These moments delighted the crowd. That was the mood of this game.

"Then if you zoom in on Dom, I think at the beginning of the season he would have played that ball to Mo, which most of the time was a very good choice because Mo can definitely score a goal as well. And now he decided to go for the goal himself and scored the goal himself." Arne Slot speaking to Liverpool FC TV

High Horseshoe

Van Dijk and Konate's main duties were to help pin Ipswich in and build the attacks from positions very high up the pitch. The "horseshoe" of passing the ball around the shape of the opposition was located very high up the pitch for Liverpool and kept them probing and stretching the Ipswich defence. Ipswich defended deep, though the depth was less exaggerated than that deployed by Brentford; the difference was only around 5 yards higher up the pitch. It was once again important for van Dijk and Konate to keep attacks going. This is in addition to Konate being a source of release passes when the opposition press at goal kicks and van Dijk striking diagonals with regularity out to Salah or Alexander-Arnold. In this game, however, van Dijk also hit passes in behind the Ipswich right-back for Gakpo on the left.

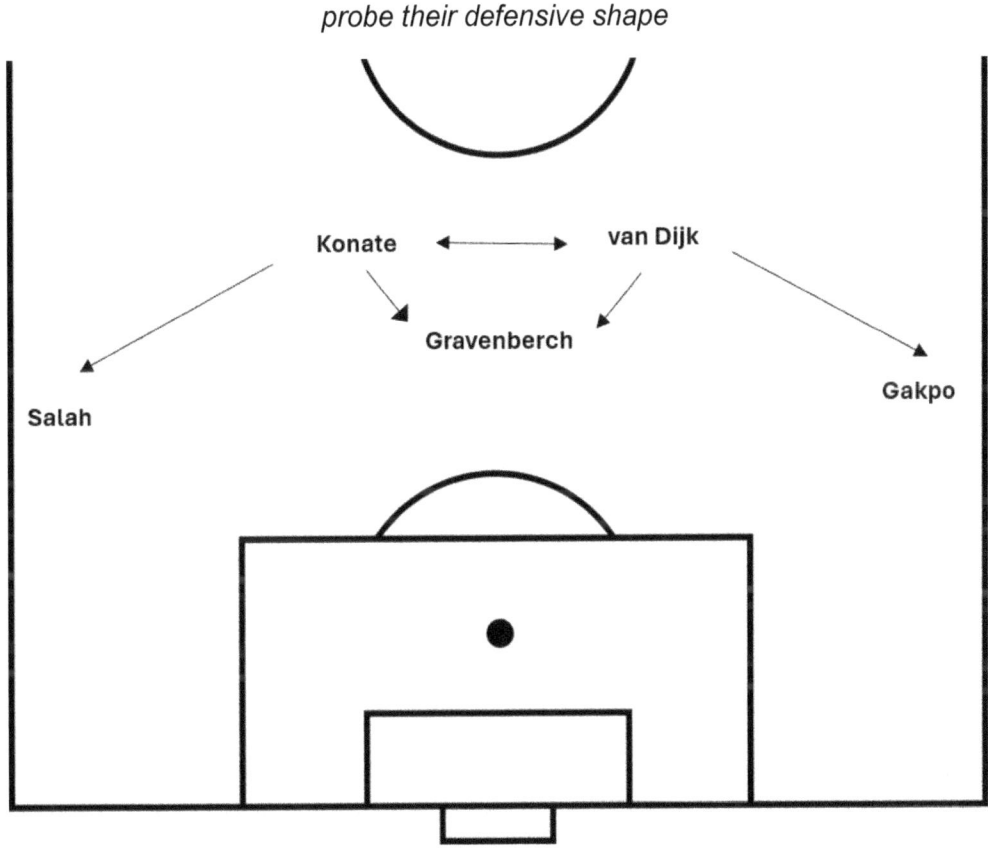

The high horseshoe used to pin opponents in and probe their defensive shape

Movement To Receive

The increase in rotations and movement from Liverpool has been important in breaking down these packed defences. Against Ipswich, Gravenberch had license to push forward and when he did so, Mac Allister filled the space left behind, ensuring one midfielder was close to the central defenders. Diaz rotated from wide with centre-forward, switching with Gakpo. Diaz also came short to receive, triggering the movement forward of Szoboszlai or Mac Allister. The whole right-hand side rotated in a triangle. If Szoboszlai was wide then Salah and Alexander-Arnold went narrow. If Alexander-Arnold was wide, then Szoboszlai would make runs through the half-space. If Salah was wide, then Alexander-Arnold or Szoboszlai would make a half-space run. One player would be inside to receive, either on the edge of the box or 10-15 yards from the box.

On occasion, the triangle had two players wide and one inside, but usually the triangle was one wide and two inside. Once, it was a rule in football to "Find the free man", and Liverpool's rotations create the free man well, but Liverpool do not simply rely on that method. The Liverpool players are happy to receive when marked and under pressure. They can protect the ball and either spin away or release to a teammate. Opponents will be drawn to the player who has received under pressure as this is a potential pressing opportunity. This moment helps create a free man elsewhere on the pitch.

Alexander-Arnold's Field Day

One member of the triangle seemed to enjoy his game more than anybody else on the pitch. Perhaps because Alexander-Arnold's defensive duties were minimal, he was able to express himself in advanced positions, and delivered dangerous crosses from the half-space and from the more conventional wide areas. Gakpo's second goal was created by a beautifully curved Alexander-Arnold cross, whilst TAA came close to scoring a couple of goals himself, with a shot from just inside the box hitting the crossbar, and a swerving 25-yard effort – struck from a central area – that went narrowly wide of the post.

Key Points

- Liverpool played with great freedom and flair after going ahead early
- Liverpool used a high horseshoe of passing to help pin opponents in and probe in attack. This was helped by the opposition pulling every player back to defend
- The midfield has reached high levels of understanding and rotates in various ways, not just with each other but also with other positions within the team
- At their best, Liverpool are happy to pass to players who are marked tightly

Game 35 – PSV – Champions League – Away – 3-2 loss

Liverpool 4-3-3

Kelleher, Bradley, Quansah, Robertson (Nyoni), Tsimikas, Endo, McConnell, Chiesa, Gakpo (Morton), Danns (Nallo)

PSV 4-4-2

Benitez, Karsdorp (Ledezma), Obispo (Nagalo), Boscagli, Mauro Junior, Bakayoko, Land, Veerman, Saibari (Driouech), Pepi (de Jong), Til (Babadi)

Scorers – Gakpo, Elliott, Bakayoko, Saibari, Pepi

The eighth game of the Champions League group stage saw Liverpool's perfect record broken by a PSV win. Slot rotated heavily and the usual patterns we see were less evident.

Chiesa Receiving Long Diagonals

Chiesa's quest for fitness and sharpness continued, completing the full 90 minutes for the first time in a Liverpool shirt. He was Liverpool's most consistent attacking threat, using his dribbling skills and ability to strike and cross with both feet. Much of Chiesa's service came from long diagonals. These diagonal passes have been a regular feature in Liverpool games this season, but what makes their presence in this match noteworthy is that the diagonals were delivered without van Dijk, Alexander-Arnold, or Salah – the usual players involved. This suggests that the diagonals are a team strategy rather than the whim of individual players.

Who Is Gravenberch's Back-Up?

From the very first game of the season, Ryan Gravenberch cemented himself into the team as one of its core components. The holding midfielder position was a problem for Liverpool and one that the recruitment team failed to solve. Arne Slot solved the problem by working with Ryan Gravenberch, and the problem now is, "What happens if Gravenberch is injured?" Depending on the opposition, the likely answer is that Alexis Mac Allister returns to the role he filled for much of the previous season. Another possible answer is 20-year-old James McConnell, and against PSV he made a rare start in the first team with so many players being rested. McConnell showed glimpses of some of Gravenberch's attributes with an ability to carry the ball forward and play progressive passes. This could make him a preferred option to the more conservative Wataru Endo.

Potential Poacher

Another player rotated into the starting lineup was Jayden Danns, who is younger than McConnell. Yet Danns looks physically well-developed and showed great maturity against PSV. His hold-up play took advantage of his physical attributes, strength and a large frame, and he also showed good link play. He has first-team goals to his name already, illustrating scoring instincts inside the box. Days after this game, Danns went on loan to Sunderland in a bid to gain valuable and regular first-team experience.

Academy Players Stepping In

On a good night for Liverpool's academy, a player further along his development continued to rehabilitate his confidence and form. Though Liverpool conceded three goals, Jarrell Quansah put in a steady defensive performance, and his on-the-ball performance was far more positive, completing all but two of the passes he attempted. His composure on the ball has hinted at the potential for Quansah to play a similar role for Liverpool as Joel Matip did during Jurgen Klopp's reign.

"Like expected I think, eventful game with many goals. I think everybody expected that before the game, for two reasons maybe. One of the reasons I think [is] two managers who always want to press high, want to bring the ball out from the back. So sometimes you see then certain mistakes – but it's always eventful. And for the other reason, because both teams, maybe mainly ours, were not playing in the set-up that we usually do, so then you see in some moments that we defend in a way that probably is not expected if we play with all of our starters." Arne Slot speaking to Liverpool FC TV

Key Points

- Long diagonal passes are not player-specific but a clear team strategy
- Though Gravenberch has stepped into the holding midfielder role this season, there is no clear back up to him that suits the way Slot desires the role to be played
- Academy players populated the line up, gaining experience and resting key players

Game 36 – Bournemouth – Premier League – Away – 2-0 win

Liverpool 4-2-3-1

Alisson, Alexander-Arnold (Bradley), Konate, van Dijk, Robertson, Gravenberch, Mac Allister (Jones), Szoboszlai, Salah (Endo), Gakpo (Nunez), Diaz

Bournemouth 4-2-3-1

Kepa, Cook, Zabarnyi, Huijsen, Kerkez, Christie (Jebbison), Adams, Brooks (Tavernier), Kluivert, Semenyo, Outtara

Scorers – Salah (2)

Liverpool travelled to one of the teams of the 2024/25 season in Bournemouth. In back-to-back games during January, they had scored four at Newcastle and five at home against high-flying Forest. Earlier in the season, they had beaten both Arsenal and Manchester City. They may not be a historic Premier League giant, but they represented a real test for Liverpool.

"Modern" Football Meets

Bournemouth's style of play has been described as one of the templates for modern football. Evolving from possession-focused positional play towards high-powered fast forward football, it is an approach that Liverpool have also been identified as playing. The terminology is not quite nuanced enough to explain how either of these teams play, though, as they place a high value on controlling possession while also looking for moments to speed up the game and attack with high intensity. Both Liverpool and Bournemouth possess fast, tricky attackers and like to be aggressive in transition. These principles created an open and entertaining game, with both teams going toe to toe.

Bournemouth were unfortunate not to land a blow with an xG of 1.6, but Liverpool ended the game with an xG of 2.5, suggesting that Liverpool were the "right" winner. On another day, however, this game could have finished 2-1 or even 2-2. Bournemouth hit the woodwork twice and Alisson made three excellent saves. One of the instances in which Bournemouth hit the post created Bournemouth's highest expected goal chance, which Kluivert slashed wide. There was also a goal disallowed for offside, which was extremely tight, further illustrating the threat of Bournemouth throughout the game.

The dribbling skills of Bournemouth players gave Liverpool problems throughout. The two wingers took on their respective full-backs with regularity, but it was

Alexander-Arnold who was given the biggest headache. Semenyo ran at Alexander-Arnold with the ball at his feet and created opportunities for himself and teammates. Semenyo was assisted by the willingness of Kerkez to overlap and attack aggressively, and Liverpool had to dedicate a lot of defensive support to help protect Alexander-Arnold, particularly in the first half. In the second half, Bournemouth seemed to focus more on attacks down their right, away from Alexander-Arnold and potentially missing a trick. Liverpool were struggling to hold themselves together for close to ten minutes after half-time, with the majority of the pressure coming from the right with dribbling and crosses.

"Not many things that we do are just by coincidence. I think it is clear that they have many good things, this team, and their left full-back is definitely a threat going forwards. Mo Salah is an incredible player but his main strength is not following the opposite full-back. But that's not the only thing. We want to keep Mo as much as we can forward, as well, because it is a risk for every team that plays us if the left full-back goes." Arne Slot speaking to Liverpool FC TV about Ryan Gravenberch playing more on the right

Ball Carrying Defenders

It was not only wingers who dribbled at Liverpool. Bournemouth carried the ball forward through their central defenders and midfielders in possession. Tyler Adams, Illia Zabarnyi, and Dean Huijsen all registered over 30 ball carries. In contrast, Salah only managed 26. Liverpool's press has struggled to stop ball-carrying defenders at times, and Bournemouth exploited this, progressing the ball through Liverpool lines with the ball at their feet. This *forced* Liverpool into a mid-block, rather than Liverpool choosing to use the mid-block as they often do when ahead in games. Liverpool are usually effective at pressing from both sides once the first pressing line is broken, but they were forced to use their recovery speed to protect their own penalty area rather than pressuring the ball.

Bournemouth Press Aggressively

The last piece of the Bournemouth template was an aggressive and effective press. Bournemouth pressed aggressively at Anfield, committing numbers to the regain. In open play, they regularly committed five players into the press, either in a 3-2 or 2-3 shape. Liverpool were forced to go back to Alisson, who went long into Salah to attempt to hold up the ball. Salah was marshalled well by Lewis Cook, yet he still ended up with two goals. Partly due to the pressure from Bournemouth but also partly because of Bournemouth's high line, Liverpool struck a large number of long balls over the defensive line, one of which resulted in Gakpo earning a penalty as he was clipped running onto the ball from deep. Salah converted the penalty for his and Liverpool's first goal of the game.

Bournemouth's central defenders carrying the ball through the Liverpool press

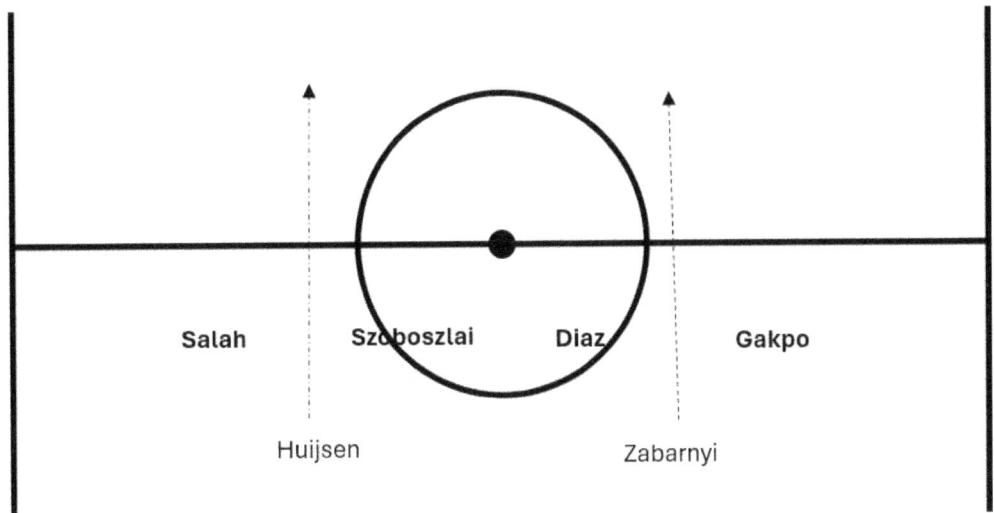

Diaz: The Axis For Attacks

Liverpool were able to counter-attack effectively, largely thanks to the excellence of Luis Diaz. They would often play forward into Diaz to act as the springboard for many attacks. Traditionally, teams will use a big, strong, Didier Drogba-type player to hold up the ball, relieve pressure, and start attacks. Liverpool are less traditional, however, and their strong target man is their winger: Salah. The link man is the centre-forward, Diaz, who comes short into spaces to receive passes into feet. The passes into him are medium range rather than the type of long, lofted invitation to 'fight for the ball' that a player such as Drogba would see. The length of Liverpool's passes meant that the ball had less travel time and was harder to cut out. Diaz could turn out and feed passes into wide players or set a ball back to trigger a longer pass behind the defence to forward running wingers or midfielders. On occasion, Diaz was able to receive and turn 180 degrees to drive directly at the defence, progressing Liverpool into Bournemouth territory.

Key Points

- A clash of two teams who mix modern styles together effectively. Possession-based positional play combining with powerful transitional football
- Both teams' wide attackers were in fine form. Liverpool had to use Gravenberch more to the right defensively to help Alexander-Arnold. Salah remained higher up the pitch when out of possession, aiding counter-attacks

- Luis Diaz performed superbly, dropping off the defence to distribute passes wide or turn and drive forward
- Bournemouth's central defenders possessed the ability to carry the ball forward. This continues to break the Liverpool press

Game 37 – Spurs – EFL Cup Semi-Final Second Leg – Home – 4-0 win

Liverpool 4-2-3-1

Kelleher, Bradley, Konate, van Dijk (Quansah), Robertson, Gravenberch, Jones (Mac Allister), Szoboszlai, Salah (Elliott), Gakpo (Diaz), Nunez (Jota)

Spurs 4-3-3

Kinsky, Gray, Danso, Davies (Moore), Spence, Bissouma (Porro), Bentancur, Sarr (Bergvall), Kulusevski, Son, Richarlison (Tel)

Scorers – Gakpo, Salah, Szoboszlai, van Dijk

Liverpool trailed 1-0 from the first leg but roared back at Anfield to reach the League Cup final. The performance was outstanding, with 26 shots to Tottenham's five. Spurs did not manage a single shot on target while Liverpool had ten, although Spurs were without their whole first choice defensive unit but close to full strength in midfield and attack. Liverpool went in with a strong lineup in an effort to overturn the deficit. This was achieved with possibly the most dominant performance of the season.

Attacking Dynamism From Bradley

A player who had his best performance was Conor Bradley. Bradley is Alexander-Arnold's understudy, but he is bursting with dynamic potential, and when he comes into the side, he doesn't weaken it. His skill set is different to that of Alexander-Arnold, which means that opponents have a different question to answer when Bradley plays. Spurs struggled to solve the problems created by the explosive play of Bradley. He is a taller, rangy figure and – at almost six feet tall – he can handle most wingers in the air and is a far post threat when crosses come into the box (attacking the far post as Robertson does from his position on the left). Bradley makes forward runs with and without the ball.

An off-the-ball movement from Bradley created Liverpool's third goal. Alexis Mac Allister received a pass from the left side in a central area in his own half, some 15-20 yards from the halfway line. When Mac Allister received the ball, Bradley was 10 yards further back, closer to the Liverpool goal than Mac Allister. Following a short dribble, Mac Allister passed the ball into the path of an onrushing Bradley and he received the ball on the extreme left of the inside right channel, almost inside zone 14. Bradley played a one-touch pass in behind the Spurs defence, creating an opportunity for Szoboszlai to stride onto and tuck into the corner. The goal was a great illustration of the explosive running of Bradley and Liverpool's counter-attacking power; their ability to turn any moment into a scoring opportunity. Bradley showed his full array of attacking weapons, using a range of turning skills, dribbling with the ball at his feet, delivering half-space crosses, and even throwing in a few nutmegs.

Liverpool Build Up With More Players

Conor Bradley had work to do in his own third, too, when Liverpool were building out from the back. Spurs stuck to their blueprint and pressed as hard as they could, but Liverpool answered this by keeping the full-backs tighter to the central defender and dropping Jones in as extra support. When opponents are pressing, it has become commonplace for Liverpool to use a 2-2-2 shape with the two central defenders, two full-backs and two of the central midfielders forming a hexagon. Opponents have often committed four or five players to press Liverpool, but very few have committed six. With Alisson also available, the hexagon plus Alisson enables Liverpool to create an overload against heavy pressure and get away by using simple passes. Add to this that Slot is happy for his centre-forward to come short, and Liverpool have many options to play through most presses. If the overloading is not working, they will use the simple route of playing long into Salah or the wide escape routes of Konate clipping down the line on the right and Robertson or Tsimikas clipping down the line on the left.

"First of all, if you play more often together, you know better what is expected. So the first time I tell them how to bring the ball out from the back against a 7-9-11 press, they were maybe like: 'OK.' But the more times you face them, the more it becomes natural for you. The more games you play, the more team meetings you have, the more training sessions you have, the better they know what we expect from them and what to expect from each other." Slot speaking about playing Spurs (from The Guardian)

Nunez Used As A Focal Point

Darwin Nunez was selected to play through the centre. He gave a physical performance, giving Liverpool an outlet in behind and also used his head as a target. Darwin and Liverpool utilised his size and strength at throw-ins, regularly aiming at his head for flick-ons and knock-downs to then pass forward, setting attacks in motion. Nunez showed his pace in the second half to win a penalty to make the game 2-0, putting Liverpool ahead in the tie. Salah turned and passed the ball in behind the Spurs defence, and although the goalkeeper looked favourite to get there, Nunez accelerated to toe the ball past the keeper and win a penalty. Salah converted, having already created the opening for Gakpo with a trivela cross.

Running Into The Half-Space

A Szoboszlai goal that was chalked off in the first half served to emphasise the relationship on the Liverpool right-hand side and the running off the ball from the Liverpool midfielders. When Salah has possession on the right, it has become a pattern for a part of the right-side triangle to make a run into the half-space. For Szoboszlai, this is a run behind the defence into a shooting position. If Szoboszlai doesn't make the run behind, Nunez makes a run into the channel for a shooting opportunity. On the left, similar runs are made from deep, mainly from Robertson. These runs help push the defence back, creating space in front of the opposition defensive line for Mac Allister and others.

Key Points

- Conor Bradley once more showed that he can be a dynamic attacking option in the absence of Alexander-Arnold
- Liverpool were able to withstand and exploit the Spurs press by keeping both full-backs closer to the central defenders plus the central midfielders, creating a six player build plus the goalkeeper
- Darwin Nunez was used directly up against a Spurs defence that was – again – short of key players. His use as a target for throw-ins had not been seen before, certainly not to such a regular extent

Game 38 – Plymouth – FA Cup – Away – 1-0 loss

Liverpool 4-3-3

Kelleher, McConnell, Quansah, Gomez (Mabaya (Nunez)), Tsimikas, Elliott, Endo, Nyoni (Kone-Doherty), Chiesa, Diaz, Jota

Plymouth 3-4-3

Hazard, Talovierov, Katic, Pleguezuelo (Palsson), Sorinola, Randell (Boateng), Gyabi, Puchacz, Hardie (Obafemi), Wright, Bundu (Tijani)

Scorers – Hardie

Arne Slot saw a trip to struggling Championship team Plymouth in the Cup as an opportunity to heavily rotate the squad. It backfired quite badly as Liverpool were beaten and hardly created anything until the very end of the match. In Jurgen Klopp's first four seasons with Liverpool, he was unable to get past the third round of the FA Cup. New managers in England often get tripped up by the FA Cup. Wholesale rotation in the FA Cup is far more risky than in the League Cup because the competition carries more significance. Here, Slot rotated heavily and paid the price.

Lacking Fluency

Liverpool were disjointed in possession and lacked the fluency of recent times. The patterns of play that have become familiar were absent, largely due to the lack of chemistry in the lineup. Similarly, the press was less organised and far slower to apply any pressure. Liverpool only looked like they might score during stoppage time when they slung balls into the box.

"Today also showed why we play with the ones we played today. These players need game rhythm as well. You saw today some of these players really need games like this to be ready for the last three months of the season." Arne Slot speaking to Sky Sports

Plymouth Play Long

The sub-par press worked against Liverpool not because Plymouth were allowed to play out with smooth football but because Plymouth wanted to go long. Two or three passes got Liverpool's press moving towards the defenders, but the press never got close enough to stop long balls into the three physical forwards of Plymouth to create flick-ons or second balls to fight for. If Plymouth won the second ball, they had territory and space to advance. If they lost the second ball, they had numbers back and sat patiently in their block. Perhaps Liverpool would have been better served by sitting back in a block and seeing if Plymouth could create or penetrate with the ball at the feet of their central defenders.

The compact Plymouth shape and how they surrounded Liverpool's pivot

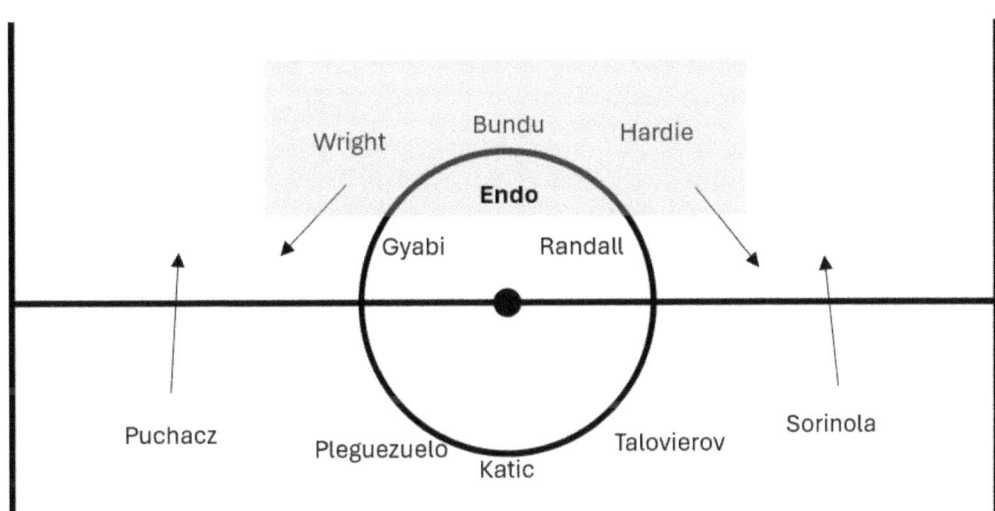

Compact Formation

Plymouth used a superbly well-organised 3-4-3 formation and were outstanding defensively. The front three didn't apply pressure until a trigger, such as a poor touch or negative pass, occurred. The front three also did a wonderful job crowding the pivot and delaying ball progression. Quansah attempted to carry the ball forward on a couple of occasions due to the lack of options, only to be crowded out. Once Liverpool did progress the ball into wide areas, a stream of crosses came in, but the three Plymouth central defenders dominated in the air and blocked efforts on goal, including one particular block on Diaz that saved a certain goal. They celebrated every header and every block, such was their determination.

Paying The Penalty

The winning strike came from the penalty spot. Plymouth hurled a long throw into the penalty area and the ball was headed towards the edge of box, where Gyabi tried to flick the ball over Harvey Elliott. The ball struck Elliott's raised hands and the referee pointed to the spot. Hardie cracked the penalty low as Kellher dived the wrong way. Plenty of time remained in the game, but Liverpool failed to create any significant opportunities.

Key Points
- The FA Cup often proves a stumbling block for managers new to English football. It is much harder to rotate in the FA Cup than the EFL Cup because of the added significance and motivation for lower league sides
- Liverpool's press was disjointed due to all the changes. Plymouth were happy to play against this as they wanted to go long into the strikers and there was room to pick up second balls. Liverpool may have been better off in a deeper block, restricting second ball opportunities.

Game 39 – Everton – Premier League – Away – 2-2 draw

Liverpool 4-2-3-1

Alisson, Bradley (Jones), Konate, van Dijk, Robertson (Tsimikas), Gravenberch (Alexander-Arnold), Mac Allister, Szoboszlai, Salah, Gakpo (Nunez), Diaz (Jota)

Everton 4-3-3

Pickford, O'Brien. Tarkowski, Branthwaite, Mykolenko, Garner (Young), Gueye (Iroegbunam), Doucoure, Lindstrom (Alcaraz), Ndiaye (Harrison), Beto

Scorers – Mac Allister, Salah, Beto, Tarkowski

The final Goodison Park derby. Liverpool were never going to win this one, were they!? With the overall Goodison record equal – at 41 wins each – there was no way that Liverpool were going to end with more wins in the Goodison derby than Everton.

Moyes and Everton Motivated

This game had been rescheduled from early December due to the storms that had lashed the country. Many considered this to be good fortune for Liverpool, but between December and February, there had been a change of Everton manager and an upturn in form. In December, Sean Dyche's Everton were tough but uninspiring, and when David Moyes returned, Everton rediscovered their energy, vigour, and ability to score goals.

The crowd certainly played their part in the game, too. Every roar helped direct decisions Everton's way; decisions that might have been 50/50. This is the nature of home advantage and one of the reasons why Liverpool's record at Anfield has been so formidable for so many decades.

Free kicks pummelled the Liverpool backline from all angles and distances. No opportunity to pressurise the defence was wasted. The majority of deliveries were struck diagonally towards the far post area of the Liverpool box, where Everton had loaded up with attackers. Jordan Pickford ventured a long way from his goal to take free kicks close to the halfway line and strike long balls, enabling Everton to add another body into the attacking mix. The one time a free kick did not go long and diagonal, it created the opening Everton goal. The far post was loaded, but instead, a pass was slipped into the space between the wall and the crowd of players. Beto sprinted on to the clever pass and slotted beyond Alisson.

Much of the match was disjointed, with the rhythm and flow disrupted by fouls and stoppages. When there was action, it was a frenetic, scruffy match, what many would say was typical of a Merseyside derby. Everton did not want or seek much possession of the ball, whilst Liverpool wanted possession but struggled to maintain and progress the ball, especially during the first half.

Everton Didn't Want Possession

In the second half, Liverpool found themselves 2-1 up and visibly attempted to slow the game down, to take any momentum out of proceedings. This almost worked until deep into added time. Everton had one final Hail Mary attack, bombing a high ball into the box. Konate leapt with Beto, the ball broke to Tarkowski, and he volleyed himself into legend status, visibly lifting the net with the velocity of his strike. Was there a foul by Beto on Konate? Quite possibly, but the script required a dramatic Everton equaliser.

Liverpool didn't necessarily deserve to win the game, though deserving to win is an inexact concept. You deserve to win the game if you score more goals than the opponent. Nothing else really matters. Of course, there are things that football teams can do to boost their chances of winning, but the greatness of the game is that nothing is guaranteed.

Second Ball Battle

Pressing is considered one of the modern keys to victory. Many teams at the sharp end of the elite-level press. They attempted to press against Everton in a 1-3 or 3-1 press in wide areas, but Everton were happy to hit balls long, over the Liverpool press and fight for the second ball in the wilds of a derby atmosphere. Here was the source of many Everton free kicks.

Everton's press was less apparent. For the majority of proceedings, Everton sat in a sound mid-block and prevented Liverpool from progressing with ease by blocking lines through compactness. Their 4-3-3 either made a line of three that prevented easy passes into the pivot or a 2-4 shape where the front two prevented passes infield. Later in the game, Liverpool attempted to use one-two combinations down the sides, but Everton snapped hard in to challenge, preferring to give away a foul than allow flowing build-up play.

"One of the reasons Liverpool played so many long balls was because of how Everton blocked Van Dijk's passing lanes from centre-back into midfield." Arne Slot speaking in the post-match press conference

The Influence Of Salah

Both Liverpool goals involved Mohamed Salah although, in general, he did very little in the game. A few tidy passes and openings were created, but the nature of the game meant that he spent most of his time fighting the full-back. Everton's shape in possession meant that Liverpool's central defenders had a lot of the ball but were unable to find passes, so they went long to Salah or behind for Gakpo, with limited success. Salah was crowded out for much of the game, double or triple-marked. Yet the first of only two real opportunities he conjured yielded Alexis Mac Allister's headed equaliser with an inswinging cross following the second phase of a corner. In the second half, he pounced on a loose ball that rattled across the penalty box to the far post. The ball was travelling at speed, but Salah had the reaction speed and assurance to control the ball with one touch and then fire into the net with his second touch. In this game, he was efficient, especially when compared to the West Ham game. The two moments he produced in the game against Everton were far more important to the team than those in games where he hasn't cashed in during relatively easy victories.

Key Points

- The last derby at Goodison Park and Everton were never going to go quietly. The team, manager, and fans were all highly motivated
- Tactically, Moyes made the game as hard as he could for Liverpool, creating a tight defensive block and a fight for second balls
- Everton were happy to let Liverpool have possession as long as they could keep Liverpool at arm's length
- Liverpool were not at their best, but Salah was able to have two impactful moments that almost won the game

Game 40 – Wolves – Premier League – Home – 2-1 win

Liverpool 4-2-3-1

Alisson, Alexander-Arnold (Bradley), Konate (Quansah), van Dijk, Robertson, Mac Allister, Gravenberch, Szoboszlai, Salah, Diaz (Endo), Jota (Nunez)

Wolves 3-4-3

Sa, Semedo (Lima), Doherty, Agbadou (Bueno) Toti, Ait-Nouri, Andre, Joao Gomes (Doyle), Sarabia (Munetsi), Cunha, Guedes (Bellegarde)

Scorers – Diaz, Salah, Cunha

After the disappointment of losing two points at the very end of the Goodison match, it was vital to Liverpool that they pick up three points at Anfield. Wolves had improved greatly after the appointment of Portuguese coach Vitor Pereira, and there were many signs that they could provide a stiff test for the Merseysiders. Liverpool have performed less convincingly against teams who play with a back three and who also use two players who perform a triple role of supporting in wide areas, occupying the number ten position, and dropping into midfield. The Wolves 3-4-3 encapsulates all these elements.

Wolves Errors

Fortunately, for Liverpool, something that has not changed since the away fixture is that Wolves are a team with good players but who make errors. Both Liverpool goals owed a lot to mistakes. The first goal came from a typical Liverpool counter-attack from left to right. As Salah squeezed the ball across to Diaz inside the box, the Wolves goalkeeper Sa advanced from his goal and clattered into Diaz, and the ball bobbled its way into the net anyway. Later in the first half, Diaz was sent through on goal and Sa again advanced, bringing Diaz down for a penalty. Salah dispatched the kick with ease.

Shotless Second Half

The narrative of the match became a now infamous second-half performance. Liverpool didn't have a single shot on target in the second half. The reaction to this was that it was a calamity and evidence that Liverpool might not be good enough to go on and claim the Premier League title. Yet the first-half performance had been excellent, dominating the game completely. The reaction to the game would have been quite different if the two halves had been swapped over, with Liverpool surging back from a difficult first half in front of The Kop end. Even though Liverpool did not have a shot on target, they did have a very tight offside decision to rule out a goal. VAR intervened as Salah received a long pass, cut inside and drilled in a finish. VAR would again intervene to overrule a penalty decision, which could easily have been given on another day. Both incidents occurred at 2-0, and a score of 3-0 would have been seen as a comfortable cruise to victory. Instead, Wolves scored and Liverpool chose to stabilise what had become a chaotic contest rather than push to extend their 2-1 advantage.

Constant Counter-Attacking Threat

Despite Liverpool's general dominance in possession, their best opportunities came through quick counter-attacks. The opening goal was a quick counter-attack ending with Diaz, and the penalty came from a quick ball forward and behind the defence. Both second-half incidents were counter-attacks, too. Klopp's Liverpool were considered to be the archetype for transition football, but under Slot there have been more counter-attacking goals scored than in the 2023/24 season.

Wolves Overload The Midfield

Transitions were almost the undoing of Liverpool at the start of the second half. Wolves managed to disrupt Liverpool's control by playing at high speed through Liverpool pressure into high attacking areas. The back three spread very wide when Wolves built up in their own half. One or two of the central midfielders would move deep alongside the central defenders, and this pushed the wing-backs high and could create a triple wide with the wide centre-backs, wing-backs, and attacking midfielder pulling wide. During the second half, Wolves picked on one of Liverpool's weaknesses from the season… dribblers breaking the pressing line, and the central defenders carried the ball forward and progressed the ball into dangerous areas. Later in the half, Alexander-Arnold was withdrawn. By inverting, he helped match up the Wolves midfield. Wolves 3-4-3 reads like two midfielders; Liverpool's 4-3-3 reads like three midfielders. However, two of the Wolves' front three drop in to create a four-man box, a 4v3. For Liverpool, Alexander-Arnold inverts and creates a four, cancelling the overload. Once Alexander-Arnold came off, the match-up appeared to be in Wolves' favour. However, Conor Bradley was far more conservative than usual, playing narrow to his central defenders and offering a glimpse into an ability to perform different functions.

How Wolves created a triple wide threat

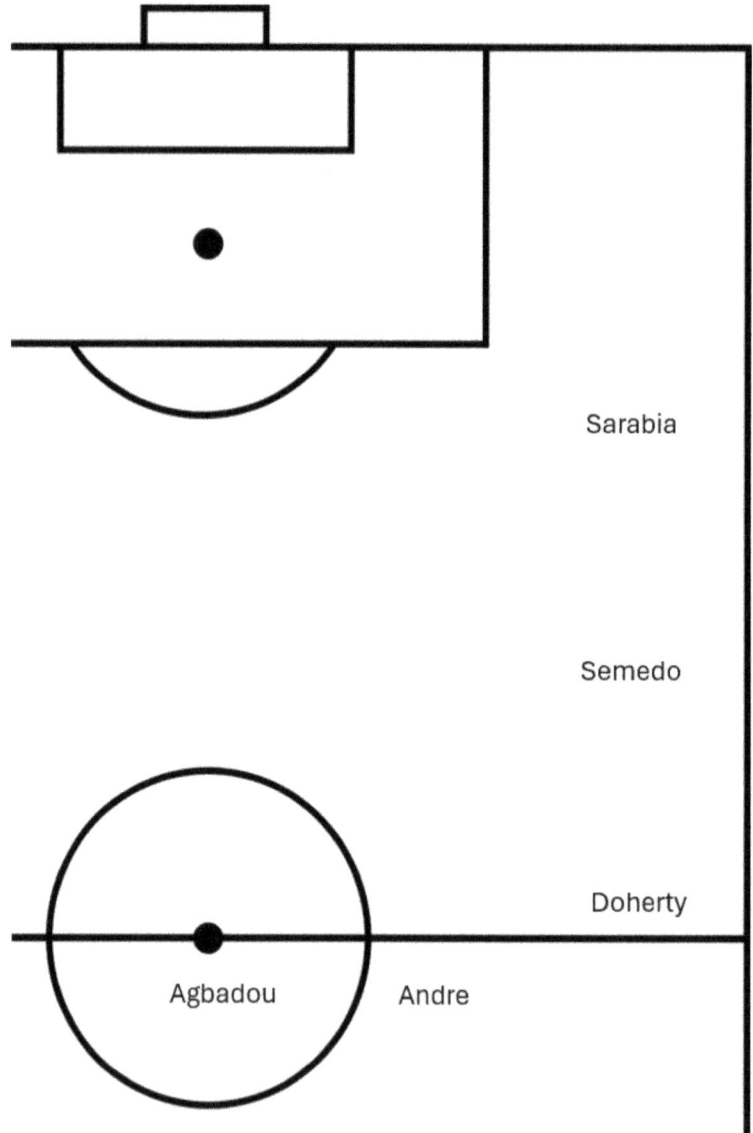

"Sometimes, as a manager, you have to be pragmatic as well and understand it is maybe not our game in terms of football, [so] then we as a coaching staff have to be ready to make decisions that help the team in those moments." Arne Slot in the post-match press conference

Jota Plays With Intelligence

Some of the credit for Liverpool's dominant first-half performance should go to Diogo Jota's performance in the central forward role. Diaz shifted wide left against Wolves, the position he filled prior to Jota's injuries. The function of a Liverpool striker is not to be the primary goal scorer, and this fact is always worth reiterating when players are being judged. The primary scorer is Salah with others weighing in around him. The striker isn't the regular target for quick balls forward to run in behind or hold up the ball; those targets are the wide players, such that Jota moves into space intelligently, pulling defenders out of position and creating overloads. Diaz's pace on the counter-attack was critical to the first-half scoreline, but it should be noted that – at times – his play in 1v1 situations can see him checking back, slowing attacks down. This may be a reason why, as the season progressed, Gakpo was preferred out wide.

Technical Leader

Credit for the result should also go to Alexis Mac Allister. Mac Allister is often overshadowed by the delightfully unexpected quality of Gravenberch or the dynamic running power of Szoboszlai. Carlo Ancelotti has described certain players as being "technical leaders". In other words, whilst some players lead by shouting and hollering, coercing and driving, other players lead through example, through their quiet determination, technical ability, tactical understanding and ability to stand up in the big moments. Mac Allister's consistent performance levels have driven Liverpool forward, and he is always one of the best performers on the pitch without bellowing instructions.

Key Points

- Wolves' errors contributed to Liverpool goals
- Liverpool's shotless second half became the narrative of the game, but two tight calls on offside and an overturned penalty would have presented a very different narrative
- Wolves used the 3-4-3 formation to create a four-man midfield and overload Liverpool in the second half
- Alexis Mac Allister has been a quiet leader for Liverpool this season with his ability and determination

Game 41 – Aston Villa – Premier League – Away – 2-2

Liverpool 4-4-2/4-2-2-2

Alisson, Alexander-Arnold Bradley (Quansah), Konate, van Dijk, Robertson, Gravenberch, Mac Allister (Diaz), Szoboszlai, Salah, Jota (Nunez), Jones

Aston Villa 4-2-3-1

Martinez, Garcia (Cash), Disasi, Mings, Digne (Maatsen), McGinn (Bogarde), Tielemans, Rogers, Asensio (Malen), Rashford (Ramsey), Watkins

Scorers – Salah, Alexander-Arnold, Tielemans, Watkins

The relentless fixture list showed no sign of let up, bouncing Liverpool from test to test. Aston Villa qualified for the Champions League in the 2023/24 season and had already claimed a win against Bayern Munich this season. Though they have been less consistent than in the 2023/24 season, they have attacking threat, a smart manager, and – in the January window – added further impressive attacking talent. Villa drafted in Marcus Rashford, Marco Asensio, and Donyell Malen. Rashford and Asensio went into the team, adding to Ollie Watkins to give an exciting attacking lineup.

Aston Villa Take Risks in Build-Up

Unai Emery decided that the best option was to work the ball into the trio of attackers and into space to allow them to attack with the ball at their feet or for them to stride on to. In their own third, Villa tried to draw Liverpool pressure onto them and then play forward, with more space created. The plan worked on occasion but was extremely risky, providing Liverpool with regains in dangerous positions. Salah's goal came from a turnover in the Villa left-back area when trying to build out. Jota regained a loose pass, entered the penalty area, and squared across the six-yard box for Salah to lift the ball into the roof of the net.

Missed Chances

Jota was unselfish in his choice to square the ball for Salah to score. The position he was in was an excellent shooting opportunity of his own. Later in the first half, he would be in a virtually identical position but screwed his shot a long way off target. Many consider Jota to be Liverpool's most clinical and efficient finisher, but his performance against Villa would question that. He had three efforts at goal in the first-half, all some distance off target. As well as the 1v1 with Martinez from the inside left channel, there was a header at the far post following an Alexander-

Arnold half-space cross, and a left-foot volley from the same area after being picked up by a midrange Konate diagonal. If you consider that the assist for Salah was a presentable chance for himself, and Jota struck the crossbar in the second half via a snap-shot from outside the box, he could have come away with five goals.

Another player who could have scored but came away empty-handed was Darwin Nunez. At 2-2, Szoboszlai was put through on the inside right channel. He could have taken the shot on himself but spotted the run of Nunez on the left side of the box, so he passed across goal and Nunez fired over the bar. According to xG, this was by far the best chance of the night. Nunez received criticism for missing, which was extremely harsh considering it was only a few weeks prior that Nunez had scored two late goals at Brentford to turn one point into three.

Passes In Behind

The position that created the Nunez opportunity came from a pass in behind the Villa defence for a runner from midfield. Jota's first-half opening also came from a long pass and run in behind. Aston Villa, under Unai Emery, have utilised a high defensive line throughout his time at the club, so opposition strikers often struggle to get away from the line and stay onside, but runners from deep are able to break the line. Liverpool played without a striker until Nunez came on as substitute, and Jones and Szoboszlai were able to make runs that tested the Villa defence.

False Forwards

Part of the reason Jones and Szoboszlai were able to make so many testing runs was the shape Liverpool used. Slot caught a lot of people off guard with the way that the team lined up, as the team sheet suggested that Jota would play through the centre as a striker and either Szoboszlai or Jones would go wide left. It was Jota who played on the left with Jones and Szoboszlai central, utilising a strikerless formation. This was a throwback to the game away to Brighton in the League Cup. Given that the primary role of the Liverpool centre-forward is to drag defenders out of position and work back defensively, it isn't a huge tactical leap to remove the striker entirely and play with four central midfielders. As mentioned, the striker in the Slot system is not the prime goal threat, with both wingers being the primary scorers. Liverpool fielded a form of 4-2-4 or 4-2-2-2, enabling Jones and Szoboszlai to play as "false 10s", creating extra bodies in midfield while also giving further license to make forward runs with double defensive midfield cover.

"Today, I liked our performance a lot – much, much, much more than I liked our performance against Wolves – from what I like the most: playing the ball, bringing the ball out from the back, creating chances." Arne Slot speaking at the post-match press conference

The high Aston Villa line and Liverpool using runners from deep to break the offside

Struggles With Crosses

Liverpool conceded two goals from crosses in the first half. The first goal was a free kick curled in from the right, with the ball headed away to the right of the box but not out of the box. Villa kept the ball alive, heading it back across the six-yard box. Contact then sent the ball towards goal, where Curtis Jones headed away from goal, but the ball only travelled to the corner of the six-yard box, where it was volleyed into the net. Jones' connection was weak and he might have left the ball for Alisson to gather.

The second goal also came from the Villa left, but this time from open play. Villa created a trio of attackers on the left, and Alexander-Arnold was dragged inside following a forward run, leaving the overlapping player free with time to pick out a cross. The delivery cleared Konate and van Dijk for Watkins to head home. Had Liverpool been more decisive in defending the crosses, both goals could have been prevented.

Key Points

- Villa took risks to play into their attacking talents, risks that Liverpool pounced upon

- Jota and Nunez have differing reputations, one a clinical finisher, the other wayward. Both missed big chances.
- Liverpool looked to take advantage of Aston Villa's high defensive line with players running in behind from deep.
- Liverpool revisited the system used at Brighton in the EFL Cup, with no striker and midfielders playing as false forwards. A system that can be both more compact and more fluid.

Game 42 – Manchester City – Premier League – Away – 2-0 win

Liverpool 4-4-1/4-2-2-2

Alisson, Alexander-Arnold (Quansah), Konate, van Dijk, Robertson (Tsimikas), Gravenberch, Mac Allister, Szoboszlai, Jones (Endo), Salah (Elliott), Diaz (Gakpo)

Manchester City 4-1-4-1

Ederson, Lewis, Khusanov, Ake (Dias), Gvardiol, Gonzalez (Kovacic), de Bruyne (McAtee), Savinho, Doku, Marmoush (Gundogan), Foden

Scorers – Szoboszlai, Salah

The form of Manchester City had fallen away dramatically by this stage of the season. When Liverpool and Manchester City met at Anfield previously, their form was wobbling, but it only got worse. City went from competing for the title to simply fighting for a Champions League place. Nonetheless, a manager of the quality of Guardiola, plus world-class players on their own patch, are enough to make even the most in-form side nervous.

Szoboszlai and Jones Create Overloads

Slot repeated the formation from Villa Park, and Luis Diaz started wide left with Szoboszlai and Jones playing in the false ten roles. The system allowed tactical flexibility with Liverpool using the pair to suffocate the centre of the pitch, dropping into a deep defensive shape when needed, but also able to occupy forward positions. The pair could help form a midfield box to retain possession while also occupying the centre-forward position when needed. Szoboszlai scored Liverpool's second goal, joining the attack to get into the box. In the second half, Liverpool scored an offside goal where Szoboszlai was put through in the right half-space, and his square ball was then tapped in by Jones from six yards out – both players having made forward runs off the ball.

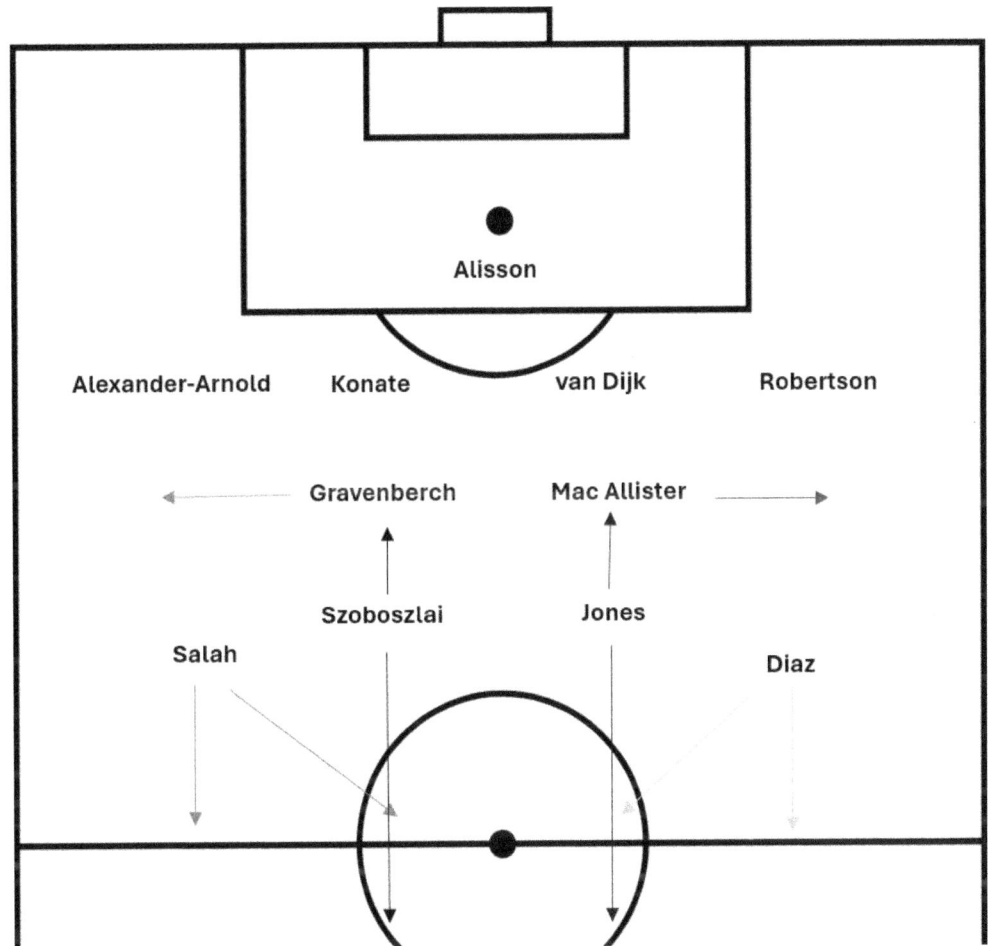

How Liverpool used a flexible 4-4-2 in and out of possession to use differing strategies within the game

Strikerless City

Manchester City also went without a striker, Erling Haaland being unavailable to even make it to the bench. Phil Foden and Omar Marmoush fulfilled the central threat for City, behaving more like a false nine and a shadow striker. Their movement asked testing questions of van Dijk and Konate during the build-up phases. Foden came short to receive and played in the space between the Liverpool back four and Gravenberch. When van Dijk followed him, space was created for Marmoush to dart into. Until the scoreline reached 2-0 to Liverpool, these movements were able to create situations where City were 4v4 with the Liverpool defence when building up. Once Liverpool went 2-0 in front, though, the team dropped deeper, compacting the space between the defensive midfielder and the back four. Foden had less room to move, and when he stepped onto the back line, van Dijk marked him easily, while Gravenberch didn't have far to look to find Foden when Foden dropped into midfield.

Pulling Strings From Deep

Kevin de Bruyne asked Liverpool some difficult questions early in the piece. When City were building in their own third, in open play, or from a goal kick, de Bruyne pulled into the right-back area. From here, he was unmarked and had time and space to spray passes. This allowed City to progress the ball with ease on the right. Liverpool didn't follow him, but once again – at 2-0 – they dropped off deeper and de Bruyne's targets for the longer passes were harder to find. He moved closer to a traditional midfield area and the phenomenon was removed from the game.

Doku Torments Alexander-Arnold

Where Manchester City threatened Liverpool all game was with their wingers. As Liverpool dropped deeper and compacted the spaces, City were able to hit switches of play from one side of the penalty box to the other, creating 1v1 situations for Doku or Savinho. Doku ran Alexander-Arnold into the ground, and FBref recorded that Doku had 51 ball carries, with 23 progressive carries. Alexander-Arnold's 1v1 defending was not fantastic, with Doku often beating him with ease (the early season signs of 1v1 defensive improvement have all but evaporated as the season progressed). Alexander-Arnold often looked off balance, and his body shape was not strong enough; he was unable to shift his feet quickly in a low-down jockeying position to match Doku. Fortunately, Liverpool offered Alexander-Arnold huge amounts of defensive support. Konate covered behind him, Gravenberch got between Alexander-Arnold and Doku, or behind him to cover him. Salah, who is often excused from defensive duties, even tracked back to help out. Of equal fortune to Liverpool was Doku's delivery lacking sufficient quality to pick out the light blue shirts

Switching From High Press To Low Block

For much of the first half, Liverpool engaged Manchester City relatively high up the pitch. The strikerless shape created a pressing box or diamond that was able to press aggressively in the corners. At Manchester City goal kicks, the shape often resembled a horseshoe, with the wide players higher and Szoboszlai and Jones deeper, between the City centre-backs and midfielders. Once the ball progressed into Liverpool territory, the shape became a low block. A little more conservative than the toe-to-toe style we had become accustomed to under Jurgen Klopp.

At 2-0, Liverpool effectively asked Manchester City whether or not they could break Liverpool down. The shift was to ultra-conservative defending; suffering in order to win. Liverpool did not engage Manchester City until the ball was close to Liverpool's defensive third, putting a ten-man screen between City and Alisson. Liverpool had clearly learned from the way Arsenal frustrated City with ten men earlier in the season and how so many teams have set up against City during the campaign. The shape was more akin to a 4-6 or even 5-5 that Diego Simeone and Atletico Madrid, at their most determined, would have been proud of. Konate and van Dijk dominated the penalty area, helping to see off City's wide threats from crosses. Without the physical presence of Haaland, the task was less difficult than it might otherwise have been. Nonetheless, the two central defenders repelled whatever came into the box – heading, blocking and clearing everything that came their way. They played with calmness, control and confidence, while their determination could be seen as they fist-bumped after every block or clearance.

Game Management

When the score was level and 1-0, Liverpool showed commitment to putting together some outstanding, fluent attacking moves, playing out from their own box to attack. The second goal was rooted in Liverpool building up in their own third. Moving the ball across the back four, Konate released out to Salah, as has been done so many times over the course of the season. Salah set to Alexander-Arnold, who clipped a ball in behind, and Salah ran onto the ball. He faced a 1v1, creating space to pass inside to Szoboszlai. A low left-foot shot through the defender's legs beat Ederson. When Alexander-Arnold clipped the pass in behind, Curtis Jones was in the centre-forward position and Szoboszlai was making a run in behind. Minutes before the goal, Liverpool had patiently built up in their own half before a longer ball advanced them into a dangerous area. Alexander-Arnold hit a pass with his left foot that set Szoboszlai away centrally. He passed out to Diaz, who ran at the defence and cut infield before finding Salah. Alexander-Arnold went from a release pass in the right-back area to overlapping Salah and provided a low cross. Liverpool always looked like they possessed enough tools to open up Manchester City, but in the second-half, they chose to put their energy into containment.

"We knew we had to defend a lot and that's what we did really well and then some good moments in the counter-attack led to us winning the game." Arne Slot speaking in the post-match press conference

Key Points

- Slot showed pragmatism, placing victory above style
- Liverpool were prepared to suffer and repel waves of attack, falling back on outstanding box defending
- Doku's dribbling tested Alexander-Arnold; once again, Liverpool helped Alexander-Arnold by doubling up whenever possible
- Liverpool managed the game superbly, playing some excellent attacking football until they went two goals in front, at which point they challenged City to break them down

Game 43 – Newcastle – Premier League – Home – 2-0 win

Liverpool 4-2-3-1

Alisson, Alexander-Arnold, Konate (Quansah), van Dijk, Tsimikas, Gravenberch (Endo), Mac Allister (Jones), Szoboszlai, Salah, Diaz (Nunez), Jota (Gakpo)

Newcastle 4-3-3

Pope, Livramento (Trippier), Schar, Burn, Hall, Guimaraes (Longstaff), Tonali (Miley), Willock (Barnes), Murphy, Gordon, Wilson (Osula)

Scorers – Szoboszlai, Mac Allister

After a tough week of fixtures on the road, Liverpool returned to Anfield against Newcastle. Their record against this opponent has been traditionally excellent, with Newcastle's last league win at Anfield in 1994. The 2025 fixture was not the one that would change that record.

Newcastle Change Approach

Newcastle gave Liverpool one of their toughest tests of the season in the 3-3 draw at St James' Park, where they used a 4-5-1 shape and aggressive man-marking in midfield. Liverpool struggled to play through the Newcastle lines until the introduction of Alexander-Arnold from the bench. Newcastle changed their approach at Anfield, however, and they used a narrow 4-3-3 with a half press. The front three and midfield three were tight together, centrally stopping forward passes, but the man-to-man approach was less evident. Liverpool returned to a 4-2-3-1 system after back-to-back games using a 4-4-2/4-2-4.

Clever Positioning From Jota

Jota was restored to the centre-forward position but he used intelligent and unusual movement to challenge the narrow 4-3-3 shape of Newcastle. The movement was unusual in that it varied from the regular movements of a Liverpool striker under Slot. We have seen the movements before, though, when Kai Havertz did something similar against Liverpool in the 2-2 draw at the Emirates. Liverpool's forward movement has tended toward dropping deep but quite central in midfield to create room for the forwards, or wide to create a 2v1 alongside the left winger. Jota moved wide but closer to the halfway line, on the outside of the narrow Newcastle shape. He was either wide on the ball side or the opposite side, giving an additional switching option. Once he received, he was able to play progressive forward passes beyond the Newcastle block.

How Jota used his movement to find space around the Newcastle defensive shape

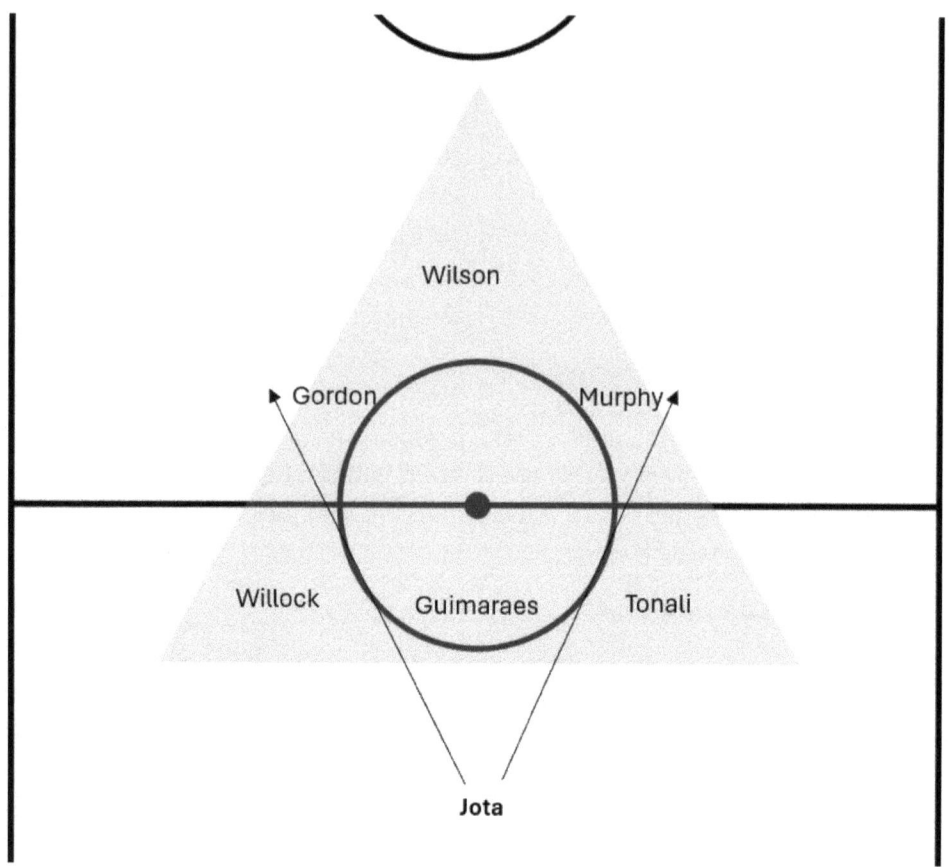

"I saw a different Newcastle tonight than a few months ago. I don't know if that is for a reason. Normally, they press in a 4-5-1 and today they did a 4-4-2 and Isak and Joelinton were not there. We can expect something different in a few weeks." Arne Slot speaking in the post-match press conference

Liverpool's Midfield On Top

Liverpool's midfield were in excellent form against Newcastle, and proved the driving force of the victory. For years under Klopp, the Liverpool midfield was functional in nature (the exception perhaps being Thiago; one can only imagine how he might have thrived in a Slot midfield). The Klopp midfield kept the game simple, helped release the wing-backs and cover the spaces. The creativity came from the full-backs or wide players. For Slot, this is not the case. The midfield is the heart of creativity, helping maintain possession while looking to combine and play forward with short, sharp passing. Both Liverpool goals against Newcastle were scored by central midfielders, and were the gloss on a showing dominated by the midfield. The signature fast passing movement and triangles were all on show! In contrast to the away game, where the Newcastle midfield suffocated their Liverpool counterparts, this time, Liverpool's trio did not give Newcastle the chance to get close to them. Their driving forward runs off the ball (looking for third-man combinations) helped to push opposition defences back, enabling Liverpool's wingers to keep onside as Newcastle's defenders had to follow the runs and drop deeper. Forward running and passing rotations require vast energy levels and Liverpool's midfield possessed both energy and quality.

Small Errors, Big Punishments

The two Liverpool goals did come with a little help from Newcastle. Not glaringly obvious errors but very small, significant, imprecise moments. On both occasions, Newcastle had packed their penalty box with defenders, yet Liverpool found enough space to score. When Szoboszlai shot, there were six Newcastle players plus the goalkeeper closer to goal than Szoboszlai. Luis Diaz dribbled at the defence, taking the ball almost in line with the six-yard box, and although the Newcastle players tracked the line of the ball, they seemingly forgot about the potential for attackers to arrive late in the box around the edge or penalty spot. Szoboszlai had significant space to shoot. Until moments before Diaz passed, Szoboszlai was marked, but the focus from Newcastle is to block the six-yard box, so they left Szoboszlai.

The same happened with Mac Allister's goal. Until the ball was passed to him by Salah from the right channel of the penalty box, he was marked. The Newcastle defender was tight to his back but then shifted a yard or two deeper. This gave Mac Allister enough space to shoot first time and punish Newcastle for their slight error.

Diaz As A Traditional Winger

Diaz's role in the opener was illustrative of the way he was deployed in this game. For much of the season, he has had license to drift and move around from the left into the centre. His positioning has been quite similar, whether playing as a winger or in the centre-forward role. In this game, though, he stuck closer to the touchline, rarely coming inside. Even with his dribbling, he went on the outside rather than cutting in.

Salah's Trivela

Mohamed Salah ended the game with another goal contribution to add to his impressive total for the season. The assist was quite a simple pass, but he worked the space well. He almost produced an assist for Diaz, too, with an extraordinary outside-of-the-left-foot trivela cross around the back of the Newcastle defence. Salah has used the trivela as a crossing method far more this season than in previous seasons and it seems to be an addition to his attacking skill set that has made him harder for defenders to play against. Salah has not only used the trivela as a chance-creating option, he has also used it to shoot himself, with one low effort saved well against Newcastle.

How and Why Does The Trivela Work?

Salah is not quite as quick as he once was. He is still fast, but he doesn't have the electric acceleration of the player who tore through on goal from inside his own half to score against Arsenal during his very first Liverpool season. The threat down the line has become lesser, but he remains a huge threat when cutting inside. Though less quick, he remains sharp with his footwork and movements, and is able to get defenders off-balance in a number of ways, all of which depend on very small, sharp touches designed to make the defender shift their positioning and balance. If defenders are too far off, Salah will pass inside and run behind or deliver an inswinging cross. If defenders are too tight, he will look to shift and create a shot or dribble infield. The addition of the trivela adds a passing or crossing option that is faster to execute, as the trivela requires very little to zero backlift. Indeed, it can be executed with little more than a jab. This allows Salah to take advantage of even the smallest window of opportunity. Defenders now have to get even tighter and Salah essentially has more angles open to him to deliver from. The defenders have fewer positions from which they can block Salah's options as the lines for the inside foot and outside foot striker are different. When dribbling, the cue for the defender – as to when a pass or shot is coming – also changes as the action to strike an inside-foot ball and a trivela are quite different. This adds more fakes to the box of tricks. A fake trivela can put a defender off balance as well as a fake orthodox ball strike.

Key Points

- Newcastle had different personnel and a different approach in the away fixture. Having suffocated Liverpool with an aggressive man-to-man press led by their midfield, this time they sat off more in a very narrow unit
- Jota used smart movement into the spaces outside Newcastle's narrow shape to create overloads and a passing option
- Liverpool's midfield were in excellent form, scoring the goals but also putting on a smooth show of passing, movement, and rotation
- Salah has added the regular use of an outside of the foot trivela pass this season; it has added to his weaponry and put defenders even further off balance

Game 44 – PSG – Champions League – Away – 1-0 win

Liverpool 4-2-3-1

Alisson, Alexander-Arnold, Konate, van Dijk, Robertson, Gravenberch (Endo), Mac Allister, Szoboszlai, Salah (Elliott), Diaz (Jones), Jota (Nunez)

PSG 4-3-3

Donnarumma, Hakimi, Marquinhos, Pacho, Nuno Mendes, Joao Neves, Vitinha, Ruiz (Zaire-Emery), Kvaratskhelia (Ramos), Dembele, Barcola (Doue)

Scorers – Elliott

Liverpool's "reward" for topping the league phase of the new Champions League format was to face the best team in France. PSG struggled early on but made it through to the knockout stages thanks to a win against Manchester City – a game they turned around from 2-0 down. After a slow start to the season and its megastar-less era, PSG had started to find a rhythm under Luis Enrique. Neymar and Messi left in 2023, whilst Mbappe left in the summer of 2024, and the superstar approach had gone; individualism had been replaced by a cohesive team ethos, with players willing to press opponents hard.

Luis Enrique's PSG: A True Team

While managers had struggled to get Mbappe, Messi, and Neymar to press, the attacking trio of Dembele, Barcola, and Kvaratskhelia pressed in an organised and aggressive manner. Indeed, the team pressed aggressively in wide areas, sending five players to press in the style that is becoming a common theme in teams who are using a pressing strategy. Centrally, the pressure is designed to direct the play wide or wait for triggers, then once the ball goes wide, the front line, one or two midfielders, and possibly a full-back close in. Hakimi stepped up high to press from full-back for PSG, while Ruiz was joined by either Vitinha or Neves to press.

PSG Press With Energy and Organisation

Liverpool's favoured wide press had little success against PSG. They showed excellent rotations to create new passing lines that Liverpool struggled to cover consistently. One of Vitinha and Neves would rotate between the central defenders, making it harder for Liverpool to cover the forward passes. The movement from Vitinha also acted as a trigger for a central defender to pull wider and the full-back to push forward. This was especially the case for Mendes, who was able to get free on the left. The trio of PSG midfielders were key to the overall dominant performance.

"It's not easy to dominate ball possession against Paris Saint-Germain because they take a lot of risk when they press. They go man-to-man all over the pitch, which makes it hard for many teams to have a lot of ball possession against them." Arne Slot in the post-match press conference

A Versatile Midfield Trio

On the surface, Neves, Ruiz, and Vitinha are quite similar. Players of medium to average build, clever and tidy in possession, with good resistance to being pressed due to their dribbling skills. This doesn't feel a great blend or great balance. Yet the blend works because each player has the classical midfield profile of being able to do a bit of everything. All three players are extremely intelligent with their movement and positioning and each player can play short, sharp passes or fire accurate passes. Each player can also rotate alongside the back line in the build, or into a pivot in front of the back line, or join the front line to link with the forwards. Indeed, they can rotate with ease, making them very difficult to mark. Though all are capable of filling different roles and functions, it was mainly Ruiz who joined the front line and Vitinha who joined the back line or acted as the pivot in front. At times, both Vitinha and Neves became pivots in front of the back line, enabling PSG to use different build-up shapes regularly.

Forward Line Rotation

Rotations were not limited to the PSG midfield three. The front line moved with great fluidity and quality, too. Bearing in mind that Enrique was the manager at Barcelona when the famed MSN attacking trio of Messi, Suarez, and Neymar were together, it should not be a great surprise that he has got the PSG three working well together. Dembele, Barcola, and Kvaratskhelia pulled the Liverpool defence all over the pitch throughout the game. Their movements and exchanges of position were difficult to cover, especially as all three have skill sets that include the ability to dribble at pace.

Ousmane Dembele was the key component, though. Having spent most of his career as a winger, Enrique has converted him to be the central player in the attacking trio. His skill set is very different to a traditional forward and he rarely spends time playing directly up against the central defenders. Dembele's movements also triggered the movements of his teammates, such that when he dropped short, the other two members of the trio would run forward. When Dembele pulled wide, whoever's side he pulled to would cut into the centre. Dembele's winger skills make him even more effective, as does his ability to strike the ball with both feet, whether this is for a cross, pass, or shot. These attributes marked him out for stardom in his early 20s, and earned a huge transfer to Barcelona, but his potential was not fulfilled. At PSG, especially under Enrique, he has a new lease of life.

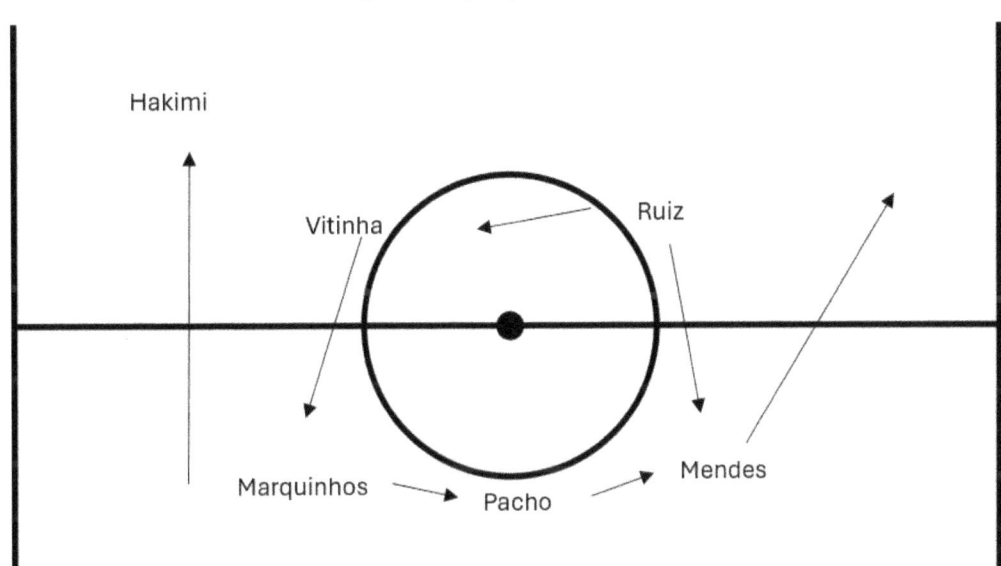

How PSG rotate their base structure to release the full-backs while also maintaining security against counter-attacks

Outstanding Alisson

The front three tested Alisson regularly throughout the game. Alisson made nine saves of varying difficulty and quality. One particular first-half sequence saw Barcola infield and Dembele running in behind Robertson. Dembele's 1v1 finish was smothered by Alisson, and although the rebound came to the feet of Barcola, Alisson prevented his progress. Another shot was blocked by defenders and, finally, Barcola fired the fourth shot of the sequence over the crossbar from eight yards out. Of the saves, this was the one that looked a certain goal. Others were excellent pieces of athleticism to keep out Kvaratskhelia: plunging low to his left after a tight dribble, diving to his right to touch away a powerful freekick. Dembele put in a dangerous cross shot from the right corner of the box with his left foot that Alisson got down well to push away with a strong right hand. PSG also had a goal chalked off for a marginal offside and a possible penalty against Konate waved away. Liverpool rode their luck.

Slot Keeps PSG at Arm's Length

Arne Slot recognised the momentum of the game when it came to the second half. In the first half, Liverpool tried to play high and press PSG. In the second half, they dropped deeper, sitting in a low block, much as they did against Manchester City. PSG dominated possession but were largely restricted to shots from long range. Indeed, Liverpool largely kept PSG at arm's length while attempting to spring counter-attacks that began close to the edge of their box. The Merseysiders have successfully attacked from these areas many times across the season, but they wasted many promising positions without even finding a shot at goal. Salah was in possession in dangerous positions, but his end product was lacking and his dribbling thwarted by the outstanding Nuno Mendes. Mendes matched Salah for speed and strength, using his body brilliantly to prevent Salah from getting past him.

Liverpool Make It Count Eventually

These promising attacks came to nothing until the very end of the game. Liverpool rang the changes, bringing on Nunez and Harvey Elliott, and Nunez used his physical presence to ruffle the PSG defence and force a pass to the right side of the penalty area. Elliott strode onto the pass and stroked the ball across the diving Donnarumma into the bottom corner. Liverpool finally made an attack count but were only able to do so thanks to a dogged defensive display and an outstanding goalkeeping performance.

Key Points

- PSG pressed Liverpool aggressively. They were outstanding at getting multiple players around the man on the ball quickly
- The PSG front line rotated and moved wonderfully
- Slot made a small change in the second half to keep PSG to shots from long- to medium-range, limiting the high-quality chances they could create
- Alisson was brilliant in goal with multiple big saves
- Liverpool had numerous counter-attacking opportunities but failed to connect the passes or get a shot away until the Elliott goal in stoppage time

Game 45 – Southampton – Premier League – Home – 3-1 win

Liverpool 4-2-3-1

Alisson, Alexander-Arnold, Konate (Quansah), van Dijk, Tsimikas (Robertson), Gravenberch (Endo), Jones (Elliott), Szoboszlai (Mac Allister), Salah, Diaz, Nunez (Jota)

Southampton 4-2-3-1

Ramsdale, Walker-Peters, Bednarek, Harwood-Bellis, Manning (Aribo), Ugochukwu (Onuachu), Smallbone (Lallana), Dibling (Sugawara), Fernandes, Sulemana, Gronbaek (Archer)

Scorers – Nunez, Salah (2), Smallbone

Southampton briefly threatened to shock Liverpool at Anfield, but – once more – Liverpool delivered an improved second-half display to overturn a deficit. The influence of The Kop is the stuff of legend, and once again, Liverpool struck the vital blows at that mythic end of Anfield.

Liverpool Use The False Full-Back

Liverpool showed an adapted build-up shape, with one midfielder dropping into the false full-back position. In Liverpool's very first structured build-up near the halfway line, Curtis Jones dropped into a narrow left-back position, pushing Tsimikas high and wide. This was the build-up pattern throughout the first half, with Tsimikas very high and wide and Diaz operating inside, close to the striker. When Diaz did receive in wide areas, he often faced multiple defenders and was well covered by Southampton. Darwin Nunez took up positions high against the Southampton back line, with Liverpool looking to use his physical presence to unsettle them.

Liverpool did create good positions and opportunities in the first half, showing some different strategies from the right half-space. In one instance, Alexander-Arnold faked to cross from the half-space, which would be his usual action, and instead cut inside onto his left foot and shot. Alexander-Arnold's left foot is strong enough and this should be an option used more often. In another instance, Ryan Gravenberch received in the half-space, using his nimble footwork to dribble into the box and force an opportunity for Alexander-Arnold, which was well saved. Gravenberch has rarely dribbled into the box, so this showed more variety of attacking play.

Curtis Jones filling the false full-back role to release Tsimikas high and wide

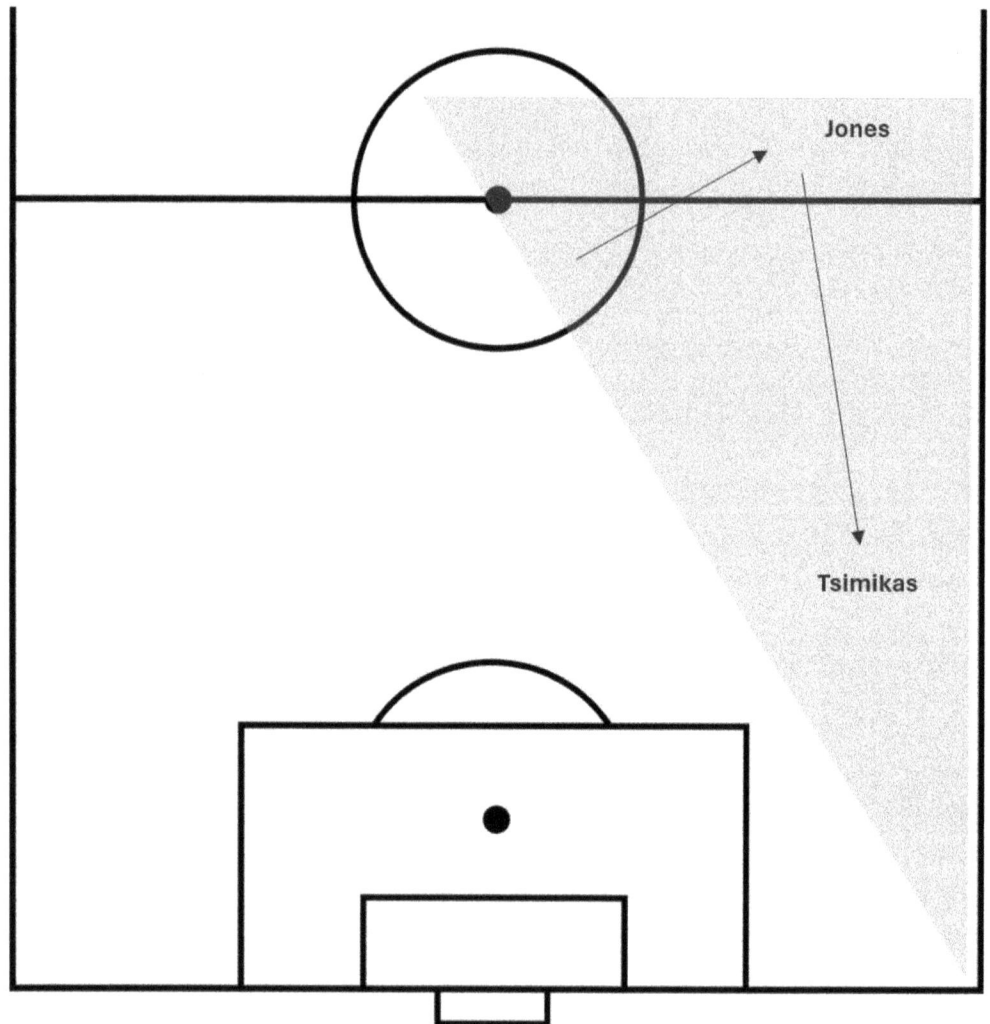

Alisson and van Dijk Err

Southampton offered very little threat, yet they went into half-time ahead. A harmless-looking ball into the penalty area led to a miscommunication between Alisson and van Dijk, and Smallbone was the recipient of the resulting opportunity, which he threaded into the back of the net. Alisson and van Dijk seem to have a mix-up each season that results in a goal. Last season, there was a very significant one at Arsenal in a 2-1 loss. This one was less damaging.

Slot Shakes The Side Up at Half-Time

Trailing at half-time enabled Arne Slot to demonstrate his ruthless side. He was sat in the stands due to being suspended following the incidents at full time in the Goodison derby, but was able to join the team at half-time in the changing room. For the second half, Tsimikas, Szoboszlai and Jones were all removed for Robertson, Mac Allister and Elliott. Slot said after the game that against PSG, they had to make tactical changes at half-time, but the changes against Southampton were not tactical and were purely to put more energy into the team. The changes paid off as Liverpool scored two goals in quick time after the break.

"If you look at the first goal, we played the ball to Diaz and all of a sudden he was on tempo trying to create something, where in the first half he kept the ball waiting, waiting, waiting." Arne Slot speaking to Liverpool FC TV

Attacking Change Of Shape

What seems an almost customary change of shape after half-time also occurred. Moving from the 4-2-3-1 system to a 4-4-2 or 4-2-4 shape, Liverpool were more threatening in the second half. On the right, Alexander-Arnold was heavily inverted, with Harvey Elliott providing width on the right, sometimes as a false right-back close to halfway and sometimes higher up, in a wing-back region. Salah was tucked inside and getting close to the centre-forward position. On the left, Andrew Robertson underlapped aggressively with Diaz, shifting from the narrow position of the first half to a more traditional wing position. A direct dribble from Diaz preceded a cutback to assist Darwin Nunez in equalising, and it was Diaz who chased a long ball over the Southampton defence to gain the penalty to make the scoreline 3-1. Diaz and Elliott stretched Southampton while Salah joined with Nunez, ensuring Liverpool had bodies in the box. Nunez won the second penalty as he pounced onto a loose ball following a cross and Salah was – once more – deadly from the spot kicks, having just missed against Real Madrid by this stage of the season.

*Note – This was an unusual instance of both teams using six substitutes. Southampton lost Bednarek to a head injury, allowing them an extra substitute. This also granted Liverpool an extra substitute.

Key Points
- Liverpool used the false full-back role to help push full-backs higher up the pitch. This was commonplace under Jurgen Klopp, but has not been seen very often during Slot's time
- Slot made multiple substitutions at half-time in response to being behind. He showed an uncompromising side to make the substitutions so quickly

- With Liverpool chasing the game against a lower ranked team, Slot again switched to two forwards through the centre and two attacking wide players. This has been a regular occurrence that has yielded results

Game 46 – PSG – Champions League – Home – 1-0 loss – Lost on penalties

Liverpool 4-2-3-1

Alisson, Alexander-Arnold (Quansah), Konate (Endo), van Dijk, Robertson, Gravenberch, Mac Allister (Jones), Szoboszlai (Elliott), Salah, Diaz (Gakpo), Jota (Nunez)

PSG 4-3-3

Donnarumma, Hakimi, Marquinhos (Beraldo), Pacho, Nuno Mendes, Joao Neves (Ramos), Vitinha, Ruiz (Zaire-Emery), Barcola (Doue), Dembele, Kvaratskhelia (Lee Kang-In)

Scorers – Dembele

After a classic smash-and-grab in Paris came a counterpunch at Anfield. Liverpool started the game fast, attacking from the off, and playing as though they had a deficit to turn around. Perhaps the deficit was one borne of ego? Though Liverpool were victorious in the only place that truly counts, the scoreboard, they came away from Paris having been outclassed. There may have been an element of needing to prove themselves to be dominant over PSG on their own patch, but this was unnecessary… the aim is to get through to the next round. The expectations at Anfield to stand toe-to-toe with PSG may also have driven the approach to the game. A draw would have been enough. A goalless draw would have been enough. Liverpool could have sat deep all game once more, inviting PSG to break them down. There was no need to attack from the off, though once PSG went ahead, the scenario changed. It was a scenario of Liverpool's making.

Liverpool Press Aggressively

Four players were sent into high positions by Liverpool to press at goal kicks – the trio of attackers plus Szoboszlai. PSG mixed their approach to the Liverpool pressure, switching between playing long and passing short. When passing short, PSG's central midfielders dropped into their own defensive third and, at one stage in the second half, all three players had dropped in to support the build-up. In open play, PSG were committed to short passing in the deep build until the ball came to Donnarumma. Donnarumma is less comfortable with the ball at his feet than other top goalkeepers, and his passes out to the full-backs, especially when striking right to left to Mendes, was hit and miss with the ball sailing over the full-back for a throw-in on a number of occasions. PSG were rewarded with their goal after controlled passing in their defensive third, with Liverpool aggressively pressing in the left-back area, there was less coverage in the centre of the pitch. Liverpool had the PSG midfielders covered, but it was the movement of Dembele that undid their defence.

Dembele Movement Unsettles Liverpool

The PSG front three impressed throughout in Paris but it was Dembele whose star shone the brightest at Anfield. Dembele intelligently moved into spaces and areas that van Dijk and Konate were reluctant to follow, and often moved to the outside of the Liverpool block to give receiving options. Liverpool's default shape is 4-2-4 out of possession when pressing, which shifts depending on who presses where and when. Szoboszlai pushes up with the front three to form the four, leaving Mac Allister and Gravenberch as the two. Depending on which side of the pitch a press occurs, one of the two deeper midfielders can step up to add to the press, leaving one to hold the middle. Dembele took up positions either side of the midfield pair or in a position where the single midfielder became overloaded 2v1 because of Dembele dropping in.

This happened for the goal.

A slow, angled pass beat the Liverpool lines and found Dembele close to the centre circle in the PSG half. Neither Liverpool central defender followed him, giving Dembele time and space to turn and drive at the defence, crossing into Liverpool territory and then passing behind the defence. He continued his run into the box to meet a low cross from the PSG right. Konate slid to intercept in front of Alisson, but the contact was minimal. The Liverpool defenders ended up entangled on the edge of the six-yard box while Dembele remained poised, balanced, and calm to roll the ball into an empty net.

Liverpool Create Chances

During the early stages of the game came arguably Liverpool's best chance. Mac Allister burst into the box in the left half-space, a position he could have shot from. Instead, he played a left-footed ball across for Salah, and Mendes superbly blocked the first-time effort. Salah wriggled into a position a few minutes later to bend a shot just wide of the left-hand post, then went back to struggling against Mendes after this. In the first game, Salah struggled to beat Mendes in 1v1 situations, and this was the situation at Anfield, too. Salah had more success when passing and running or looking to slot teammates in on goal.

In the second half, Liverpool had a rare counter-attacking opportunity. PSG controlled transitions well over both legs, constantly creating a deep trio with either a full-back or midfielder alongside the central defenders while a midfielder sat in front of this unit. Liverpool were able to get away with the ball at Salah's feet, and he slipped a pass between the PSG defenders for Diaz to run onto. Diaz was completely free with a chance to strike first time with his left foot, but he cut in on his right, and the defenders recovered to snuff out the threat.

The movement from the PSG front three

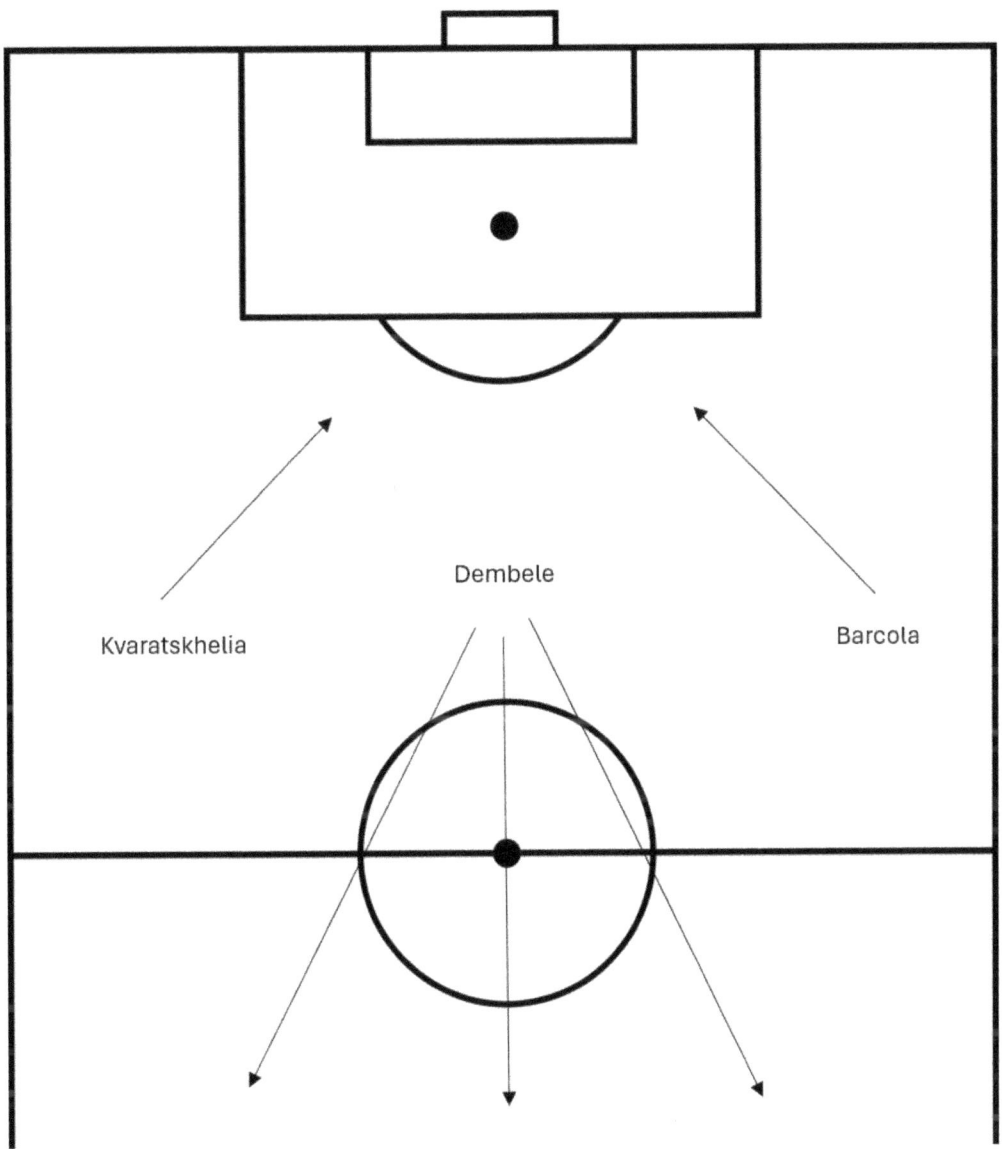

Diaz Takes On Hakimi 1v1

PSG were under pressure in the second half but kept Liverpool at arm's length. Diaz was a key attacking source as Liverpool largely focused their attacks on the left side. This may have been because of how well Mendes played Salah.

Diaz took on Hakimi in 1v1 situations, creating numerous set-piece opportunities and one 'almost chance' from open play. An almost chance because, ultimately, offside was called. Diaz received a pass beyond the PSG back line on the left of the box; he cut back onto his right and picked out Alexander-Arnold on the edge of the area. The first shot was saved by the goalkeeper. The shot pushed out to Alexander-Arnold again, this time with his left foot striking the inside of the post. The next rebound cut across the six-yard box and was tapped in by Szoboszlai. Then the flag went up for offside.

Largely, PSG defenders were able to block or cut out similar dangerous positions. In many respects, this was similar to how Liverpool dealt with PSG in the second half of the first leg, threatening from set-pieces, mostly from corners and one particular, simple movement. Players started close to the goalkeeper and then pulled away to the edge of the six-yard box to be picked out by an outswinging corner. Diaz, Jota, Quansah and van Dijk all had efforts from this movement, which we saw as far back as AC Milan in the Champions League group stage.

There was one other set-piece opportunity. A free kick won on the left side delivered by Robertson to the right side of the PSG area. Quansah attacked the cross and headed the ball against the inside of the post. Robertson was a sharp attacking threat from open play, with quick footwork and a stream of crosses reminiscent of his apex under Klopp. The difference seems to be that he has struggled to play to this level when having to start successive games with a short break in-between.

Liverpool Run Out of Energy

Liverpool spent the second half on top until the final stages. When Liverpool were chasing and needed to find the extra push to win, they faded instead, running out of gas. Rather than piling on the pressure in the latter stages, it was PSG who grew more comfortable and controlled, able to use the possession style of the first leg to control the remainder of normal time and extra time. Liverpool hardly recorded an attempt of note in the extra 30 minutes, while PSG rattled off a number of attempts, mostly longer-range and comfortably saved by Alisson.

"In overtime, I thought Paris Saint-Germain was a bit better than us in this half-hour and then it comes down to penalties and they scored four, us one and we lost." Arne Slot speaking at the post-match press conference

Donnarumma The Shoot Out Master

The penalty shootout played out at the Anfield Road end. PSG slotted their attempts while Nunez and Jones missed the penalties as Donnarumma made his intimidating presence felt. Two saves for Donnarumma, making the most of his wingspan to win yet another penalty shootout. When this tie was completed, the BBC asked, "Why is Donnarumma so good at saving penalties?" He had faced 103 penalties in normal time and shootouts and saved 24. He stands, arms spread, filling as much of the target as possible. A six-foot-five-inch frame helps.

Key Points

- Mendes proved to be Salah's toughest opponent of the season, with Salah struggling to beat him in 1v1 situations
- Liverpool switched their attacking focus to the left and Diaz, with some success
- The PSG forward line once again showed excellent and intelligent movement. Dembele was their star contributor and the difference-maker

Game 47 – Newcastle – EFL Cup Final – Neutral – 2-1 Loss

Liverpool 4-2-3-1

Kelleher, Quansah, Konate (Jones), van Dijk, Robertson, Gravenberch (Chiesa), Mac Allister (Gakpo), Szoboszlai, Salah, Diaz (Elliott), Jota (Nunez)

Newcastle 4-3-3

Pope, Trippier, Schar, Burn, Livramento, Guimaraes, Tonali, Joelinton, Murphy (Krafth), Barnes (Willock), Isak (Wilson)

Scorers – Chiesa, Burn, Isak

Liverpool's hopes of winning a treble vanished in just a few days. The PSG loss eliminated the club from the Champions League, and it is quite possible that their physical and mental efforts over extra time and penalties left them out of energy for the cup final against Newcastle.

Newcastle Stifle Liverpool

Liverpool had totally dominated Newcastle at Anfield a few weeks earlier, but the game at St James' Park had been a struggle, especially in the first-half, with an energised Newcastle pinning Liverpool back. The key to Newcastle's excellence was their midfield trio of Tonali, Joelinton, and Guimaraes. They man-marked the Liverpool midfield and did so once again, making it extremely difficult for Liverpool to find and create the extra man to play out to. Newcastle employed a man-to-man press in their 4-3-3 shape, which led to the commitment of seven players against the Liverpool build-up. Newcastle suffocated Liverpool for the whole of the first half, with the Merseysiders not creating a shooting opportunity until moments before the half-time whistle. At St James', Liverpool were behind at half-time but able to summon energy and quality from the bench. Alexander-Arnold came on at half-time in the 3-3 draw to grab two assists and unpick Newcastle's 4-5-1- block. He was injured in the PSG game and unavailable for the cup final. Slot needed to find other methods to unlock Newcastle.

Too Many Problems To Solve

Slot has shown himself able to find a number of solutions to Liverpool's half-time issues across the season. In this game, there were a lot of problems to address. The personnel were not on their game, which is usually solved by bringing on high-quality substitutes. Slot demands more energy at half-time, which is addressed through requesting more crosses, higher counter-pressing, and earlier passes forward. The solution is successful because players have the energy to give. It was very clear from the early stages of this game that Liverpool struggled to match Newcastle's energy levels. There was little in the tank, even from the starting players.

Some of the eventual substitutes did show more energy, but Slot was slow to turn to Elliott and Chiesa, seeming not to trust them as much as other players. He attempted to change tactics to get on top of Newcastle, which led to shape changes through the second half, with Liverpool seeming to lose some structure with little attacking benefit. The cohesion with the systems used was lower than the usual preferred systems. This can be overcome with energy, but the lack of energy was the initial issue that remained unsolved.

Tactical Shift One

Slot started with a 4-2-3-1. After conceding the second Newcastle goal, the shape became a 4-2-4, with Gravenberch taking up the half-back position: a central defender when Liverpool were out of possession and a central midfielder when in possession. Gakpo came on and took a wide left position, with Diaz moving into the centre. Gakpo had still not fully recovered from his injury, yet was brought on before Chiesa.

Tactical Shift Two

The next set of changes saw Liverpool move into a system that was something akin to a 3-2-5, though the precise nature of the system is hard to define, even after a number of viewings of the match. The system and personnel were on the pitch without a true form. There is a question raised by this… when does fluidity become a formless mess? Well, this comes awfully close to the answer. Quansah, van Dijk and Robertson made up the Liverpool back three. Elliott took up a role wide on the right, while Gakpo played wide left. Salah, Nunez and Chiesa were the three central strikers. Liverpool put in a barrage of crosses to little effect. Their breakthrough came beyond the 90th minute from an unorganised passage of play following a Liverpool set-piece. Elliott regained the ball and threaded a pass through for Chiesa to slip the ball into the corner. The changes created chaos in the game, but they felt like a dice roll.

Newcastle Punish Set-Piece Mismatch

Newcastle made the most of set-pieces throughout the game. When you have the tallest player on the pitch, it makes a great deal of sense to utilise him. Dan Burn is two meters, and Newcastle saw that Liverpool focused on defending the zone in the centre of the penalty area. Dan Burn was sent to an area outside the far post and was marked by Alexis Mac Allister, but whilst Mac Allister is not bad in the air, he is a full 25 centimetres shorter than Burn. This led to Burn connecting with almost every corner, including the opening goal, where Burn planted a powerful header back across goal and into the bottom corner. The mismatch was not addressed by Liverpool until Mac Allister came off in the second-half and Quansah picked up Burn. When Liverpool had attacking corners, their best header of the ball – Virgil van Dijk – was marked by Burn.

The positioning of Dan Burn vs Alexis Mac Allister at the far post on corners

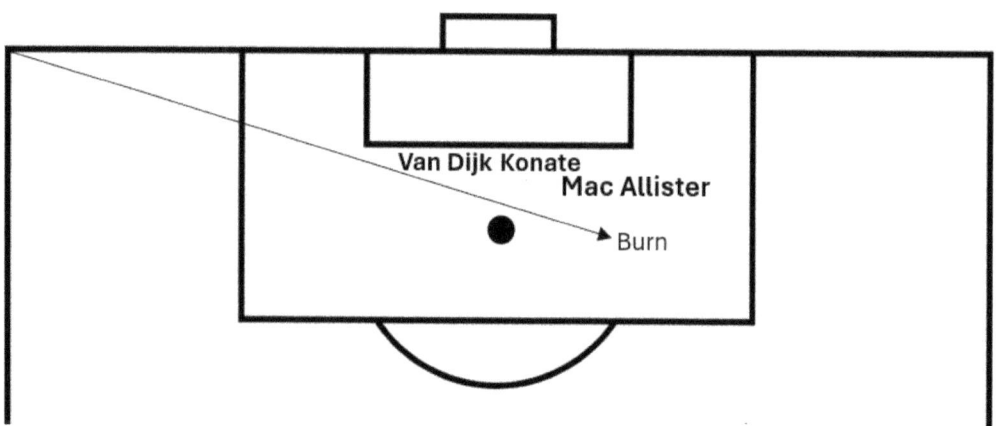

"We play zonal, so we have five players zonally close to our goal. So, if the ball falls there, it is always one of the five stronger players that are going to attack that ball. And we have three players that man-mark and Macca [Alexis Mac Allister] is one of them." Arne Slot speaking at the post-match press conference

Key Points
- Newcastle reverted to the man-orientated pressing system that was used the first time these two sides met during the season. Liverpool struggled to break through this pressure
- The mismatch between Burn and Mac Allister at the far post was exploited by Newcastle as Liverpool stuck to their zonal marking system, refusing to move their best headers of the ball away from the centre
- Arne Slot attempted to make tactical changes to get Liverpool back into the game, but none created the consistent attacking threat that was required

Game 48 – Everton – Premier League – Home – 1-0 win

Liverpool 4-2-3-1

Kelleher, Jones, Konate, van Dijk, Robertson, Gravenberch, Mac Allister, Szoboszlai, Salah (Endo), Diaz (Gakpo), Jota (Nunez)

Everton 4-2-3-1

Pickford, O'Brien, Tarkowski, Branthwaite, Mykolenko, Gueye (Iroegbunam), Garner, Doucoure (Chermiti), Harrison (Ndiaye), Alcaraz (Young), Beto (Broja)

Scorers – Jota

Is a Merseyside derby the best or worst game to return to action with? After back-to-back Cup losses, Liverpool had a break of well over two weeks to stew on those defeats, but also to allow some players to recharge their batteries. A game with Everton always carries high emotions and expectations, so it is an easy game to get the players up for, but it is the sort of game where the opponents can prevent a fluid and flowing performance.

As Liverpool won the game 1-0, it has to be viewed as the best game to return with, but as expected, Everton battled and scrapped to keep the game competitive. Liverpool struggled to find any real attacking rhythm.

Everton Play Long

Everton prevented Liverpool from pressing by constantly playing long balls forward for Beto to fight for. At goalkicks, Pickford either fired the ball forward himself or played a short pass, which was quickly followed by a long ball. In open play, the story was very similar. Konate and van Dijk largely dealt with the long balls, apart from on two notable occasions in the first half. The first was a goal correctly ruled out for offside when Beto got beyond Konate and van Dijk in the right-hand channel and tucked a finish beyond Kelleher. He was clearly offside. The second occasion was the best opportunity for either team in the first half, possibly the whole game. A long ball forward was not won by Konate, and the second ball was passed in behind by Everton. Beto's touch gave van Dijk an opportunity to regain, but he missed, allowing Beto through on goal. The finish from the edge of the box struck the inside of the upright and bounced to safety.

The Liverpool defence dealt with Everton's long balls and crosses with comfort. Kelleher punched away late corners under heavy pressure, and van Dijk and Konate headed away the crosses. One long throw cleared the central defenders, resulting in a shot that was blocked by defenders reacting well. A late cross cleared Konate and van Dijk but was athletically hooked away by Curtis Jones with an Everton forward ready to pounce.

Jones at Right-Back

Arne Slot had chosen Jones at right-back for this fixture. Neither Alexander-Arnold nor Bradley were fit enough to make the matchday squad. Jurgen Klopp used Joe Gomez as an auxiliary defender across the back line, but Slot has only been willing to use Gomez at centre-back. Gomez was not an option in any case due to injury. In the Cup final against Newcastle, it was Quansah who started at right-back (as he did at St James' in the league). Quansah was a substitute for this game. Most likely, Slot was not satisfied with the contributions of Quansah in possession. Knowing that Everton would be likely to grant Liverpool over two-thirds of the possession (it turned out to be closer to three-quarters), Jones' abilities in possession were deemed of greater value. Though Jones didn't break lines with passes and dribbles, his press resistance and smoothness in possession helped Liverpool build up with security. Defensively, he was less tested than might have been expected. Everton tried to attack his side early on, but this strategy faded away.

Gravenberch Attacking The Half-Space

Being a central midfielder by nature, Jones was able to invert effectively during Liverpool's build-up. In early phases, Jones was positioned higher up the pitch than Gravenberch, Mac Allister, and Szoboszlai, and the Liverpool midfield trio operated with some slight tweaks to their usual roles, with Gravenberch attacking the half-spaces more than Szoboszlai, who was rarely on the right or making runs into the half-spaces, whilst Jota made the runs in behind more often. Jota had the freedom to roam from his centre-forward position, and when he vacated the centre-forward role, it was largely Mac Allister who filled the position. In the second half, Gravenberch was more central and closer to the defensive line; his first-half role had seen him using dribbling and shooting skills in the half-spaces to attempt to unlock the Everton defence.

Liverpool getting Gravenberch into the half-space to shoot or dribble at the Everton defence

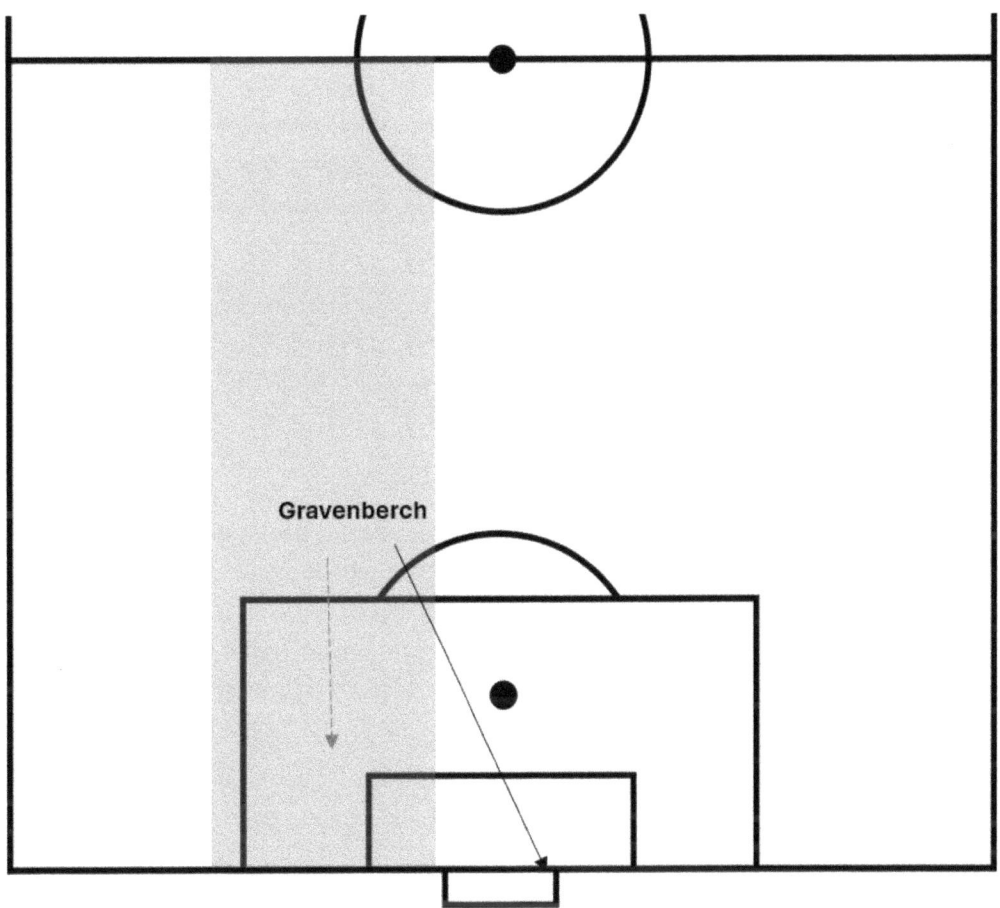

Everton Seek To Frustrate Liverpool

Everton sat in a deep, low, defensive block. Their 4-2-3-1 shape becoming a 4-5-1 with the ball in the middle third and then a 6-3-1 when the ball entered their defensive third. Everton paid special attention to Salah, surrounding him with as many as four players. Liverpool countered this by attacking on the left, hitting diagonals, and switching play across to Diaz to create 1v1s. Liverpool made runs into the half-spaces, which had to be tracked, and this made it harder for Everton to double up on Diaz. His fast and sharp twisting footwork returned. The international break seemed to do Diaz good, as he looked full of energy and was involved in the controversial Liverpool goal. Gravenberch played a forward pass to Diaz, who was behind Tarkowski and in an offside position. The ball never reached Diaz as Tarkowski intercepted. Had he not, and Diaz received the ball,

Everton would have received a free kick. Instead, Jota counter-pressed the ball and then combined with a now-onside Diaz as the combination moment was deemed a different phase of play. Jota dropped his shoulder and danced past two players before wrong-footing Pickford with his low shot. The goal was very similar to Jota's finish against Fulham to grab a late point. Though Diaz was offside, the law deemed him not to be involved as he did not make a move to play the ball. Liverpool, Diaz, and Jota did nothing outside of the laws of the game, and the officials followed the laws correctly. Unfortunately, the laws themselves are problematic.

"If you want to talk about tactics, you first have to match their work-rate, and that is what we can do, because we have shown in all the games we have played until now that we are a team that works really hard as well." Arne Slot speaking at the post-match press conference

Possession To Defend

Once Liverpool went in front, their intent became to take the edge out of the game through the use of short passing and possession. Liverpool completely dominated possession after the goal, with the intent of starving Everton of opportunities. The strategy worked until the final few minutes when nerves inevitably took over. Liverpool were deep, allowing Everton pressure and crossing opportunities, which Liverpool repelled.

Key Points

- Konate and van Dijk defended a stream of long balls
- Curtis Jones moved from midfield to right-back. Everton didn't test him defensively, and Jones helped Liverpool dominate possession
- Ryan Gravenberch took on more attacking responsibility in a bid to break down Everton's defensive block
- Diaz was an attacking spark, looking refreshed by the international break

Game 49 – Fulham – Premier League – Away – 3-2 Loss

Liverpool 4-2-3-1

Kelleher, Jones, Konate (Bradley), van Dijk, Robertson (Chiesa), Gravenberch, Mac Allister, Szoboszlai (Elliott), Salah, Gakpo (Diaz), Jota (Nunez)

Fulham 4-2-3-1

Leno, Castagne, Anderson, Bassey, Robinson, Berge, Lukic (Reed), Sessegnon (Traore), Pereira (Smith-Rowe), Iwobi (Tete), Muniz (Jimenez)

Scorers – Mac Allister, Diaz, Sessegnon, Iwobi, Muniz

Fulham broke Liverpool's unbeaten run in the Premier League, a run that stretched back to the defeat at home by Nottingham Forest. Liverpool went in front early, but then had a dreadful 20-minute period, and spent the rest of the game playing catch-up.

Fulham Attacking The Makeshift Right-Back

Curtis Jones was selected at right-back once again, but his experience in this game was in stark contrast to the Everton game. The left side is one of Fulham's strengths. Antonee Robinson had ten assists in the Premier League prior to this match, Alex Iwobi had seven goals and four assists prior to this match (he added one to each of those tallies during the game), so this was the perfect mix of a strength lining up against a weakness.

Against Everton, the main concerns for Jones were in-possession, whilst against Fulham, he was stretched and tested out-of-possession as Iwobi moved inside from a left-sided starting position, and Robinson ran in behind on the outside. Jones was pulled out of position and spent most of his time making recovery runs to cover defensive areas. Two of Fulham's goals involved the Liverpool right side. For the first goal, Jones was unable to deal cleanly with a cross from the right under very light pressure. The second goal was scored by Iwobi after Robertson gave the ball away during build-up play, passing from left to right. Jones was caught upfield and unable to get back into a position to affect the play.

Robertson and Robinson Comparisons Yet Again

Robertson's double error for the Iwobi goal was not helped by the comparisons made between him and Fulham captain Antonee Robinson. Robinson is explosive and creative – as Robertson once was – and people are perceiving that Robertson no longer is. Robertson, having only one assist across all competitions, seems to suggest that he is not the player that he was, the player who racked up three Premier League seasons with double-digit assists. Robertson remains a threat, though, with dynamic underlapping energy. He just can't do it twice a week any more. He has swung from very good to very poor, with the pattern connected to the weeks when he must play with little rest.

"It wasn't 45 minutes of disaster, but the errors we made, I think is something we're not used to. One of the reasons why we are in the position we are in, is that we don't make a lot of mistakes." Arne Slot speaking at the post-match press conference.

Fulham Aggressive 4-2-4 Press

Fulham pressed aggressively in the first half. Both teams attempted to press, but Fulham were more successful, and they used a 4-2-4 shape to apply pressure. The two teams' press structures, especially in the front line, were very similar, with the attacking midfielder or no.10 stepping into the line to close down. Fulham had more snap and aggression in their press, with Muniz outstanding. It was noticeable that he curved his runs to close down the defender and prevent a forward pass into Gravenberch.

In the second half, Fulham didn't press as hard, and Gravenberch adjusted his position to receive between the Fulham players, helping Liverpool get out. Once Liverpool changed their shape entirely, the Fulham press had fallen away due to the game state and possibly fitness. Liverpool improved their own press by pushing an additional midfielder up to stop Fulham's ability to bypass the Liverpool press and find their double pivots.

A six-player structure was used by Fulham to press and also to build up. The system was a 2-4 shape with the full-backs wide to receive and the pivots open. Fulham's pivots – Berge and Lukic – were both able to get free whenever Fulham shaped to pass to the full-backs. The pivots could play forward or drive forward, and this was how Fulham progressed the ball for their opening goal, driving through midfield before passing into a wide area.

How Fulham carried the ball forward through their pivots

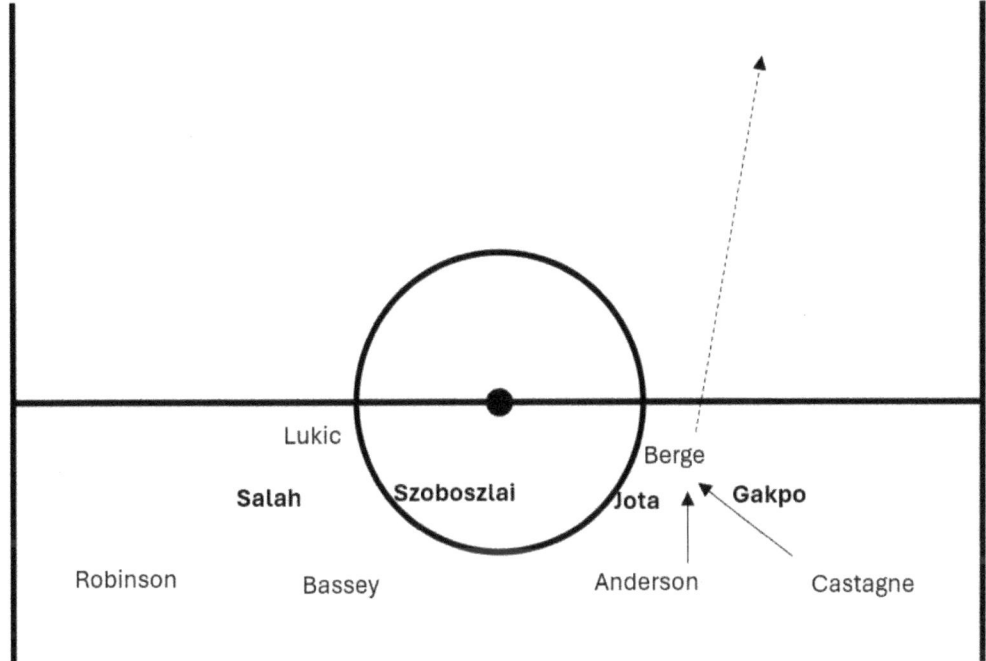

A Specialist Right-Back Improves The Performance

Arne Slot has shown that he likes to be proactive when Liverpool are behind. Eager to change the personnel or team structure in the quest to score, Ryan Gravenberch was moved into central defence, into the half-back position. This enabled Liverpool to get an extra player into midfield when in possession, as he could step forward, much like he did at Forest. Not long after Bradley and Elliott came into the team, moving Curtis Jones back into midfield. At this stage, Liverpool were piling the pressure onto Fulham, scoring through Diaz and hitting the bar with Elliott. Liverpool were able to pin Fulham in and swarm the penalty area with runners from midfield.

With 15 minutes remaining, Slot decided to make another change. He switched to three at the back, with van Dijk the central defender, Gravenberch the left centre-back, and Bradley the right centre-back. The wide centre-back roles were hybrid positions, allowing Gravenberch and Elliott to push forward. The extra attacking changes did not hurt Liverpool, but they did little to improve them either. Was this a case where Slot pushed too hard? Liverpool had Fulham on the proverbial ropes anyway. Did the changes disrupt Liverpool's momentum and prevent the equaliser? We can never know, but there can be negatives to being proactive.

Against Newcastle in the EFL Cup Final, there were numerous changes in shape that did very little to improve Liverpool, but in that game, there was a lack of threat. That was not the case at Fulham in the second half.

Key Points

- Liverpool having a makeshift right-back coincided with Fulham being at their strongest on their left side. Jones struggled defensively at Fulham
- Bradley returned during the second half and Liverpool's performance improved, looking more balanced
- Fulham pressed Liverpool in an aggressive 4-2-4 shape. Liverpool struggled to bypass this press in the first half
- Fulham's double pivots made it difficult for Liverpool to press. They were prepared to dribble the ball forward

Game 50 – West Ham – Premier League – Home – 2-1 Win

Liverpool 4-2-3-1

Alisson, Bradley (Quansah), Konate, van Dijk, Tsimikas (Robertson), Gravenberch, Mac Allister, Jones (Szoboszlai), Salah (Endo), Diaz, Jota (Gakpo)

West Ham 3-4-3/3-5-2/4-2-3-1

Areola, Todibo (Guilherme), Mavropanos, Kilman, Wan-Bissaka, Soler (Fullkrug), Ward-Prowse, Paqueta, Scarles (Coufal), Bowen, Kudus

Scorers – Diaz, van Dijk, Robertson (OG)

Liverpool's title march received a well-needed boost after the loss at Fulham. Arsenal had lost an opportunity to put Liverpool under pressure by drawing at home with Brentford the previous day and – until van Dijk's late winner – Liverpool looked as though they might let Arsenal off the hook and fail to win in back-to-back Premier League games for the first time this season. The game began with a celebratory atmosphere as the long-running saga of Mohammed Salah's contract came to an end just days before the game, with Salah signing on for another two seasons.

Liverpool Attack West Ham From Wide

Salah had a celebratory first half as Liverpool dominated the vast majority of the half, with threats from both wings. The space behind the wing-backs and outside the wide central defenders was targeted for long passes out from defence. In the early stages of the construction of this Arne Slot team, it was a regular happening to see Konate clipping balls into Salah or behind the defence for Salah to outstrip his full-back with a mixture of strength and elusive acceleration. Twice in the first half, Salah got away from the defender following this type of moment. The first time, Salah wriggled inside onto his left foot and flashed a shot wide of the post. The second time, he used his body to spin the defender and race into a position to strike a low trivela cross to the far post. Diaz arrived to slot the ball in for the lead.

When Liverpool have the ball in their own half, Konate and van Dijk are a significant distance apart, and we can regularly see van Dijk telling Konate to get wider. With Konate outside the width of the box, van Dijk stays within the width of the box. Liverpool's right-back is often much higher up the pitch than the left-back until the ball has been advanced into the final third. With the ball in the opposition half, Konate and van Dijk are much tighter together in an effort to control the spaces for opposition transitions.

How Liverpool used long passes into the space behind West Ham's wing-backs

van Dijk

Wan-Bisska

Scarles

Salah   Kilman   Mavropanos   Todibo   **Gakpo**

Liverpool's Right Puts West Ham Under Pressure

Salah and Diaz were both threats during the first half, but Salah had little involvement during the second half. The right side of the Liverpool team was the most threatening in the first half, and it was not just because of Salah. For the first time in many weeks, Liverpool were able to field an actual, natural right position, with Conor Bradley returned to the starting lineup. Curtis Jones was able to return to a midfield role, giving Liverpool better balance to the team.

Bradley offered a dynamic presence with his aggressive off-the-ball underlapping movements, driving forward and running with the ball at his feet. He also offered an additional penalty box presence, as he loves to attack the far post on crosses. Bradley's return to the lineup allowed Liverpool to rest Szoboszlai and move Jones, who had a much more comfortable performance than in his last outing. In the second half, Conor Bradley tired and was replaced by Quansah. The removal of Bradley was one of the reasons Liverpool were less threatening on the right side in the second half, taking an effective foil away from Salah as well as the attacking threats that Bradley himself carries.

Energisers

Luis Diaz asked questions of the West Ham defence throughout the fixture. In the first half, the long passes into the area behind the wing-backs created 1v1 opportunities for Diaz, who utilised his sharp footwork and fast hip action to create crossing and shooting opportunities. Diaz continued to torment the West Ham flank in the second half, and his defensive energy – working back and helping protect his own wing – was unrelenting. Since the return from the last international break, it has been the energy of Diaz and Mac Allister that has lifted the team. Their contributions have helped to mask a few players' lack of top form and keep the lead in the title race healthy. After West Ham equalised in this game, Alexis Mac Allister had an electric few minutes, crashing into tackles, counter-pressing, shooting, and winning corners that he then delivered. The all-action sequence from Mac Allister resulted in the corner from which van Dijk headed the winning goal.

Potter Changes West Ham's Strategy

Since the clubs' last meeting, West Ham changed manager from Julen Lopetegui to Graham Potter. His changes slowly worked West Ham back into the match. Their initial formation utilised a back three with wing-backs and, once again against Liverpool, West Ham started without a recognised centre-forward, relying on Kudus and Bowen moving into the forward positions. There was the potential for a fluid front line of three, but West Ham were largely starved of possession in the first half and there was little pressing from the London team, using a mid-block and engaging only once the ball was close to the halfway line. This strategy gave Konate the space to drop passes behind the back line. In the second half, West Ham pressed Liverpool, denying them the time to play in behind so easily.

Switch From Back Five to Back Four

The first change that allowed a foothold into the game was to shift to a more aggressive pressing strategy. From early in the second half, West Ham used a 2-2-2 press with Bowen and Kudus close together. The press was especially aggressive when the ball was in wide areas, preventing Liverpool from playing through the centre or dropping longer passes behind the back line with as much ease.

Ten minutes later, West Ham switched from a back five to a four, further covering the weakness that the wing-back system presented with the space between the wing-backs and the back four. Wan-Bissaka switched from right wing-back to left-back, taking up high positions, and a ball behind the Liverpool defence found a running Wan-Bissaka. His cross created a mix-up between van Dijk and Robertson, resulting in an own goal after van Dijk's clearance struck Robertson and nestled in the bottom corner. West Ham had started to dominate possession with the change of shape, and the 4-2-3-1 pulled their pivots back closer to their central defenders when building up from their own half. The fluidity of the forward line that didn't work in the first half now came to the fore in the second half, coming away from the front line to create overloads in midfield. West Ham also took lessons on board from Fulham vs Liverpool, getting their pivots onto the ball and driving through Liverpool's lines. This has been a weakness for Liverpool all season, with opponents able to carry the ball through the first line of Liverpool's defence.

Alisson Makes Saves When Needed

Alisson's performance was vital to this victory. West Ham had one dangerous sequence in the first half, resulting in a double save by Alisson to keep out a 1v1 and then recovering to tip a chip onto the crossbar. In the second half, he had to rush from his line to prevent Bowen from scoring a 1v1. The two 1v1s were excellent opportunities, and the saves from Alisson – highlighting his speed from the line – were critical in securing Liverpool's victory.

Key Points

- Liverpool attacked the spaces outside the three central defenders of West Ham's back-five system
- Konate and van Dijk split very wide in-possession when deep in their own half. In the opposition half, they were tighter together and closed the gaps for opponents to counter-attack, helping to pin West Ham in
- West Ham changed their system and began to control possession, putting Liverpool under pressure
- West Ham's pivots carried the ball from deep to break Liverpool's defensive lines

Game 51 – Leicester – Premier League – Away – 1-0 Win

Liverpool 4-2-3-1

Alisson. Bradley (Alexander-Arnold), Konate, van Dijk, Tsimikas, Gravenberch, Mac Allister, Szoboszlai (Elliott), Salah, Gakpo (Jota), Diaz (Jones)

Leicester 4-2-3-1

Hermansen, Pereira (Justin), Faes, Coady, Thomas, Ndidi (Skipp), Soumare, El Khannouss, De Cordova-Reid (Buonanotte), Mavididi (Monga), Vardy (Daka)

Scorers – Alexander-Arnold

Arsenal's win against Ipswich meant that anything but a win risked injecting some jeopardy into the Premier League title race. Leicester needed to win to avoid relegation, and they worked hard, but Liverpool dominated the game as expected. Liverpool put themselves into a position where a win in the next match would confirm them as champions.

Finishing

Liverpool created many opportunities in the game, but their finishing was not quite deadly enough. With two minutes on the clock, Salah hit both posts with an effort Opta rated as 0.3 xG. The sequence that led to the eventual winning goal featured Salah and Jota hitting the post then the crossbar, with efforts both ranked at 0.2 xG. The Alexander-Arnold strike itself ranked at a lowly 0.015 xG. Liverpool totalled 2.57 team xG for the game. For context, when Liverpool won 7-0 at Crystal Palace in 2020, they recorded 2.8 xG. When Liverpool scored seven at Rangers in the Champions League in 2022, their xG was 2.4. Liverpool created well, but their finishing didn't quite match!

Fast Passing

In recent games, Liverpool had struggled to find their fluid, fast passing rhythm. Against Leicester, this returned and Salah's early chance was created with two line-breaking passes, including a one-touch pass into Diaz, who spun and passed behind the defence in two touches to find Salah. Liverpool used short, fast progressive forward passes to attack at speed, and this was especially noticeable in wide areas as both Tsimikas and Bradley combined with one-twos to progress possession, following the pass with an underlap or overlap. At times, the pass from the interior to the wide player didn't end with a return pass but a 'round the corner' helping pass, enabling the point of attack to be switched across to the opposite side of the pitch.

Twin Attacking Full-Backs

An evolution of the team under Arne Slot has been a willingness to unleash both full-backs at the same time in attacking areas in a bid to overload the penalty box. Committing both full-backs forward is dependent on the factors of game state, opponent quality, and opponent tactical approach. One full-back will generally be tight to the central defenders in the build-up stage, but once the ball has progressed into the final third, one full-back will be in the half-space to receive on the side of the pitch with the ball, either to cross or break the line into the penalty box. The opposite full-back will attack the box as a target for crosses. Alexander-Arnold is the exception, as he inverts or stays in the opposite side half-space to receive, which suits his ability to create with a pass or shot. Tsimikas also usually plays the role differently, with more overlaps and less box crashing due to his crossing ability but, at Leicester, he was crashing the box, almost scoring as Liverpool sought to break down Leicester.

With Leicester defending deep and with no real out ball, it was easy for Slot to switch the team structure into a diamond backline. Gravenberch was the head of the diamond, van Dijk the left side, Konate central and deepest, and Bradley or Alexander-Arnold to the right. With the ball on the opposite side, players rotated around. Bradley or Alexander-Arnold left the diamond with Tsimikas in on the left side. Konate picked up the right side of the diamond, and van Dijk sat at the base. The full-back not involved in the diamond structure pushed up high in the half-space, adding to the attacking options. As the ball progressed further into the opposition half, the full-back left the diamond structure, with Konate and van Dijk positioned as a tight pair, pinning opponents in.

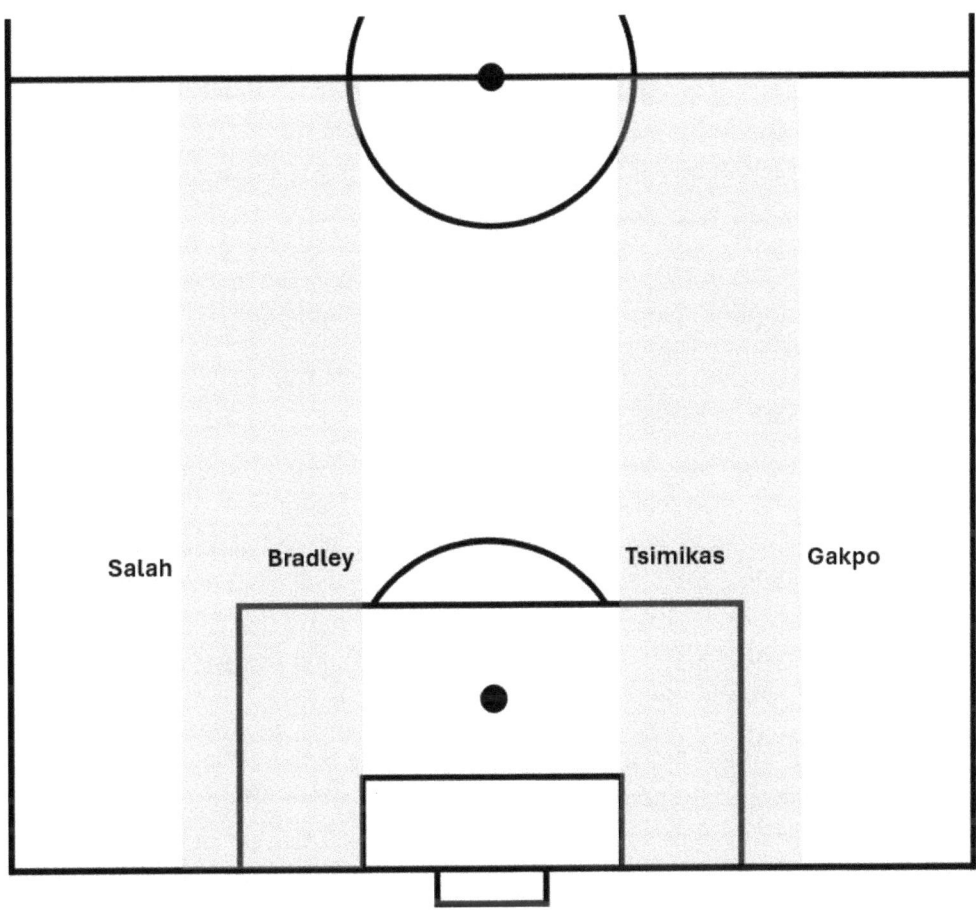

The positioning of Liverpool's full-backs to flood the half-spaces at the same time

Alexander-Arnold's Left Foot

This was Trent Alexander-Arnold's first goal in senior football with his left foot, in his 350th club appearance. Which would be no surprise for a normal right-back. Of course, Trent is not a normal right-back. His left foot is not as good as his exceptional right foot, but it is strong enough to switch the play. Alexander-Arnold has often used his left foot to escape situations where he has been pressed, with long balls behind opponents or switches out to Robertson. He also takes up positions in the half-space where a touch inside creates shooting opportunities with his left foot. He has come close before, but he finally scored in game 350, after a spell on the bench, at a time when the team badly needed a goal and a time when discussions about his future have impacted his standing amongst the fan base. Fantastic timing.

Pressing Structure and Strategy

Liverpool pressed Leicester aggressively from the beginning of the game, immediately using a five-player press in either a 3-2 or 2-3 structure. Alexis Mac Allister joined as the fifth player. The full-backs and Gravenberch were poised to jump on any passes out to full-backs. When goalkeeper Hermansen was in position, Diaz had an extreme curve on his run to close down and stop passes out to the right. Hermansen had to go long and straight with his right foot or clip diagonally with his left, both of which led to turnovers.

Once Liverpool hit the front, they persisted with pressing but less aggressively, switching to the four-man block, leaving Alexis in midfield covering the centre while Gravenberch continued to jump to the Leicester full-backs.

Individual Qualities of Forwards

All of the Liverpool front line were able to display their key attributes during this game, and each one brought different challenges for opponents. Luis Diaz may not be the most efficient finisher, but his movement is clever and he can manipulate the ball quickly in tight areas. He moved away from the front line into deep midfield positions and out to both wings, creating overloads on both the right and left. Other players filled the space he vacated. Gakpo pushed into the centre when Diaz was in central midfield areas or wide on the right.

Gakpo returning on the left gives Liverpool a different threat. The ability to cut in and shoot is possessed by both Diaz and Gakpo, but Gakpo has scored more regularly using this move. His right foot delivers very effectively to the far post, with good height and curve. Plus, he has the added option to dribble on the outside and cross left-footed. Gakpo created a good far post chance for Salah in this manner.

Salah's attacking threats are multi-fold, but one that is less often discussed is his ability to get free on the far post. Lurking outside the eye line of the full-back before attacking the space where the ball will drop over the head of the full-back. Inswinging crosses impact the body shape and position of full-backs, and the defender has to shift their body early to track the line of the cross, enabling the attacker to escape the view of the defender. For an outswinging cross, the body position of the defender is slightly less challenged, with the defender able to see the ball and the attacker for longer.

Possession Pauses

Liverpool use possession in many different ways. As a defensive tool, they starve opponents of opportunities to create. When managing the tempo of a game, they slow the pace and take energy out of the match. They also use ball possession to pause the game, particularly when players are out of position. On a number of occasions, Liverpool regained possession after a set-piece and played a number of short passes that didn't really go anywhere, but enabled the defensive spine of the team to get back into position. Liverpool's fluidity retains a central core to continue their control of the game situation as much as possible.

Key Points

- Each Liverpool forward has their own individual qualities, carrying different attacking threats
- Liverpool have been willing to use possession as a defensive tool as well as an offensive one
- Liverpool's fast, fluid passing and movement returned
- Trent Alexander-Arnold has a highly effective, highly underrated left foot

Game 52 – Tottenham Hotspur – Home – Premier League – 5-1 Win

Liverpool 4-2-3-1

Alisson, Alexander-Arnold (Endo), Konate, van Dijk, Robertson. Gravenberch, Mac Allister (Nunez), Szoboszlai (Jones), Salah, Gakpo (Jota), Diaz (Elliott)

Spurs 4-3-3

Vicario, Spence, Danso, Davies, Udogie, Bergvall, Gray (Sarr), Maddison (Kulusevski), Johnson, Tel (Odobert), Solanke (Richarlison)

Scorers – Diaz, Mac Allister, Gakpo, Salah, Udogie (OG), Solanke

Liverpool confirmed their status as Premier League champions with a thumping win at Anfield against Tottenham Hotspur. Arsenal had drawn in their midweek game against Crystal Palace, meaning that a draw would have been enough to confirm the title. In many ways, this was the perfect occasion against the perfect opponents. As has been well documented, when Liverpool won the League in 2020, they did it in an empty stadium due to the COVID restrictions. This time, they had the opportunity to win it in front of a packed stadium against an opponent committed to playing attacking football. This was always going to be a spectacle, and the party at the end of the game was certainly epic.

Open Spurs

Tottenham came to Anfield and played as everyone expected 2024/25 Tottenham to play. They attempted to press Liverpool high up the pitch, play short and progressively in their own half, and get bodies forward when attacking. None of this worked well for them. When they attempted to build at the back, Liverpool were largely able to pick them off. Liverpool especially helped themselves to Vicario's clipped passes out to the Tottenham left side.

The Liverpool press was especially aggressive on their right, pushing high into the corner with Gakpo not actively involved in the press, but ready for the moment the ball went back to the goalkeeper. Gakpo was positioned between the deepest left-sided Spurs player to receive and the player occupying a left-wing position. Vicario looked to clip the ball over Gakpo into the wing position, but Gakpo is a big target to clear and he picked off these passes. (He was also able to pick them off when Liverpool pressed the Spurs left.) Diaz pressed aggressively almost on his own, attacking the receiver wide but also curving his runs to encourage a pass back to Vicario. From there, Vicario tried to clip the ball forward, and Gakpo again picked off the passes. In the second half, Liverpool pressed from a slightly deeper starting position with many central turnovers, one of which saw Gakpo pinch the ball and create a 2v2 against the Spurs back line, the move resulting in a shot on target from Szoboszlai.

Spurs' attempts to chip the ball wide with Vicario, but turning the ball over

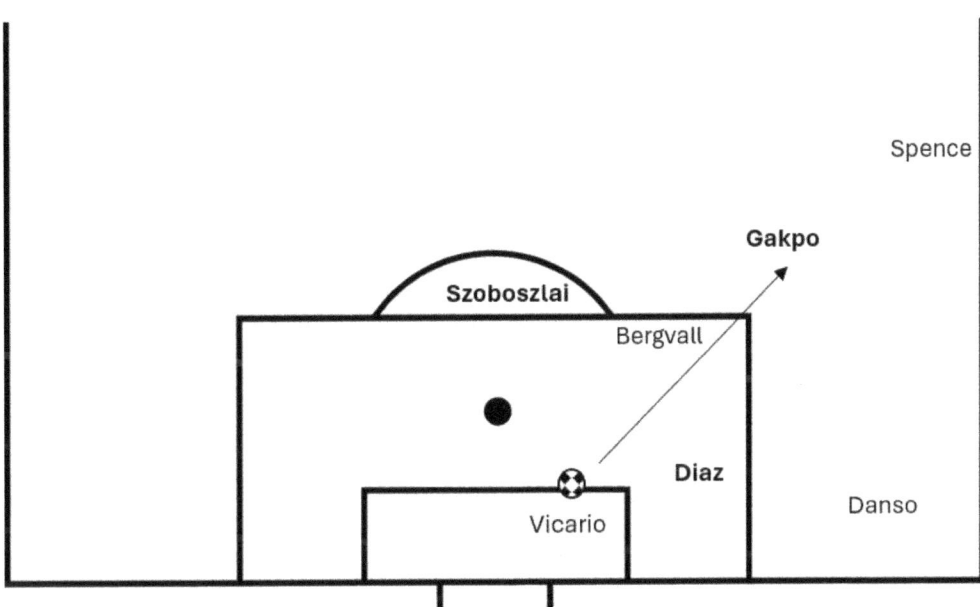

Form Players Make The Difference

Alexis Mac Allister scored Liverpool's second after a counter-press in the Spurs' right-back area close to the touchline. As Tottenham tried to pass their way out of trouble, Gravenberch leapt onto a ball rolled from the corner diagonally towards the Spurs area, getting his body between the intended recipient and the ball, and nudged a pass to Mac Allister who then smashed a left-foot shot into the roof of the net from the edge of the box. This goal put Liverpool 2-1 ahead (having gone behind) and kickstarted the Anfield party.

Since the final international break of the season, Mac Allister has been in fantastic form. His midfield displays have been perfect for an all-round midfielder. The ability to tackle strongly, pass the ball tidily while also being able to split a defence, run in behind opponents and track back, rotate with teammates and score goals was plain to see. He has scored two spectacular goals, one at

Fulham and now against Spurs. When others have seemed to lack energy at times, Mac Allister has brought energy in bundles.

As has Luis Diaz. With the rest of the forward line suffering a dip in form, Diaz returned from the international break full of vim and vigour. Overall, Diaz has been patchy this season, with extreme highs and lows; his play has been hesitant, and has seen him cutting back and forth when dribbling without releasing a pass, shot or cross. In the last month, though, he has been back to sharp and decisive form. Diaz pounced for the equaliser, sliding in at the far post, reacting faster than everyone else. The build-up for the goal was a great example of Liverpool using half-space runs. Salah received the ball wide on the right and Szoboszlai – knowing that Salah would try to find him making the run into the half-space – then slotted a ball across the six-yard box.

Slick Passing and Movement

There were signs in the game against Leicester that the slick passing from earlier in the season had returned to Liverpool's play. Part of the passing play can be connected to what might be termed "back to basics", with one-twos in wide areas and right-side release passes particularly prominent. Konate, Alexander-Arnold, and Salah had heavy involvement in ball progressions. Konate played passes of medium- to long-range from a wide position into Salah along the line. He and Alexander-Arnold combined for one-twos but perhaps not in the manner that might be expected. Konate passed to Alexander-Arnold wide and then made a forward run to receive the ball close to the touchline, an inside-out one-two movement that got Konate roaming forward in space on the right side.

Playing Forward Early

Part of the way that Tottenham play is to have a very high defensive line. Throughout the first half, it was very clear that Liverpool looked to play in behind them quickly to attack the space. The balls in behind were either to wide players or players running in behind from deep (mainly Szoboszlai and Mac Allister). A very similar ploy was used at Villa Park, where Aston Villa used a high line.

In the second half, the Tottenham line was a little deeper, and Liverpool had fewer runners behind. Instead, the players were in front of the defensive line. Liverpool used their excellent box defending to regain and counter from deep, driving into open spaces with the ball or playing into the feet of Salah, Jota, or Gakpo. Liverpool's fourth goal came as Kulusevski dribbled at the penalty area. Three players surrounded him, cutting off the entry point into the area. Szoboszlai drove forward with the ball at his feet and picked Salah out to the right as Liverpool flooded forward with numbers. Salah cut inside and drilled a low shot in at the near post. It was fitting that Salah scored by cutting in and shooting left-footed in his classic manner. In the second half, there seemed to be an almost obsessive need to create a goal for Salah, with Gakpo and Nunez turning down fantastic shooting opportunities to pass to him.

Liverpool Weaknesses

Tottenham did identify some areas to go after Liverpool. They played long behind Robertson, resulting in a number of challenging foot races and the corner from which Solanke scored. Madisson's outswinging corner went to the far post, much as Newcastle's corner went to the far post for Dan Burn's header in the League Cup final. Solanke's header was not as far from goal, but it exploited the same factors. Liverpool's best headers of the ball mark zonally in the six-yard box, leaving other players to mark man-to-man, which can result in mismatches.

Key Points

- Liverpool used Gakpo to pick off the Tottenham goalkeeper's distribution
- Liverpool played forward early to exploit the high Spurs' defensive line and to counter-attack quickly
- There has been a noticeable weakness for Liverpool when defending far post corners. Their zonal marking set-up can be taken advantage of by positioning a powerful header of the ball away from van Dijk and Konate, who are in a central position

Game 53 – Chelsea – Away – Premier League – 3-1 Loss

Liverpool 4-2-3-1

Alisson, Alexander-Arnold (Bradley), Quansah, van Dijk, Tsimikas (Chiesa), Endo (Mac Allister), Jones, Elliott (Szoboszlai), Salah, Gakpo, Jota (Nunez)

Chelsea 4-2-3-1

Sanchez, Caicedo, Chalobah, Colwill, Cucurella, Lavia (Gusto), Fernandez (James), Palmer, Neto, Madueke, Jackson (Sancho)

Scorers – van Dijk, Fernandez, Quansah (OG), Palmer

After being confirmed as Premier League champions, Liverpool's next game came at Stamford Bridge against Chelsea. Chelsea gave the Liverpool players a guard of honour before kick-off, but the respect (rightly) ended there.

Slot chose to rotate the line up, giving starts to players who haven't always been first choice. This decision must have been driven by sentiment with an element of keeping players fresh for a game where the result isn't that important to winning the league, but will matter to Liverpool in terms of pride… the home game against runners-up Arsenal. Losing at home to them will leave a small blot on Liverpool's record.

Fast Start for Chelsea

Enzo Fernandez put Liverpool in front in the third minute. After that, Cole Palmer's positioning challenged Liverpool's pressing shape as Chelsea built up in their defensive third. Plamer moved closer to the central defenders and wide of the midfield cover. Curtis Jones attempted to track Palmer's movement but slipped at a crucial moment, so Palmer drove forward and then passed wide to Neto. From wide, Neto forced the Liverpool defence back, cutting a low ball across the box close to the penalty spot. The Liverpool defence had overcovered to the near post and six-yard box, leaving Fernandez open to control, and he tucked a low shot into the bottom corner.

Cole Palmer gave Liverpool problems throughout the match. He had gone months without a goal, and there were question marks over his form, but he was back to his best. He carried the ball forward with tight control and at speed on numerous occasions, including turning away from Conor Bardley and hitting the far post from a narrow angle during the second half.

Palmer was not the only player to worry Liverpool with dribbles at the defence. Madueke, Neto, Lavia and Caicedo also had moments taking on Liverpool players successfully. A clever Palmer pass created the low cross that led to the chaos of the Quansah own goal. Finally, Palmer tucked away a stoppage-time penalty to end any hopes of a Liverpool fightback. Palmer's positioning was aided by Caicedo's movement from right-back, as he moved forward from the right side of the defence into the right half-space beyond the Liverpool midfield. This drove the deepest Liverpool midfielders away from the space Palmer wanted to occupy. Curtis Jones attempted to cover the space for the opening goal but was unable to get there in time, slipping as he attempted to follow Palmer's movement. Jones also slipped as he and Palmer competed for the ball in the build-up to Chelsea's second goal.

Players Off Their Game

A number of Liverpool players struggled during this game, especially during the first hour. It would be very tempting to suggest that the players had spent time celebrating during the week between beating Spurs and facing Chelsea, but it may be best not to look for such a cheap excuse. Liverpool put together slick passing moves during the first half, but the moves collapsed after a poor pass or touch. Harvey Elliott gave the ball away often. Nothing was sticking with Salah when passes were fizzed into him. During the first half, a deflected cross looped into the Chelsea area and Diogo Jota in yards of space, but Jota neither controlled the ball nor got a shot away, the ball bouncing off him and harmlessly out of play. This was the encapsulation of Liverpool for much of the game.

Jarrel Quansah's performance could be described as a curate's egg. Largely, he was steady, yet all three goals conceded involved Quansah. For the first goal, he was dragged out of the centre to cover the near post, a part of the group of players who over-covered. The second goal was his own goal, but he was not at fault for van Dijk clearing the ball against him. Then, it was Quansah who conceded the penalty with a trip on Caicedo. However, Szoboszlai had sold him short with an under-hit pass, and Quansah had taken a knock moments earlier when repelling a Chelsea counter-attack.

Errors Creeping In

Defensive errors have become more common with Liverpool in the latter part of the season. At Fulham, there were mistakes from Robertson that were punished. Against Southampton, West Ham, and Chelsea, there have been mix-ups involving the generally impeccable Virgil van Dijk. The first mix-up saw van Dijk and Alisson allow Smallbone in to score, putting Southampton ahead. Liverpool bounced back to win 3-1. The second was a van Dijk clearance hitting Robertson for a West Ham equaliser. Then there was his clearance that struck Quansah and nestled into the net. Virgil van Dijk responded against both West Ham and Chelsea with a headed goal from a corner, with the header against West Ham the winner. A good response each time, but against Chelsea, it was not enough.

Liverpool Take Control

The possession percentages were in Liverpool's favour for most of the game but Liverpool struggled to create until the final 30 minutes. Bradley came on for Alexander-Arnold and drove at his full-back. Mac Allister and Szoboszlai came into midfield, enabling Liverpool to play better forward passes and also lifting Curtis Jones' levels. Darwin Nunez added a hungry presence in the box.

Yet the chances created were not converted. Liverpool struggled to cut through the middle of Chelsea, and their main threat came from inswinging crosses towards the far post. Salah picked out Nunez, who headed a long way wide when well-placed six yards out. More confirmation bias for those who believe Nunez has let Liverpool down more times than he has helped win games. Salah also headed wide at the far post from a Gakpo inswinger from the left side. Liverpool overloaded the right side and attacked the far post. At one stage, they had four players on the right side of the box with Gakpo cutting in. Three players attacked the far post while one hung out to the edge of the box. Gakpo faced a makeshift right-back in Caicedo, running at him in the first half and attacking the space behind. In the second half, the space behind was restricted, so Gakpo cut in and curled crosses to the far post instead. Chelsea were able to survive the threat and come away with three points to aid their quest to qualify for the Champions League.

Liverpool overloading the far post

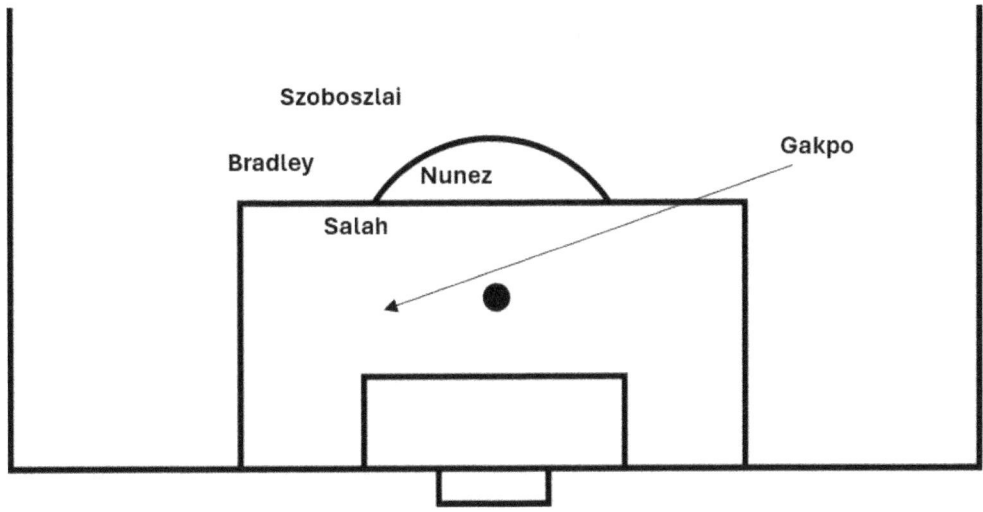

Key Points

- Endo played in a more attacking style, breaking lines with and without the ball
- Cole Palmer caused Liverpool problems with movements into pockets of space
- Liverpool used inswinging crosses and far-post overloads

Game 54 – Arsenal – Premier League – Home – 2-2

Liverpool 4-2-3-1

Alisson, Bradley (Alexander-Arnold), Konate, van Dijk, Robertson, Gravenberch (Elliott), Jones (Nunez), Szoboszlai, Salah, Gakpo (Mac Allister), Diaz (Jota)

Arsenal 4-3-3

Raya, White (Calafiori), Saliba, Kiwior, Lewis-Skelly, Odegaard, Partey, Merino, Saka (Zinchenko), Trossard (Tierney), Martinelli

Scorers – Gakpo, Diaz, Martinelli, Merino

At various stages in the season, this fixture was circled with the words "title decider". Arsenal were unable to keep pace with Liverpool, however, and the game carried no significance other than pride. Arsenal gave Liverpool their guard of honour before kick-off at the end of a difficult period for them that saw their last hope of a trophy ended by PSG in the Champions League. Arsenal would have to lift themselves to put in a good showing at Anfield.

Pressing

Both teams are excellent at pressing the opposition. Liverpool have been smart and aggressive but possibly over-reliant on their ability to recover with speed once the pressing line is broken. Arsenal are the pressing masters of the Premier League, using different pressing shapes within games. While they do not always win the ball high up the pitch, they are expert at forcing opponents to play long balls that can then be mopped up.

Liverpool had Arsenal in trouble during the first half using traps in wide areas. When building up in their defensive third, Arsenal pulled a centre-back into the left-back area with the left-back high up. Liverpool invited the pass into the central defender, closed off the pass inside to central midfield, and blocked the pass down the line into feet. This resulted in several turnovers.

Luis Diaz was extremely sharp in closing down the central defender in these situations and in other 1v1 pressing opportunities, regaining possession on a number of occasions. Arsenal fixed this issue in the second half by keeping their central defenders closer to the goalkeeper in the build and pulling the full-backs deeper to occupy the wide area. Arsenal weren't caught again until Merino was sent off. Liverpool made a change to their shape and system, playing with Jota and Nunez. Szoboszlai was also nearby and the free of them pounced on a Raya goalkick pass. Merino lunged into not one but two challenges, picking up his second yellow card of the game. The press and pass created pressure and panic.

Arsenal Pressing Shapes

Arsenal mainly used a 2-3 shape to press Liverpool. This 2-3 was flexible, moving into a 3-2, and two-man orientated shapes – the 2-4 and 3-3 – wherein another central midfielder joins the press.

Liverpool were challenged by the pressing, as many teams have been. Arsenal can press by directly pressuring players in one moment and indirectly pressuring players by threatening their next pass in the next moment. All while being close enough to the player in possession that their next touch could be the moment they come under intense pressure and lose the ball. Alisson almost lost the ball in the first half when he played against a pressing player only for the ball to loop kindly into his arms. Curtis Jones did lose the ball close to his own goal when he took an extra touch and, suddenly, he was converged upon. Fortunately for Liverpool, there were too many Arsenal players around the ball to get a quick shot away. Liverpool got away with it.

Shifting Build-Up Shapes

The pressure from Arsenal forced Liverpool to come up with different solutions. Jones and Gravenberch came in much tighter to the central defenders to receive, sometimes being between them in the quarterback position that was once deeply associated with Xabi Alonso and Andrea Pirlo. This acted as a double pivot, which we have rarely seen from Liverpool this season, but which Slot often used at Feyenoord.

Another unusual solution to help Liverpool play out came from Konate in the first half. He has regularly received the ball in the right-back area with the actual right-back pushed higher, either on the outside of wide or inverted on the inside. Konate then finds a short pass or plays long into Salah. On this occasion, he drove forward with the ball, eating up territory with each stride and creating an attacking position.

Arsenal Movement

A lack of a genuine striker has often been cited as the reason why Arsenal failed to keep pace with Liverpool in the league this season. Not having a centre-forward has made Arsenal and Arteta be more creative with their attacking movement. Trossard, Martinelli, Merino and Odegaard all move and shift positions to stretch and create spaces in opposition back lines. In this game, Trossard and Martinelli exchanged on the wing and through the centre. Trossard pulled short and Merino filled the centre-forward position. Odegaard, meanwhile, is free to float from the centre to the wings to offer support. The movements impacted all of the Arsenal goals, with Trossard pulling wide and Martinelli getting into the box to head in for 2-1.

In turn, Bradley gave Trossard too much space to cross while Konate and van Dijk allowed Martinelli to drift into space and the equaliser for Arsenal was scored by Merino, poaching in the centre-forward position as Odegaard cut in from the right and fired a shot. Alisson pushed the effort onto the woodwork but Merino reacted first to score. The movement of players into midfield areas has given Liverpool problems when pressing this season, but Konate followed Trossard, tracking his movements into midfield areas and making it harder to pick him out with easy passes.

Attacking The Half-Space

Liverpool's second goal was a result of how they aggressively run into the half-space. Salah received the ball close to the halfway line and struck a pass with the inside of his foot to a forward-running Szoboszlai. The run was made from deep into the half-space, followed by a low cross slid in by Diaz. It was very similar to the goal scored in the last home game against Spurs.

The goal was also the result of a fast counter-attack from deep. A similar counter led to the opening goal as Gakpo was played in behind. The initial attack only created a throw-in, but the throw was taken quickly, catching Arsenal out of position and allowing Gakpo to head in unmarked.

These counter-attacks have been a hallmark of Liverpool's play this season. The Premier League stats centre has Liverpool on 14 goals from counter-attacks this season, with Spurs second on 10. Liverpool crowd their own penalty box when defending, regaining the ball and then pushing forward at speed. Often, the ball is at the feet of Szoboszlai, who uses his own speed to drive forward with the ball. Gravenberch and Mac Allister will also regain, though they are more likely to play a long pass to the wingers who will be pushing forward. Liverpool hit Arsenal with counter-attack after counter-attack in the first half from these positions. In the second half, Arsenal prevented a number of these opportunities by surrounding the player on the ball quickly and stopping the exit routes.

After Merino's red card, Liverpool had opportunities to win the game, and Robertson put a far-post volley just wide. Liverpool had overloaded the far post with three players, and Arsenal covered two of the three but left Robertson free. He couldn't steer the volley on target. In stoppage time, Robertson swept home at a corner, after a header was blocked and the ball dropped to Robertson in the six-yard box. The flag went up for a foul by Konate. Had there been more riding on this game, the decision would have been debated forever more. As it was, a draw was enough for pride to remain intact.

Key Points

- Konate tracked the movement of Trossard, preventing him from finding space in midfield and creating an overload
- Liverpool exploited the right half-space with runners to create chances
- Both teams pressed aggressively using varied pressing shapes and traps
- Liverpool counter-attacked quickly from their own defensive third, but Arsenal found a way to stop this, counter-pressing their own turnover to make the breakaway very difficult

Game 55 – Brighton – Premier League – Away – 3-2 Loss

Liverpool 4-2-3-1/4-3-3

Alisson, Bradley (Endo), Konate, Quansah, Tsimikas, Gravenberch, Elliott, Szoboszlai (Jones), Salah, Gakpo (Diaz), Chiesa (Nunez)

Brighton 4-2-3-1

Verbruggen, Wieffer, van Hecke, Webster, Estupinan, Baleba, Ayari (Gomez), Minteh (Hinshelwood), Gruda (O'Reilly), Adingra (Mitoma), Welbeck (Howell)

Scorers – Elliott, Szoboszlai, Ayari, Mitoma, Hinshelwood

Liverpool's extended victory lap continued with an entertaining loss at Brighton. Slot gave starts to fringe players once again, with Quansah and Chiesa in the starting lineup. The manager also took the opportunity to tinker tactically, possibly giving glimpses of next season's concepts.

High Pressing

Both Liverpool and Brighton pressed aggressively. Both teams were happy to be pressed because – if they got through the initial pressure – there were opportunities to combine and create semi-transitional attacks... the fast forward flowing play that we have seen regularly from Liverpool this season.

Brighton's press was particularly aggressive. The main thread of the pressing style was man-to-man, but this created different pressing shapes including a 3-2 and a 1-4. At one stage, Brighton had seven players pressing in the Liverpool half (Liverpool had pulled deeper in an effort to create an overload against the press. Brighton followed, creating a seven man pressing situation). Unsurprisingly, Liverpool then went long, as a 3v3 had been created in the Brighton half.

Liverpool pressed with their four-player shape, adding in a 1-4 shape when pressing in wide areas. Brighton were able to play swift one-touch football and escape in wide areas. This was a feature of both teams play. When the lines were broken, 5v4 and 4v3 attacks were created, with fast attacks that required intense recovery runs from the players who had been bypassed. This made for an attractive, fluid game of football where both teams carried a goal threat whenever they went forward.

The opening goal of the game came from a move that started in the Liverpool half, with pace injected into the attack as Salah volleyed a one-touch pass into the path of Conor Bradley. Bradley attacked the half-space and cut a ball back for Elliott to finish from six yards.

Influenced By PSG?

There have been subtle hints that Liverpool are looking to build up slightly differently. For much of the season, Konate and van Dijk have positioned themselves with a large distance between them and Alisson behind, making a flat and wide triangle. In recent games, though, one of the central midfielders has dropped in between Konate and van Dijk to receive. A second central midfielder is located within a relatively close distance and at an angle to receive. The player between the central defenders has rotated, much as PSG did against Liverpool. For PSG, it was Vitinha and Ruiz who dropped in. For Liverpool, it was mostly Szoboszlai and Elliott receiving. For most teams, the defensive midfielder drops in, but Gravenberch often took up a different position.

Building Out with a Right Side Triangle

Ryan Gravenberch often took up a position in the right-back area to help with the build-up. Konate was tucked inside more than he had been for much of the season, with Gravenberch further outside and Bradley tucked infield, higher up the pitch. Liverpool could create an overload on the right and Gravenberch could also carry the ball forward from the right-back area, as he did in the second half with a mixture of dribbling and improvised one-touch passes creating attacking opportunities.

Ruthless Play Changes Games

A 3-2 defeat could easily have been a victory. With the score 2-1 to Liverpool, a huge opportunity was missed by Salah. Gakpo had broken free of his marker and driven into the box. His low, square pass found Salah six yards out but, to the shock of everyone, Salah managed to scuff the ball wide.

Brighton then struck twice, attacking the Liverpool right side. Welbeck was involved for the equaliser, combining with Mitoma (his shot was saved but Mitoma followed in). Danny Welbeck's movement had given Liverpool problems all game, playing as an intelligent false nine and pulling towards midfield to create space behind. In Liverpool's last game, Konate followed Trossard. A first time pass found the run of Ayari, joining from deep, running beyond the Liverpool backline to finish low into the corner. Welbeck had positioned himself closer to Quansah, who did not follow. The pass went over Konate's head into the run of Ayari.

Brighton found a winner when a low cross from their left picked out Hinshelwood at the far post. Hinshelwood was unmarked and finished easily. Brighton had thrown bodies forward into the Liverpool box, as they had done all game, symptomatic of both teams' willingness to attack.

Liverpool creating a triangle in the build-up on the right

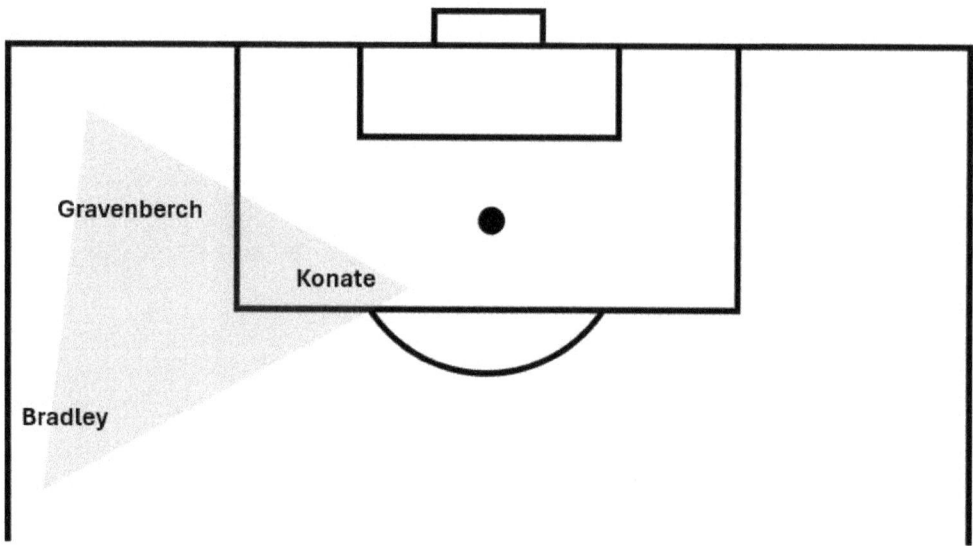

Key Points

- Both teams baited the opposition press in order to create flowing semi-transition attacks after breaking through the pressure
- Liverpool changed their build-up play, dropping Gravenberch into the right-back position to create a triangle
- Liverpool rotated a central midfielder between the central defenders during deep build-up, possibly influenced by PSG

Game 56 – Crystal Palace – Home – Premier League – 1-1 Draw

Liverpool 4-2-3-1

Alisson, Bradley (Alexander-Arnold), Konate (Jota), van Dijk, Robertson (Elliott), Gravenberch, Jones, Szoboszlai, (Nunez) Salah, Gakpo, Diaz (Endo)

Crystal Palace 3-4-3

Henderson. Richards, Lacroix, Lerma, Munoz, Hughes (Esse (Franca)), Kamada, Mitchell, Sarr, Mateta (Nketiah), Eze (Devenny)

Scorers – Sarr, Salah

Liverpool's extended victory lap (have I mentioned that already?) continued with a 1-1 draw at home to Crystal Palace. We were treated to a very rare double guard of honour, with Liverpool receiving from Crystal Palace and then giving to Palace for their FA Cup win. This was a game about ceremony as the Liverpool fans inside Anfield were desperate to see Virgil van Dijk lift the Premier League trophy after the game.

Arne Slot named a strong lineup, very close to his first choice lineup. Only Bradley came in for Alexander-Arnold and Jones for an unfit Alexis Mac Allister. No sentimental selections in this match.

Liverpool pressed high and hard. The front three effectively went man-to-man with the Palace back line, with the fourth member of the press marking Crystal Palace's pivot. After a couple of short passes, Palace would go long into Mateta, a strategy that worked in the FA Cup final but which yielded little success at Anfield.

Counter-Attacking Palace

Where Crystal Palace offered constant threat was on the counter-attack. Their strategy was to defend deep, crowd the penalty box, and spring forward. Their defensive lines were compact, and when the ball was in wide areas, the wing-backs and wide players showed Liverpool attackers infield to a very crowded area. Liverpool created crossing opportunities which Palace were happy to defend as the wing-backs were on the alert for passes out to the Liverpool wingers. With the Liverpool full-backs tucked infield, the wingers were positioned wide, outside the Palace shape. However, the wing-backs of Crystal Palace were able and primed to intercept the passes to the wingers, creating a number of counter-attacks in the first half.

Impact Of Liverpool's Full-Backs

When Liverpool were building up in the first half, both full-backs were often closer to the central defenders to help create an extra man against the Palace front three. Once the ball progressed into the Palace half, Robertson and Bradley both inverted, with Bradley high in the half-space on the right, and Robertson tucked in closer to the central defenders. When the ball progressed closer to the Palace box, both full-backs occupied the half-space.

Unfortunately for Conor Bradley and Liverpool, this was an ungainly performance from the young right-back. His touch, passing, and dribbling were far from smooth. One instance of a misplaced pass created Sarr's opening goal for Palace as Liverpool attempted to build in their defensive third. Alisson passed out to Bradley, who was under some pressure, but his ball infield was very loose. Mitchell turned quickly and fed a pass into the inside left channel and Sarr received. He opened his body and bent a right-foot shot low past Alisson. The central defensive pairing of van Dijk and Konate were slow to close the gap, but Palace were swift in their execution.

Farewell to Trent

Against Arsenal, the boos for Trent Alexander-Arnold were uncomfortable; the reaction to his announcement that he would be leaving on a free had been hostile. Thankfully, he received a much better reception when coming on at half-time against Crystal Palace and during the trophy ceremony. In the second half, he treated the fans to his fine array of passing, playing a number of defence-splitting passes to break lines plus one sumptuous 50-yard ball behind the defence, curved perfectly into the path of Darwin Nunez. Nunez effort was saved brilliantly by Henderson. Liverpool will find it very difficult to replace Alexander-Arnold's passing skills.

More Tactical Changes

With Liverpool behind, Arne Slot made the shift to take off Konate, push Gravenberch into central defence and bring Jota on. Liverpool briefly had a front five with Gakpo, Diaz, Nunez, Jota, and Salah all on the pitch together.

Then came the red card. Gravenberch controlled a long high ball out by Palace and brought it down by the halfway line but Kamada nicked in and stole the ball. As he was set to sprint into acres of space, Gravenberch committed the foul and received a straight red card.

Slot had to reshape again. He kept a back four but – when in possession – Endo pushed to the right and Alexander-Arnold moved into midfield. A diamond of security in the buildup. Liverpool still pushed two wingers and two strikers up against the Palace back line and attacked with intent, and Jota worked back out of possession… his industry led to the equaliser. Jota won possession close to the right corner of his own box, and Liverpool picked up the second ball. The attack was repelled but Jota picked up the third ball, feeding a pass wide to Nunez. Nunez crossed and Gakpo won the far post header, nodding down to Salah who smashed a volley in off a Palace defender.

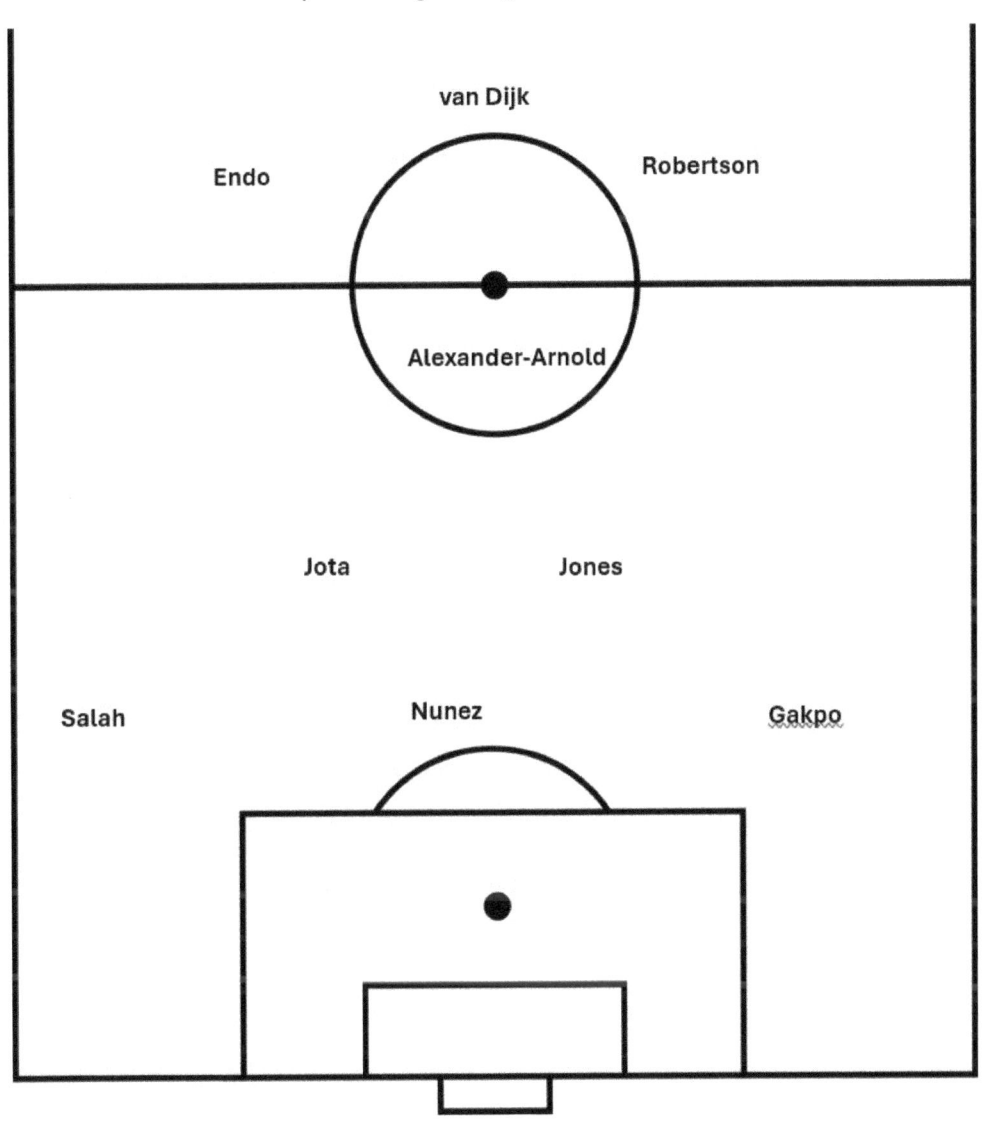

Liverpool reorganising down to ten men

Key Points

- Crystal Palace were a constant threat on the counter-attack
- Crystal Palace's organisation forced Liverpool infield and into a barrage of crosses
- Once again, Slot showed that when down to ten men it is still possible to be positive and attack
- Alexander-Arnold displayed his wonderful passing range and showed what Liverpool will miss next season

A Stunning Achievement

Liverpool pulled off a true masterstroke by choosing Arne Slot.

When he was appointed as the successor to Jurgen Klopp, no one was expecting a Premier League triumph. Manchester City had won four successive league titles and looked as strong as ever. Arsenal had pushed City close in the 2023-24 season and looked ready to step in should City slip up. Liverpool had challenged during the 2023-24 season but faltered during the run-in, then lost their iconic manager. Slot and Liverpool would be fascinating to observe as they rebuilt. Many thought the best they could hope for was Champions League qualification, yet they finished top of the pile.

The final points tally of 84 was the lowest since Leicester won the title in 2015-16. However, Liverpool only took two points from their final four league games after sealing the top spot with a 5-1 win against Tottenham. At that stage, Liverpool were recording 2.4 points per game. For the final four games, they recorded 0.5 points per game. Had they not gone on an extended victory lap and maintained their points game form, the final total would have been 91 points, an extremely respectable tally.

Liverpool were able to claim the title without pushing all the way to the end because none of the competition could keep pace. Arsenal finished second. Manchester City and Chelsea briefly threatened. Yet Liverpool went top of the league when they beat Brighton on November 2nd and were never removed from that position as the lead just seemed to keep growing. Teams had opportunities to close the gap but never seemed to take them.

Early success came from introducing concepts a few at a time and then slowly layering additional ideas. Slot didn't hit his players with too much learning at the same time. The plus-one concepts with the defensive and midfield units were embedded in the early days. In the build-up phases, Liverpool always tried to have one player more than the number that the opposition pressed with. This was achieved through inverting full-backs, dropping both full-backs closer to the central defenders, or having midfielders tighter to the defenders in the build. Inverted full-backs helped create a solid rest defence shape, enabling Liverpool to control transitions. The left full-back underlapped with adventure and aggression while Alexander-Arnold, at right full-back, took up a less advanced role to take advantage of his passing and playmaking skills. When Bradley was at right-back, his movement and play were more similar to that of the left-backs.

Liverpool's right-hand side was vital in building out and playing forward. Many early goals and attacks came from the use of Konate playing forward from a right-back area. Liverpool were happy to bait the opposition press to create space to attack into. Konate could play in behind, clip a pass to Salah to hold up the ball against a full-back, or punch a pass into a midfielder, especially Gravenberch in the pivot role.

Ryan Gravneberch was one of the stories of Liverpool's season: a player who was rarely used by Klopp, and certainly not used in the pivot role that Slot gave him. Liverpool found themselves a pivot that the transfer market could not deliver. Gravenberch protected the defence well, but most importantly was his ability to receive and turn, dribbling past players and giving momentum to attacks being built from the Liverpool half. Later in the season, we saw Gravenberch's flexibility, playing a half-back role. Being a central defender when the team was out of possession then pushing into the pivot when the team was in possession.

Tactical flexibility and pragmatism were themes of Slot's triumphant first season as Liverpool manager. The expectation was that Slot would be a possession-heavy coach with a desire for controlled football. Many considered him to be a disciple of Pep Guardiola. There was some truth to this. Slot certainly wanted control, but he displayed different means of control and, at times, sacrificed control for chaos in order to crack open an opponent.

Slot's formation of choice was a 4-2-3-1/4-3-3 hybrid. The system was not a pure 4-2-3-1 because of the role performed by the number 10. This was mainly Szoboszlai, with Jones filling in. The player in the 10 worked extremely hard without possession, leading the press and making recovery runs. A pure number 10 would be considered a creator, while Szoboszlai and Jones often played more like box-to-box midfielders. Playing in this style enabled Liverpool to swap into a flexible 4-4-2, which was practised in the league cup against Brighton before being deployed against Aston Villa and Manchester City in important league games. This system enabled Liverpool to switch between high pressing and defending deep. Slot was happy to play the game situation. Sitting back and looking to play on the break when ahead or switching to extremely aggressive attacking formations, often playing a 4-2-4 with twin strikers and wingers to chase the game. This could be taken even further by moving Gravenberch into the centre of defence, able to join the midfield and push five players into attack. The smart pragmatism of Slot was evident on a game-by-game basis, mixing patience and chaos. Slot gave the appearance of a man steeped in tactical knowledge with the ability to apply this knowledge.

At the start of the season, Liverpool used one basic form of pressing – a 4-2-4 press based on the front three being joined by the number ten. The pressing evolved, using 2-3, 1-4, or a purely man-orientated press. The press was most effective and aggressive in wide areas. Full-backs and holding midfielders jumped into pressing positions, enabling Liverpool to attack teams when their shape was open. Liverpool's press was not flawless, as the first line could be bypassed with passes, especially when full-backs were used to stretch the pressing four. When this happened, Liverpool used powerful recovery runs to then pressure the ball from both sides: a second chance to press. The press could also be exposed by players dribbling through the lines (a weakness that was exposed throughout the season). These flaws didn't lead to the concession of many goals, but they show an area that Slot and Liverpool might be able to improve next season.

Arne Slot was able to improve the performance levels of a number of players. Gakpo and Diaz had their best scoring seasons at Liverpool. Diaz was unleashed as a central striker, playing the false nine role. He also created wide overloads, and his movement triggered runs by Szoboszlai, Jones, and Mac Allister into the centre-forward area. Gakpo was able to cut in and shoot with his right foot with regularity, but he offered threat on the outside with his left foot, plus his height could dominate full-backs at the far post.

Then, there was Mohammed Salah. His quality has been evident since arriving in 2017, and he had a wonderful scoring season, scoring 32 league goals and 44 goals in all competitions. He has never matched that scoring season, but at one stage during the 2024-25 he appeared to be on course. Salah recorded his second-best league scoring season with 29 goals, which earned him a record-equalling fourth top scorer award (tied with Thierry Henry). He also recorded 18 assists, giving him a combined tally of 47 goal contributions, tying the record with Andy Cole and Alan Shearer, though both recorded their totals in 42-game Premier League game seasons, while Salah's tally came in a 38-game season. Salah showed his trademark plays, cutting inside and shooting while also adding other plays to his repertoire. The inswinging far post crosses fitted with a general strategy of half-space crosses to the far post. Salah also used the trivela far more regularly than he had in previous seasons.

Salah also acted as Liverpool's target man. Long passes that were designed to relieve pressure were aimed at Salah, using his upper body strength to pin full-backs, holding them off while players supported, or spinning them to break away. For Slot, his wingers are the strikers, while the striker operates as an additional midfielder, with more defensive responsibilities. Salah had far fewer responsibilities in this regard. A conversation between Salah and Slot came to light, during which Salah requested that he work back less defensively, expending his energies going forward. He promised a higher goal return. Salah certainly delivered. His passing range has appeared to expand over the seasons, too, and this season, he sent passes into the half-space, opening up opposition defences. Szoboszlai and Bradley were willing runners into that area, looking for shots and low crosses. Finally, Salah showed his ruthless streak from the penalty spot (albeit missing one against Real Madrid in the Champions League), his Premier League record was a perfect nine out of nine.

While Jurgen Klopp was Liverpool manager, the team was renowned for fast breaking football. Yet, Slots's Liverpool scored 14 goals from counter-attacks (Spurs were second in the Premier League with 10 goals). When Liverpool were last Champions, in the 2019-20 season, they scored 11 goals from counter-attacks, and it was the last time they reached double figures for counter-attack goals. Liverpool defended deeper than under Klopp, protecting the edge of their box, and regaining possession before swiftly breaking away. Often, a midfielder or the central striker would emerge with the ball to drive forward or hit a longer pass into one of the wingers. The powerful, dynamic running of the side kicking in as they stream forward in numbers.

Arne Slot married together the principles of Jurgen Klopp with his own concepts, slowly moving closer to the concepts used at Feyenoord. In the final games of the season, we saw further experimentation, using a double pivot in the build-up, for example, hinting at things to come. With new signings on the way to further strengthen a title-winning squad, there may well be further success coming to Arne Slot in the near future.

www.ingramcontent.com/pod-product-compliance
Lightning Source LLC
Chambersburg PA
CBHW060935170426
43194CB00026B/2963